family
its craft.

Selected ories

Selected Letters of Stephen Vincent Benét

Books by Charles A. Fenton

The Apprenticeship of Ernest Hemingway

Stephen Vincent Benét: The Life and Times of an American Man of Letters, 1898-1943

Editor

The Best Short Stories of World War II

Selected Letters of Stephen Vincent Benét

University of Pittsburgh
Bradford Campus Library

Selected Letters of
Stephen Vincent Benét

Edited by Charles A. Fenton

New Haven, Yale University Press

1960

© 1960 by Yale University Press, Inc.
Set in Caledonia type and
printed in the United States of America by
the Vail-Ballou Press Inc., Binghamton, N.Y.
All rights reserved. This book may not be
reproduced, in whole or in part, in any form
(except by reviewers for the public press),
without written permission from the publishers.

Library of Congress catalog card number: 60-11231

To Norman Holmes Pearson

Acknowledgments

THE debts which I had already acquired and inadequately acknowledged in connection with an earlier book about Stephen Vincent Benét have been renewed and enlarged in the preparation of this edition of his letters. To all those creditors—the owners of his correspondence, the librarians, the generous keepers of so much remembered material about him, and in particular to his widow, Rosemary Benét—I am once again more obligated than I can properly say.

The Introduction, which has appeared in somewhat different form in *The Virginia Quarterly Review,* is reprinted here with the editor's permission.

Durham, North Carolina   C.A.F.
February 1960

Introduction

THE principal objective of this volume has been to select from Stephen Vincent Benét's extensive correspondence a cross-section which will reveal his character and illuminate his profession. Like, however, most writers save the most cynically commercial or the most devotedly experimental—like, indeed, most men who practice their vocations with exasperated devotion—Benét's temperament and work were so fully complementary that they can't properly be separated.

A volume of his letters might have been chosen, for example, from his correspondence with young writers. It would have been an absorbing handbook for other writers and for teachers of composition and fiction, but much of it would have been inevitably repetitious; young writers and their dilemmas, both technical and personal, are as unvarying as the vocational and private problems of apprentice lawyers, politicians, scholars, pilots, or left-handed pitchers.

An alternative volume might have been selected from Benét's correspondence with his literary agent, the late Carl Brandt. This was a tempting plan, for we know very little about such relationships and their role in American writing. But the advantages of such a selection to the literary historian would have been diminished, it seemed to me, by the partial quality of its portrait of Benét as both writer and person. About one-quarter of his existing letters to Carl Brandt are nevertheless included in this present selection; the high proportion of the Brandt letters, as compared to the number to his family and friends, supplies what I think is an accurate index to the importance of the association.

Family, friends, vocation—or friends, vocation, family, or vocation, family, friends, the sequence and their relationship were virtually interchangeable and interdependent—these, in fact, were the ingredients of Benét's life. He was nowhere more characteristically American than in the equality of emphasis which he gave to those three elements. Had he been more ruthlessly proprietary about his vocation, he might have written more poetry and fewer trivialities for the slick magazines; had he neglected his friendships and cherished his family less, on the other hand, both his fiction and his verse would very likely have had fewer of the homely intimacies which seem increasingly his durable strength. Family, friends, vocation—these, then, were the major pillars of his life. These are the compartments which the present selection attempts to represent and clarify.

And yet this isn't really accurate. There was a fourth element which bound the other three together and which weighted every aspect of his life until eventually it killed him. This was his deep feeling about his country, and I have tried too to include correspondence which will illuminate the relationship. He was not a professional patriot, nor was he a noisy one. To his normal reticences he added an even greater reticence about his affection for

viii

America. His patriotism, though it is implicit in much of his work, was not really for publication. It is most movingly present in his diary and in the memories of a few friends with whom he occasionally discussed it. "News from Manila very bad," he wrote in his journal on December 31, 1941. "Hardly know what to expect of 1942—but God preserve the United States!" This was the same characteristic which Archibald MacLeish remembered later, many years after Benét's death: "Steve was more conscious of being an American than any other man I ever knew." And yet you will find some of this element among the letters, particularly in the final years when he felt his country simultaneously threatened by domestic intolerance and overseas totalitarianism.

Often, of course, he was writing in his letters about the same general topics or experience or attitudes. I have tried to eliminate such repetition by omitting passages essentially duplicated in other letters. These omissions—indicated by the conventional ellipsis dots—are the only ones. The misspellings—Benét was a rapid and careless typist—have been silently corrected. Idiosyncrasies of punctuation have been retained (except when they create an ambiguous phrase or sentence), but Benét's usage in regard to italics, capitalization, quotation marks, and hyphens has been normalized.

Benét rarely dated his letters; he was a prompt correspondent and generally replied within a few days. Many of the letters can be firmly dated, however, from the postmarked envelope; most of the others can be dated from parallel passages in letters written at about the same time, or from entries in his diary, where he often noted the letters he had answered on a particular day.

Brackets are used only in those occasional cases where there is doubt about the date.

There is a ponderous irony, of course—which Benét would have enjoyed—in the necessity for a declaration of the principles of editorial selection of a contemporary writer's letters. For there is a legend that nobody writes letters any more. Not long ago a well-known New York editor explained why he had once rejected an enviable opportunity to write the biography of a famous contemporary.

"No letters," he declared with absolute and, it later developed, wholly incorrect conviction. "There can't possibly be any letters. Nobody writes letters any more. Notes, memos, telegrams that get lost. No letters."

So goes the myth: nobody writes letters any more. It is an interesting if unimportant myth so far as twentieth-century American writers are concerned. The very senior literary man was a superb vessel: he had accepted and was extending all aspects of the myth.

One school argues that the telephone has destroyed the fine and ancient art of correspondence; this is persuasive doctrine, representing as it does that familiar, sanctified bromide about the displacement of traditional values by a technology. Others maintain that the new mobilities of car and plane have made correspondence unnecessary; this is merely a more gaudy version of the telephone theory. Then, of course, there is in each generation a third group which has its inclusive explanation for all change; call it the curmudgeon doctrine. Bad manners, this group tells us; the younger generation has bad manners.

Well, if the myth were an accurate one—which it clearly is not, as the Postmaster General's annual budget demonstrates—we might employ the one myth to consolidate another, which has to do with the inalienable separation of the American writer from American society. For if nobody writes letters any more, except American novelists and poets and playwrights, then surely this is additional evidence of the notorious gulf between the artist and the layman. Even the habits of writers are different, this myth out of myth might argue. Very strange people, writers.

And yet not such strange people at all, if we remind ourselves of the importance of mail call during a war, of the development of the V-Letter for troops overseas, of the soldier bent above his writing pad in barracks, or at a table in the doubtful privacy of a PX or NAAFI. In time of war all men save the most orphaned are writers; in time of war they are separated from their friends and families and business associates. For the professional writer, however, this is almost the normal condition of his working life.

Unless he lives in a writers' colony, which few productive writers inhabit after a single youthful experience, his friends are scattered in many states and several continents. Unless he is one of the handful whose entire and sufficient income is produced by their serious work, he is frequently separated from his family while he pursues a more available if less appetizing dollar in Hollywood, at writers' conferences, on the lecture circuit, or in servitude to a visiting professorship. Unless he lives in Manhattan, as only the least and the most successful can afford to, he must correspond with his publishers and his editors and his agent and, a few of the most successful, with their lawyer and their tax man. He writes letters because he must, and in a majority of cases, I think, he also writes many of the letters because he wants to. "I am writing," says Benét in 1935, in a letter to his friend Christopher LaFarge, the fellow poet who lived a few streets from him in New York and who had asked Benét to read his current project, "because it's easier for me to think on paper."

Benét's letter-writing began when he was a small boy —separated periodically from his family, like most American middle-class boys, by summer camp or boarding school or vacation—and continued without interruption until, almost literally, the very day of his death in March 1943. Had he died at midnight, in fact, instead of at three in the morning, it would have covered that final day as well. In a lifetime that included all the major busyness of most nonliterary American generations—a frantically extracurricular collegiate experience, war, gay expatriation, purposeful courtship, marriage, careerism as competitive and arduous as any American vocation, parenthood, and all the attendant glories of rent, tuition, life insurance, and the grocer—in that kind of lifetime Benét somehow found time to write at least 1400 letters which have been preserved and subsequently located. He surely wrote, at the very least, twice again that number which have either permanently vanished or temporarily eluded their collectors.

Perhaps Benét was exceptional among contemporary writers. Perhaps he wrote more letters than most of his colleagues because of the important role friendship played in his personal values, or because a tradition of letter-writing is characteristic of the Regular Army in which he was raised, or because his well-known generosity to the young and unknown made him vulnerable to their suits and manuscripts.

Perhaps—but the published evidence of American scholarship during the past several decades seems instead to show that rather than being exceptional in this respect he was characteristic. From the papers of those who were, roughly speaking, his contemporaries there have already appeared collections of the letters of writers as dissimilar in their habits and aspirations as Sherwood Anderson, Sinclair Lewis, Ezra Pound, Hart Crane, Ellen Glasgow, Stuart Sherman, Thomas Wolfe, Gamaliel Bradford, Edna St. Vincent Millay, and Theodore Dreiser, to say nothing of the partial publication in biographies and critical treatises of portions of the correspondence of Fitzgerald and Hemingway and Dos Passos.

The letters of all these writers, needless to say, reveal a different impulse toward letter-writing behind each separate stream of correspondence. They wrote letters because they were decorous invalids like Gamaliel Bradford or desperate wanderers like Hart Crane, or literary talent scouts and impresarios like Pound, or self-elected entrepreneurs like Lewis, badgering his publisher for more advertising and bigger ballyhoo. And yet, as their letters as well as these letters of Benét remind us, they also wrote them because for most writers it is as natural to discuss by mail as it is for their fellow men to discuss by voice. A writer's letters are apt to be full of the same gossip and invective, non sequitur, and occasional clarity and splendid illumination, each in somewhat larger measure, that other men deliver across the back fence or to a bartender.

You could make a plausible argument, in fact, that many a writer has substituted his correspondents for his saloon-keepers. This is in most cases an acquired habit rather than an instinctive one, and it is learned painfully, by domestic trial and professional error. A major vocational problem for the average writer is how to stay out of trouble and off the streets when his working day ends. He shares the dilemma with all mankind, but for him it is more acute; his working day, in appearance at least, is more brief and his opportunities for relaxation are more ample. It's an exceptional novelist or poet who can put in, effectively, more than four or five consecutive hours at his desk. He will very likely return to it at various times during the remainder of the day, to revise or admire or detest, but from 8 to 12 or 1 to 5 or midnight till dawn is apt to be his working day.

As a rule, however, he is neither physically nor mentally exhausted after that four-hour stint; often, indeed, he may be as wound up as an actor or an entertainer after a performance. Only rarely, on the other hand, as most writers discover, can an additional four hours be regularly and genuinely fruitful. And this, not artistic perversity or cultural separation or constitutional instability, is as much as any other single factor the reason they become amateur gardeners, salty mariners, solitary walkers, periodic drunks, vengeful book-reviewers, village adulterers, or excellent if irregular correspondents.

And, as Benét points out in another of these letters, "writing is a habit." It is no easier to break than other mortal habits, and both more rewarding and more complex than most. If a novel is stuck or a short story bogged down, the habit of writing from 8 to 12 or 1 to 5 nevertheless remains. At the very least, even if the writing is a letter instead of a current project or assignment, there is the comfort of being at the desk and writing something. Writing, similarly, as natural instinct and psychological therapy have demonstrated, is a kind of self-lubricant; perhaps the act of writing a long letter will loosen whatever is stuck or bogged down. Writers, like crapshooters, develop their own private rituals. For some it will be music, for others silence, for still others the careful, preparatory tidying of the desk; for most of them correspondence plays a varying part in this ritual of composition.

For Benét his correspondence was all these things and it was also both a part and an extension of his private and his public lives. Portions of each of these lives, like so much of himself, were a heritage of the boyhood he had spent as both son and grandson of career officers in the United States Army. Thus in his own maturity he created and cherished an intimate cluster of personal loyalties and permanent friendships. His attitude toward these friendships, and the way in which he tended them, were remarkably similar to the pattern of lasting relationships among the families of any regular officer corps. His private life was centered on a fixed cadre of friendships.

They were, as in the regular army, friendships of long standing whose origins were frequently in a single situation of the past. Often, in Benét's case, they commenced either at college or in young expatriate manhood, just as in his father's case they were rooted in the single intimacy of duty shared twenty years earlier at some provincial Arsenal. Separated from these friends by, in the one case, subsequent military assignment, or, in the other, adult domicile, both the Benét who was a soldier and his son who was a poet employed their correspondence to keep the friendships green. In the same way that Colonel Benét might meet his former comrades only on brief official visits to Washington, so his son encountered some of his own friends only by coincidence, on a train to Chicago, at a beach in Rhode Island, in the lobby of the Yale Club in New York. The correspondence, however, was unbroken; it was valued immensely by the old friends and it was prolonged by Benét as much from his awareness of that value to them as for his own pleasure in the friendship.

Other of these old friends, of course, were trebly linked to him, by professional bond and geographic proximity as well as by ancient claim. His literary and artistic friendships were remarkable for their durability. All his life he was the cherished companion and resilient prop of such colleagues as Archibald MacLeish, Robert Nathan, Douglas Moore, Charles Child, Christopher LaFarge, and Philip Barry. His friendship with John Farrar, begun at Yale in 1915, not only survived but was even enriched by their further, traditionally difficult relationships as Broadway collaborators, as author and editor when Farrar was successively with George H. Doran and then Doubleday, Doran, and finally as author and publisher when Farrar established his own house of Farrar and Rinehart.

Here too, as is indicated by these selections from his letters to these professional colleagues, Benét was both a thoughtful and a joyous correspondent. The temptation, in fact, is to describe Benét as a correspondent in those same pietistic, saintlike terms by which some of his friends almost emasculated him as a man after his death. Here, fortunately, are the letters, to restrain and confirm their editor, and more particularly to display the vigorous dissent and sturdy anger which were as much a part of Benét as the sweet tolerance and serene wisdom.

His letters, indeed, are peculiarly revealing for the very reason that they were written with warmth and spontaneity and, often, with haste. They were not the careful compositions which literary men sometimes write, discreet as politicians, one eye warily on posterity and the other on the immediate impression. In his letters he stated what he thought and what he felt, just as in his personal and private relationships he said with candor and directness exactly what he judged he had to say. A man who valued privacy, for others as well as himself, Benét somehow avoided the inhibition of emotion which often accompanies such reserve. He prized emotion in his own work and in the work of other writers; he neither diluted nor rationed it in his correspondence or his friendships.

We see these same qualities in the letters to the young poets and novelists whom his public luster and private generosity attracted. The concept of master and pupil, on the other hand, was thoroughly repellent to him; he did not cultivate himself as sage or them as protégés. He felt, as I think is demonstrated by these letters to Muriel Rukeyser or Paul Engle or George Abbe or any of the younger writers, that writing was a craft in two senses of the word: a writer owned membership in the literary guild as others, say, might have membership in the community of scholars. In his own guild he insisted that membership should not duplicate those communities of literature and scholarship which never transcend the local community of a single coterie or a single university.

Thus he sponsored and responded to a variety of literary schools and practices; he did not require literary visas and aesthetic blood tests. He was not as cheerily indiscriminate as the colleague who once told him, over the wine at the American Academy of Arts and Letters, that he had never met a writer he didn't like, but neither did he ever deny good work because of partisan commitment or personal distaste. He practiced, though the comparison would have startled him, something of the same kind of rigorous guild evangelism that Ezra Pound maintained through a similar network of correspondence. They worked different sides of the street yet both of them recognized the obvious but elusive truth that any avenue has two sides and a middle and a fundamental interdependency between the three parts.

Like Pound too—like any responsible member of any mature profession—Benét maintained these responsibilities at the cost of his own work and his own leisure. Not only, it's also worth remarking—to prolong this bizarre parallel a little further—was he committed to a heavier burden of domestic responsibility than Pound, but he had inherited and acquired more expensive tastes than could be satisfied by expatriate and avant-garde frugalities. He found innumerable compensations in the help he gave to younger and contemporary colleagues, and in the friendships which were thereby established and maintained, but the help was given and the letters were written, after all, on his own time, not on the company's or the guild's.

When his work was going well, Benét often wrote the letters in the evening. From September until June, during most of the 1930's and early 1940's, he and his family lived in New York, in comfortable, rented houses in the East Sixties; the working day he preferred ran, generally, from late morning to mid-afternoon. This kind of schedule allowed him a number of the small comforts and large pleasures which he valued. He could thereby, for one thing, sleep later in the morning and stay up longer at night. "Oh God," he wrote his wife one year from Iowa, where he was lecturing, "how early everybody goes to bed!"

He could also, on this kind of working schedule, spend the late afternoon and early evening with his wife and three children, if there were no letters to write or deadlines to meet, and during the rest of the evening they could, several nights a week, have dinner or go to the theater with another couple or two from among the many friends of their active social life. He could also, on this kind of schedule, take a long walk before he began work in the morning, often through Central Park and around the basin, sometimes down Second Avenue as far as Herald Square, occasionally uptown to the East Nineties where Farrar lived or further on to the Morningside Heights apartments of Douglas Moore and Hervey Allen.

He could do all these things on that kind of schedule, and some days he was actually able to do them, but more often than not his current short story required extra work, or there was a lecture to write, or a review to finish, or a cocktail party to launch a friend's new book. Always there were the meetings—a meeting of the National Institute of Arts and Letters' committee on grants, or a meeting of the Century Club's admissions committee, or during the 1930's a meeting of an antifascist organization, or during the 1940's a meeting of a civilian propaganda agency. Always too there were the younger colleagues with their manuscripts and the older ones who merely wanted to draw on his strength and enjoy his wit.

"I should have written before," he says in a 1940 letter to his mother, to whom he wrote regularly and at length once a week, from the time his father died in 1928 until her own death in 1940, "but this week has been a mess. Or not so much a mess as just full of people. One afternoon—Joy Davidman, the last Yale Series poet,[1] and Norman Rosten, a nice young playwright." Benét thoughtfully and animatedly strung out the chatty exposition and trivial details for the entertainment of his mother, bored and semi-invalided at the end of an energetic life.

"Davidman had six weeks in Hollywood which she didn't like a bit except for the MGM lion. It was a lion-cub which they are training up to take the former MGM lion's place (same having deceased) and she played with it every day. Well, she has a new book of poems—will I look at the mss.—yes—Rosten has a play for radio—I try to give him some advice on it.

"Next afternoon, Eddie Weismiller, another Yale Series poet, then a Rhodes Scholar, now teaching at Harvard. He & his sister were in the Black Forest when war broke out, they got the last train out of Germany, the last train

1. Benét was editor of the Yale Series of Younger Poets for the ten years from 1933 until his death. See, for example, his letters to George Parmly Day and Eugene Davidson of the Yale Press and more particularly those to and concerning the various winners and losers of the annual contest—Shirley Barker, Muriel Rukeyser, James Agee, Frank Guenther, and Norman Rosten.

from Geneva to Paris, the last boat across the Channel. His sister then managed to get a seat on the Yankee Clipper, the transatlantic plane—and suddenly discovered the plane, instead of leaving from Southampton was to leave from the Faroes—is it? anyway from off the Irish coast. So Eddie & his sister spent 24 hours in a train that was evacuating Irish slum-dwellers from London to Ireland—no rest, no food, and no notion if they'd be on time or not—but he finally got his sister on the plane. It's a good story and he tells it well. Also, he now has an instructorship as Harvard, so I don't have to worry about him. He beams solemnly at me from behind his glasses & asks me if I realize how I've completely changed the course of his life. Unless I'd published [his] book, he'd never have had the Rhodes—etc. Well, that's pleasant to hear, and I give him advice about *his* new book.

"Another afternoon ———— comes in to talk about an idea for a Rivers book.[2] Delighted to see him and he is, as usual, long-winded. Then Johnny [Farrar] and I and King Gordon [of Farrar & Rinehart] decide what to do about *The Delaware* which has just come in, in mss. And a publicity man from the National Institute of Arts and Letters comes in—just to get acquainted and see if I have any ideas for the furtherance of the Institute. I do my best and dig up an idea or so, and make a date to have lunch with Henry Canby and call a meeting of a committee—and—oh well! Yes, I am grouching—I am frankly grouching. I like doing it, really—and you know it and I know it.

2. Benét was also a co-editor from 1939 until 1943, with Carl Carmer, of Farrar and Rinehart's Rivers of America series. See his "Ballade Irregular of Rivers Unbooked," *Saturday Review of Literature*, 25 (December 12, 1942), 15.

"But in the last week or so I have advised a gent to get married and a gent to change his publisher and a gent to rewrite the Lincoln portion of his book, and they are all very nice but they never know when to go home. Well, that is a characteristic of youth. I remember, as a Freshman, going to Minot Osborn's house for lunch and staying till 11.40 P.M. I didn't want to stay that long, and while they were cordial, they certainly didn't want me to. But I just couldn't get out of my chair and remark, 'Well, I guess I'll be leaving.' Or rather I did do that, once or twice, and each time the Osborns would say politely, 'Must you go?'—so I'd stay. If Minot hadn't taken the dog out for a walk finally—and me with it—I would probably still be there.

"Meanwhile—to revert to last week—I was having a little sinus and [Dr. Ralph H.] Boots would look at it and think he'd drain it and then he'd look at it and think he wouldn't. Finally he didn't, to my great relief, as having it drained always makes me feel as if they were building the Panama Canal in my nose. And in the midst of this, a story had to be written—and got written, at least in first draft. And now things will be clearer—at least when I have looked at the 30 manuscripts submitted *this* year to the Yale Series of Younger Poets, which, at the moment, are downstairs in a packing box.

"Today the exterminator has been here as the roaches were getting to be a problem. Rachel [his youngest child, eight years old at this time], however, wept for the cruelty of it all. 'Why does he have to exterminate the poor roaches?' she said. 'Couldn't I just hit them over the head with a hammer?' I couldn't see how this would make an essential difference to a roach—but it seemed to, to her. And tomorrow, for my sins and because I promised to, months ago, I must go up to Boston and read a poem at a dinner of the Signet Society. But when that's done, I mean to take a rest . . ."

And so, if he were to get through days of that sort, which were characteristic of most of his days from the success of *John Brown's Body* in 1928 until his death fifteen years later, and if he were also to conceive and complete the demanding short stories which he called his bread-and-butter writing and the poetry which he valued, the letters had at best to be answered in the evening. They came to him from friends, and from those he had neither met nor heard of but who regarded him as their friend because they had been moved by his work, and they came from cranks of every variety. They came, as nearly as one can judge, at the rate of about twenty a week—leaving aside, that is, all those others which concerned his own affairs, and which of course had to be dealt with too—and he answered them all.

He'd let them accumulate for about a week; then he would attack the steadily growing pile. "In evening," he noted in his diary in 1938, "write 18 letters and clear up correspondence." Often one night a week was not sufficient, particularly after he had been away with his family in Rhode Island or Connecticut during the summer, or on a lecture tour, or after their annual Christmas visit to his wife's relatives in Richmond. "In evening," he notes in September 1936, "try to catch up on correspondence." Two nights later he worked on them again—"Write letters."—and again the next night: "Do odd jobs, letters, etc." In July 1940 it took the better part of six days to answer conscientiously the letters of condolence after his mother died. He even got around eventually to those letters which get pushed aside in the guilty hope that eventually an answer won't be necessary. "Clean up a lot of old correspondence," he wrote in his diary in April of that same year.

That he got his main work done the staggering bibliography of twenty-three years as a professional writer reminds us: five novels, two long poems, ten volumes of verse, and a hundred and fifty published short stories, several of them already classics of the national literature and at least a dozen more which will always be anthologized and reread. To say nothing of the radio scripts, literary journalism, prefaces, plays, book reviews, lyrics, reader reports, Hollywood scenarios, and operettas.

He never kidded himself, on the other hand, that the letters were either his principal obligation or an excuse for work undone. "Do up some letters in afternoon," he noted in 1942. "Don't get much real work done." It's also true, I think, that he borrowed the time for most of these letters at a greater cost than most writers; during a major part of his poignantly brief maturity he worked under an awful urgency which most men are spared until they can better afford it. From 1930 until his death in 1943 he was rarely in even moderately good health, and during long periods of those thirteen productive years he was in considerable physical pain. You'd never guess it from these letters.

LOCATIONS

The Yale Collection of American Literature, Sterling Memorial Library, Yale University, is the holder, under varying conditions of gift, purchase, and restricted deposit, of the original Benét correspondence with the following individuals and firms: Charles Allen, Shreve C. Badger, Rosemary (Carr) Benét, William Rose Benét, Henry S. Canby, Thomas and Rachel Carr, John F. Carter, Jr., Malcolm Davis, George Parmly Day, William C. DeVane, John Farrar, Bernhard Knollenberg, Sinclair Lewis, Helen McAfee, William Lyon Phelps, Allan M. Price, Phelps Putnam, Samuel C. Slaymaker, and Chauncey B. Tinker; Brandt and Brandt, Inc., addressed variously to Bernice Baumgarten, Carl Brandt, Erd N. Brandt, Homer Fickett, Nannine Josephs, Frieda Lubelle, Lilla Worthington, and Collier Young; and Doubleday, Doran, Inc., addressed variously to Page Cooper, Daniel Longwell, and Harry E. Maule.

The letters to Eugene Davidson are in the files of the Yale Series of Younger Poets, Yale University Press; the letter to Carl Lohman is in the Secretary's Office, Woodbridge Hall, Yale University.

The letters to Philip Bellinger, Mrs. James Walker Benét, Col. James Walker Benét, and Laura Benét are owned by Laura Benét.

The letters to Hervey Allen are deposited in The University Library, The University of Pittsburgh; to Joseph Auslander and Douglas S. Freeman, in the Library of Congress; to the Board of Directors of the American Academy of Arts and Letters, Walter Damrosch, Felicia Geffen, Arthur Train, and Mrs. William Vanamee, in the American Academy of Arts and Letters; to Roy W. Cowden and Bennett Weaver, in the Hopwood Room, University of Michigan; to John Dollard, in the University Archives, William Rainey Harper Memorial Library,

University of Chicago; to Paul Engle, in The Lockwood Memorial Library, University of Buffalo; to James T. Farrell, in the Library, University of Pennsylvania; to Ellen Glasgow and Guy Holt, in the Manuscripts Division of The University of Virginia Library; to Frederica Field and Robert Grant, in the Harvard College Library, Harvard University; to Elizabeth Manwaring, in the English Poetry Collection, Wellesley College Library; to Harriet Monroe, in the Harriet Monroe Poetry Room, the University of Chicago Library.

The letters to C. D. Jackson are in the files of *Life;* those to William Maxwell and Katherine S. White, the *New Yorker;* and to Edward Weeks, the *Atlantic.*

The letter to John Drinkwater is owned by C. Waller Barrett.

The letter to Margaret Mitchell is owned by the Margaret Mitchell Marsh Estate.

The following letters are in the possession of the original recipients or their heirs: George Abbe, Philip Barry, Van Wyck Brooks, John Winchester Dana, Basil Davenport, Russell Davenport, J. Raymond Derby, William Dieterle, Louis Finkelstein, Valentine Mitchell Gammell, John F. Hagen, Henry R. Hallowell, Mrs. John M. Harlan, Miles Hart, Pierre Hazard, Marion L. Joest, Andrew D. Talbot Jones, Christopher LaFarge, Florence Locke, Dean B. Lyman, Jr., Robert E. McClure, Douglas Moore, Pauli Murray, Mrs. Richard Myers, Robert Nathan, Egbert S. Oliver, Edward Bliss Reed, Selden Rodman, Norman Rosten, Muriel Rukeyser, H. Emerson Tuttle, John H. Ware, and Margaret Widdemer.

Calendar

THIS calendar of Benét's life is a hybrid, being neither adequately chronological nor fully bibliographical nor amply biographical. Its function is merely to supplement the letters by providing, in so compressed a form that no single consistent principle of selection can be detected, a handful of the significant moments and achievements of Benét's private, public, and professional lives. For detailed bibliographies and a critical biography see Gladys L. Maddocks, "Stephen Vincent Benét: A Bibliography," *Bulletin of Bibliography and Dramatic Index,* 20 (September 1951, April 1952), and Charles A. Fenton, *Stephen Vincent Benét: The Life and Times of an American Man of Letters, 1898–1943,* Yale University Press, 1958.

1898   July 22. Born, Bethlehem, Pa., third and youngest child—brother of Laura and William Rose —of Capt. James Walker Benét, U.S.A., and Frances Neill Rose Benét.

1899   Captain Benét and family to Watervliet (N.Y.) Arsenal.

1904   January. Captain Benét promoted to major; to duty for one year at Rock Island (Ill.) Arsenal.

1905   Major Benét and family to Benicia (Cal.) Arsenal.

1910–11 September–June. Attends Hitchcock Military Academy, San Rafael, Cal.

1911   August. Colonel Benét and family to Augusta (Ga.) Arsenal.

1911–15 Attends Summerville Academy, Augusta, Ga.

1915   August. "Winged Man" (*New Republic*).
September. Enters Yale College.
December. *Five Men and Pompey.*

1916   March. "The Hemp" (*Century Magazine*).
December. Elected to the editorial board, *Yale Literary Magazine.*

1918   April. Elected chairman, *Yale Literary Magazine.*
June. Completes junior year in good standing, resigns from Yale College.
July. Enlists in the Army of the United States. Honorably discharged.
September. *Young Adventure.*
October–December. Office of the Counselor, Department of State, Washington, D.C.

1919   January. Readmitted, Yale College.
June. Awarded B.A. degree. An editor, *Yale Book of Student Verse, 1910–1919.* Editor, *Tamburlaine the Great* (acting version).
July–October. Copywriter, Hoyt's Agency, Manhattan.
October. Admitted Graduate School, Yale University.

1920   January–December. Poetry in *Ainslee's, Parabalou, S4N, Literary Digest,* New York *Evening Post, Yale Review, Contemporary Verse.*
June. Receives M.A. degree, Yale University. Awarded traveling fellowship, 1920–21.
June–August. Works on first novel, *The Beginning of Wisdom.*
September. To Paris.
September–November. Completes *The Beginning of Wisdom.*
November. Meets Rosemary Carr.

     January–June. Works on second novel, *Jean Huguenot.*
1921   March 17. Engaged to Rosemary Carr.
June. Returns to U.S.A.
July–October. Carl Brandt becomes his literary agent. Writes third novel, *Young People's Pride,* also first commercial short stories; first sales, to *Metropolitan, Cosmopolitan, Delineator.*
November 26. Marries Rosemary Carr, in Chicago. To Europe for honeymoon.

1922   May. Benéts return to New York.
November. "The Ballad of William Sycamore" (*New Republic*).

1923   February. "King David" (*Nation*).
February–November. Short stories, *Harper's Bazaar, Ladies' Home Journal, Everybody's, Redbook, Cosmopolitan.*
September. *Jean Huguenot.*

1924   April 6. Birth of daughter, Stephanie Jane.
        May. "Uriah's Son" (*Redbook*). Republished as
        an O. Henry Memorial Prize Story.

1925   March. "Mountain Whippoorwill" (*Century
        Magazine*).
        March–June. Short stories, *Liberty*, etc.
        October. *Tiger Joy.*

1926   January–June. Short stories, *Collier's, Good
        Housekeeping, Elks' Magazine, Country Gen-
        tleman;* first fictional use of American his-
        torical material.
        May. Awarded Guggenheim Fellowship for
        1926–27.
        July. To Paris, with wife and daughter.
        September 28. Son, Thomas Carr, born in
        American Hospital, Paris.
        September–November. Working on *John
        Brown's Body.*

1927   March 9. Guggenheim Fellowship renewed for
        additional six months.

1928   March 30. Death of Colonel Benét, in West-
        town, Pa.
        August. *John Brown's Body.*

1929   May. Pulitzer Prize for poetry.
        August. Benéts return to U.S.A.

1929–30 December–February. In Hollywood, script-writ-
        ing for *Abraham Lincoln.*

1930   February–December. Ill throughout most of this
        period; variously diagnosed as arthritis, rheu-
        matism.

1931 May. "A Life at Angelo's" (first sale to *Saturday Evening Post*).

June. *Ballads and Poems.*

October 22. Daughter, Rachel, born in Manhattan.

1932 January–November. Short stories in *Maclean's, Harper's, American,* etc.

February. "An End to Dreams" (*Pictorial Review*). Awarded O. Henry Memorial Prize, best American short story of year.

1933 July. "Metropolitan Nightmare" (*New Yorker*)

September. With Rosemary Benét, *A Book of Americans.*

1934 April. *James Shore's Daughter.*

1935 February–December. Reviewing books regularly for New York *Herald Tribune, Saturday Review of Literature.* Continues these associations throughout remainder of life.

April. "The Professor's Punch" (*Pictorial Review*). Republished as an O. Henry Memorial Prize Story.

May. "Nightmare, with Angels" (*New Yorker*). "Ode to Walt Whitman" (*Saturday Review of Literature*).

July. "Nightmare Number Three" (*New Yorker*).

September. "Litany for Dictatorships" (*Atlantic*).

October. "Selection from *Western Star*" (*American Prefaces*). "The Curfew Tolls" (*Saturday Evening Post*).

1936   April. "Notes to Be Left in a Cornerstone" (*New Yorker*).

June. *Burning City.*

October. "The Devil and Daniel Webster" (*Saturday Evening Post*). Awarded O. Henry Memorial Prize, best American short story of year.

1937   March. With Douglas Moore, *The Headless Horseman* (operetta).

May. "Daniel Webster and the Sea Serpent" (*Saturday Evening Post*).

June. Honorary degree, Yale University.

September. "Johnny Pye and the Fool-Killer" (*Saturday Evening Post*). Republished as an O. Henry Memorial Prize Story.

October. *Thirteen O'Clock* (short stories).

1938   April. "Nightmare for Future Reference" (*New Yorker*).

May. "Into Egypt," "Jacob and the Indians" (*Saturday Evening Post*); "O'Halloran's Luck" (*Country Gentleman*).

1939   May. At the Martin Beck Theatre, *The Devil and Daniel Webster,* libretto by Benét, music by Douglas Moore, production by the American Lyric Theatre.

November. *Tales before Midnight* (short stories).

1940   May. "Freedom's a Hard-Bought Thing" (*Saturday Evening Post*). Awarded O. Henry Memorial Prize, best American short story of year.

June. "Nightmare at Noon" (*New York Times Magazine*).

July 8. Death of mother, Frances Neill Benét.

September. Son, Thomas Carr, enters Phillips Exeter Academy, to prepare for Yale.

October. "The Most Unforgettable Character I've Met" (*Reader's Digest*)—Benét's brief, effective memoir about his father.

November 5. "Americans United," an address written for the Council For Democracy and delivered by Raymond Massey at a Madison Square Garden mass meeting.

1941   May. Purchases the Whistler House, Stonington, Conn., as summer home.

July. "Listen to the People" (*Life*).

September. Daughter, Stephanie Jane, enters Swarthmore College.

1942   February. "The Bishop's Beggar" (*Saturday Evening Post*).

May–November. *A Child Is Born, Dear Adolf, Selected Works* (2 vols.), *They Burned the Books.*

December. "The Prodigal Children" (*Saturday Evening Post*).

1943   January. "A Judgment in the Mountains" (*Country Gentleman*).

March 13. Dies.

June. *Western Star.*

1944   May. Pulitzer Prize for poetry.

Contents

A specimen of Benét's handwriting appears on page 58, and a typewritten letter is reproduced on page 297.

Boyhood and Adolescence
(1908-1915)

Stephen vincent benét was born at Bethlehem, Pennsylvania, on July 22, 1898. His father, James Walker Benét, was then a captain in the United States Army, Department of Ordnance, on duty at the Bethlehem Iron Works. Captain Benét, a career officer who had graduated from West Point in 1880, was himself the son of a regular army officer, Brigadier General Stephen Vincent Benét (1827–1895). General Benét was Chief of Ordnance from 1874 until his retirement in 1891.

By the time the first of his youngest child's boyhood letters was written, in 1908, Captain Benét had become a lieutenant colonel and received command of the Benicia Arsenal in California. The Colonel and his family— his wife, their daughter Laura, and their two sons William Rose and Stephen Vincent—lived pleasureably in the spacious quarters at Benicia until 1911, their warm and literate unity interrupted only during the academic year by Laura's absence at Vassar and William's at Yale. The letters from Stephen to his mother—leaving aside those from military school in 1911—were written either during her annual visits to relatives in Carlisle, Pennsylvania, or on the summer holidays he sometimes spent traveling with his sister.

During most of this period Stephen was educated, like so many of the nomadic children of prewar army and navy officers, by the celebrated Calvert Correspondence System; he received additional tutoring from his father and sister. In the fall of 1910, however, he was sent to board at the Hitchcock Military Academy. A physician had persuaded the boy's parents that Stephen would profit from the comradeship of his contemporaries. Benét was unhappy and wretched at Hitchcock, though he made good use of the experience in his first novel, *The Beginning of Wisdom* (1921). He was reprieved from a second year at Hitchock when the Colonel was posted in 1911 to command of the Augusta (Ga.) Arsenal. In Augusta the boy attended happily, as a day student, the nearby Summerville Academy. He also began writing precociously the verse which culminated in his first book, *Five Men and Pompey,* composed in Augusta when he was seventeen and published in the early winter of 1915 during his freshman year at Yale.

TO PHILIP BELLINGER [1]

> Benicia Arsenal
> Benicia, California
> December 9, 1908

Dear Philip:—

The most interesting lesson I have had was about Robin Hood, the archer of Sherwood Forest. I would have liked to have been like him. He led a merry life

1. Philip Bellinger was the younger of the two sons of Capt. Thomas Bellinger, who was stationed at Benicia Arsenal during this period as Colonel Benét's adjutant.

sleeping under the trees, shooting deer when you wanted to eat, having contests in archery, taking from the rich to give to the poor, tying people on mules. A life for a king himself. Doubtless the king would have liked to have stayed in Sherwood. I would have liked to have been in the tower with a .22 caliber revolver, when the nun was bleeding him (Robin) to death. Face at the window! Collapse of nun! bandages for Robin! See!

Also when he died I would have erected a monument like the Bunker Hill one over his grave.

Then I would have an old Egyptian embalm him so that in 1904, the newsboys would yell, "Extra, Extra. Robin Hood's body found embalmed. Wuxtry."

Your Affectionate Friend,
S. V. Benét

TO MRS. JAMES WALKER BENÉT

Benicia Arsenal
Benicia, California
[July] 1909

Dear Mother:—

I am having a fine time here. I play tennis every day with Laura [and] Mrs. Platt. Laura, Billy, Mrs. Platt, Miss Wedgeworth and I went in swimming yesterday. I did not stay in very long because of the coldness of the water. Mr. [Sinclair] Lewis has gone to the city to get a job. I now have 850 stamps and about 1200 duplicates. Prince has something the matter with his ear & is unhappy at present. My poem which I sent to the [St. Nicholas] Competition got in too late and so did not qualify.

William writes in the summerhous[e] in the garden. He

has fixed it up with books and a chair. In there are also some wasps who have built a nest there.

[*Thumb prints affixed here.*]

The thing above is my thumb-print.

Your Loving Son
Stephen

TO MRS. JAMES WALKER BENÉT

Camp Ahwahnee
El Portal, California
July 25, 1909

Dear Mother:—

I went up Glacier Point yesterday and got on a rock where I could look down on the whole big valley. I have met some nice kids here. The valley is certainly the most Beautiful Place on earth and I would like to stay there always. We saw the place where the poor man got lost. I hope you are having a good time in the East though you are so far away that I hardly know. The squirrels are so tame that they will almost eat out of your hand and if you were here everything would be all right.

Your loving son. Tibbie

TO MRS. JAMES WALKER BENÉT

Benicia Arsenal
Benicia, California
September 13, 1909

Dear Mother:—

We miss you very much. The house is very lonely without you. We play tennis nearly every day now. Father and I beat Billy and Capt. Platt.[2] I am teaching Laura

2. William P. Platt, a graduate of West Point in the Class of

4

and Mrs. Platt to play. They're very good pupils. Father gives me examples in decimals every day.

Prince is rather smelly and is not allowed to come in very much.

The Bellingers will be back in a few days and I expect to see them. I have catalogued all my soldiers and I have over 400.

Laura is going to begin school again soon. Tell me when you are coming.

Yours   Devotedly
Stephen

TO MRS. JAMES WALKER BENÉT

Hitchcock Military Academy
San Rafael, California
[December] 1910

Dear Mother:—

There was a show last night given by the big boys and if I hadn't forgotten to bring it over I would send you the program. I will send it tomorrow. I am on my third model in shop and when I come back on the 21st I expect to bring it and my second model with me. About two weeks ago I asked you to send me an extension for my light. You said that you had written to Dr. Hitchcock about it and he said he would see. I have not got it yet so if you would either get one or ask Dr. Hitchcock if I can have an order to go down to San Rafael and get one. Would you also ask him if I could draw skating money twice a week. There is a rink down in San Rafael and I have improved my skating. I guess in about 2,000,000 years I

1901, had been posted to duty under Colonel Benét at the Benicia Arsenal on June 1909.

shall learn to dance but as it is I have no hope of learning now. Of course I have only had two lessons. Thank you ever so much for the lovely apples. I ate so many I am afraid I will turn into one.

I changed my seat at the dining-room and instead of sitting at Miss Daly's table I sit at Mr. Rose's. I like the change.

With love for ever and ever and ever and ever and ever.

Tibi

TO MRS. JAMES WALKER BENÉT

Hitchock Military Academy
San Rafael, California
April 3, 1911

Dear Mother:—

I got over all right Saturday [to San Francisco], went up to Bill's house and found him in bed. We had lunch about 12 and then went over to the beach. We had a fine swim there and went to Dr. Platt at 3.30. He says that appointment on the 15th will not be necessary but to come some time in August or September.

I wonder if I could go to the city next Saturday. What do you think? Several of the boys go nearly every Saturday. Anyway we come home the 12th and have about a week—and then it's only a month to the 20th when we stop for good.

I am about half through the box with the cover and may bring it with me on the 12th. How is Mrs. Platt? Has the Captain come back yet? Santa Rosa won the track-meet at Vkiah. We came in fifth. Have you any new good books? We have confirmation class tonight *I think*.

Tibi

TO SINCLAIR LEWIS [3]

Highlands, North Carolina
August 1912

Dear "Tom Graham":—

Thank you very much for the book.

It's swell, one of the best boys books this year, indeed the best.

Are you going to write a sequel? I guess you are for you let the villain escape! Miss Granicle who has been visiting us says she will present a copy to the Benicia library. So you see how famous you are!!

I wish there was a Santa Benicia. It would be much better than Hitchcock. I wish you were up at the Islington [Hotel], though the country isn't equal to California, but there's fine swimming and walking.

Thanking you again and sending you the *best* congratulations from Mother, Laura, Miss Granicle & myself

I am

Your Friend
Stephen Benét

TO MRS. JAMES WALKER BENÉT

Highlands, North Carolina
[August] 1912

Dear Mother:—

I am a mut not to write to you before but there has been so much to do.

3. Lewis, a classmate of William Rose Benét at Yale and a frequent guest at Benicia, had presented Stephen with a copy of his *Hike and the Aeroplane,* published in 1912 under the pseudonym Tom Graham.

Yesterday we walked up Satulah in the morning and went down the Walhalla road in the afternoon. Today we walked 8 miles in the morning. In the afternoon Laura took tea with Louise Bascom, and I saw the Farnsworths for an hour or so. They sent best regards. Tomorrow we are going to Garnet Park with the Sloans.

I have written a poem and by the way *Please send the St. Nicholas* if you are holding it. The competition closes on the 10th and I don't know the subject yet.

There are only 8 (counting us) left at the Smith House. The food is not very good.

Tell Father Roosevelt will sweep the country.

What do you think of the Balkan Trouble?

The riot must have been nasty. Laura has had you shot, hanged, blown up and I don't know what else.

I thought you had a cook. Laura says, "We will stay till otherwise informed."

We are all very well. Lollie [Laura] is swell.

Stephen B.

TO WILLIAM ROSE BENÉT

Augusta Arsenal
Augusta, Georgia
[January 15] 1915

Dear Bill:—

You are certainly terrifically good! It was awfully good of you to get those books for me and I do thank you ever and ever so much! "The Congo" is fine! Lindsay is a great poet. How I love "But gentle will the Griffen be" and "Dirge for a righteous kitten" and the one comparing Gloriana to the "white, sweet Russian" ["Yet Gentle

8

Will the Griffin Be," "A Dirge for a Righteous Kitten,"
"On Receiving One of Gloriana's Letters"] and indeed
all the Moon Poems and the Christmas Tree and The
Santa Fé Trail and The Firemen's Ball and The Congo!
I never knew he could do such graceful delicate things.
The war-poems are not so good, though the epilogue is
fine. The "Big black bucks in a wine-barrel room" has
been running in my head all morning. *Magic* [a play by
Chesterton] is fine too. The place where the red light
turns blue is a great moment, great, GREAT. There certainly are devils. The poem I am sending is about a sort
of half-devil. I like him pretty well though he is very
blasphemous and turgid. It is a splendid edition of
Rossetti. I like him more and more. "Soothsay" is a fine
poem—and nobody ever did sonnets like "The House of
Life." Except you and Eugene Lee Hamilton. How many
great men lie buried in the Victorian Anthology! Men
like Mangan and Sir Samuel Ferguson and John Davidson (though I suppose he is better known than the
other two). . . .

Who would have thought Wilson, the cultured scholar,
the polished gentleman, could have made such a speech
as he did on Jackson Day! Lord! the cheap wit, the oily
glad-hand hail-fellow-well-met manner, the undignified
virulence toward the newspapers and the Republican
party, the plain statement, unsurpassed by any insolent
the-public-be-damned mandate of any corrupt boss, that
any member of the Democratic Party who dared oppose
ANY measure of the President's would be regarded as a
traitor to his country! Croker or Tweed would never
have dared to make such a speech.

The war seems to be going fairly well except for the

"Dacia" affair. That looks suspiciously like an Ethiopian in the timber-heap.

Poor old Italy! This is a bad time to have an earthquake.

Dinner is calling.

> Yours, with much, MUCH gratitude, for France
> STEPH

TO WILLIAM ROSE BENÉT

> Augusta Arsenal
> Augusta, Georgia
> May 29, 1915

Dear Bill:—

> HOORAH!
> HOORAY!
> FOR FRANCES ROSEMARY!
> FOR THE TWENTY-NINTH DAY OF MAY
> IT WAS A JOYFUL DAY!
> WHEN THE QUEEN DID ENJOY HER OWN AGAIN!

A million million congratulations! Has James [William's oldest child] said "How-do" to her yet? There might be a slight difference in their politics, though: she is evidently a staunch Royalist, while James, with his sociable nature, is, I think, a good deal of a Republican. If she lives to be as lovely as her mother, though, she will be a prodigy. And just think, you can start right in chanting "Arma, virumque cano" to her! What color are her eyes and hair? Aunt Agnes is much aggrieved that you did not telegraph these too! It is a lovely and beautiful name, one of the loveliest, for a lovely and beautiful child (She couldn't be her mother's child or yours without being that) Rose Mary! I have sung of women in six cities!

Henceforth I shall sing of you alone! My heart (and not the first heart or the last that will be there) is at your feet! Henceforth I ride for you alone!

The New Republic paid me fifteen (Count 'em, FIF-TEEN) lucious dollars for Icarus.⁴ I feel terribly cocky. I put on my hat with a boot-jack. An uncle of a niece. The possessor of fifteen dollars. What more could anybody want? I send you a short but bluggy play. I think it and "Five Men" are the best things I've done (I talk, Heaven help me as if I was a Shakespeare—but that's the effect of Rose Mary and the fifteen)

My Yale exes. begin the 23rd and last four days. There are TWELVE of them. God help me!

This is a very silly letter—probably because I am very happy. Good-bye. My very very very VERY VERY best love to Mother, Teresa [Mrs. William Rose Benét], Thy self AND ROSE MARY. Tell Teresa I hope she will only be sick enough to enjoy to the full the seventh heaven that con-valescence can sometimes be, full of lazy golden days, and lovely things on trays and soft-voiced people read-ing aloud to you.

Stephen Vincent Benét

UNCLE

TO MRS. JAMES WALKER BENÉT

Augusta Arsenal
Augusta, Georgia
June 1915

Dearest Mother:—

Nothing much has happened this week, except study. Twelve examinations! which I probably will not pass.

4. Stephen Vincent Benét, "Winged Man," *New Republic, 4* (August 7, 1915), 20.

Well, maybe not quite that—but if I passed in Geometry, Algebra or Physics—well, I would be surpised!

. . . The Smith-Harper wedding came off last night with great eclat. Dan was there, of course, looking, Father says, quite senile. The Carpenters have gotten off for California. Gee! Don't you wish! .... Laura is reading Conrad's *Victory* and liking it very much. It certainly is a *great* book. Dumas' *Memoirs* are a mine of treasure! I must study. Much love to all.

Your loving Son
S.V.

Young Manhood (1915-1920)

BENÉT matriculated at Yale in September 1915, having been successfully tutored at Augusta during the summer for the make-up exams. With the exception of wartime service in Washington in 1918 and a period in New York as a copywriter in the summer of 1919, he spent the next five years in New Haven. He received his B.A. in 1919 and his M.A. in 1920.

His affection for Yale was limitless and unashamed, tempered by irony but firmly compounded of the rich friendships he formed there and the literary fertility which its prewar renaissance encouraged and rewarded in him. He became a deviate legend in the collegiate world whose heroes were more characteristically the athlete, the rake, and the pious deacon. He wrote prolifically for and held office in both the *Yale Literary Magazine* and the *Record;* his fertility spilled over into unpublished drinking songs and gay satires of the local scene.

All his life Benét valued and preserved the friendships first formed at Yale, with John Farrar and Archibald MacLeish, Douglas Moore, Philip Barry, with Phelps Putnam and Shreve Badger and the Carter brothers and Effingham Evarts and scores of others. To each of them he presented a different side of his multiple personality: with Badger he schemed in the precinct politics of the senior societies; with Putnam he exchanged irreverent and robust poetic metaphor; with Farrar he was the young and briskly professional careerist.

Benét was the most celebrated member of the Class of 1919. Uncomplainingly he later wrote odes and salutes for the innumerable class books; he labored for his senior society long after its absurdities had surpassed, for him, its doubtful validity. In 1936, when the new Yale was being constructed out of the Harkness millions, he was appointed an Associate Fellow of Calhoun College; he shrewdly counseled another generation of undergraduates concerning the literary life.

He even considered an academic career, returning to Yale in the autumn of 1919 for a year of graduate study; by June he was appalled at the material poverty and eager for social and intellectual liberty. From the Yale Graduate School, however, he received not only Henry Canby's excellent instruction in composition but also the splendid bounty of a $500 traveling fellowship. From another of his professors, the late Edward Bliss Reed, he borrowed an additional $500 for his year in Paris. Yale, traditionally indifferent to the creative artist, was nevertheless a generous benefactor to Benét.

TO COLONEL JAMES WALKER BENÉT

New Haven, Conn.
September 1915

Dear Father:—

Well, I went around to Merritt [Alfred K. Merritt, Registrar of Yale College] today and he smiled consolingly (he's a very decent fellow really) and said "Nothing doing!" in polite terms. Call around some time at the end of the week he said and maybe then there'll be a vacancy. Everything's jammed up at present. I asked him what time to call and he said vaguely, oh some time near the end of the week or along there—a vacancy *might* happen any day. But all the same the accent is on the *not!*

Well this isn't a bad place here—large, airy etc— lighted only by gas, but Mrs. Conway is going to put a drop-light on my table—the trouble is it's somewhat off the center—a block above York [Street], where Pierson Hall and the other Freshman dorms. are. I can get my typewriter out of Pierson of course but the other things— well "there they might as well stand till they doon fa'!" I wish I hadn't been so darn precipitate about the furniture—but it was 10% off for cash in 10 days and at that time I had no doubts—God knows why!

. . . By the way about that $80.00. You sent me 50 and Bill sent me 30 (16 of which was yours and 14 his.)

Trunk (bringing it here & storage)	.75
Meals (Sunday night to Tuesday night)	2.30
Furniture (Damn!)	41.00
Telegrams	.87
Books (10 text etc.)	13.43
Athletic ticket (*Not* my Freshman ticket. I have to pay 15.00 for that)	4.00
Fountain pen	2.15
Magazines (A monstrous heap!)	1.60
Nail scissors, drugs etc.	.85
Short changed (unfortunate)	.25
Sundries (ha, ha)	.57
	67.77

80.00
67.77
———
12.23

Cash on hand therefore—

12.23. But 1.40 of this was mine personally originally —the last of the Hemp.[5]

∴. Cash on hand—

10.83 which is correct.

I deposited the check with the New Haven Bank and promptly drew a check for $14.00 and sent it to William as it's his. I will therefore account for this with the $100.00 as if I subtracted it from the remains of the 80.00 it would leave me with a minus 4.00—at which the brain reels!

An allowance—I don't know anything about amounts. What did my admirable brother get? Whatever you think best. . . .

I send you a poem I am sure you will appreciate—it's from *The Trimmed Lamp,* a nutty Chicago paper. Bill sent it to me—with comments. Honestly a scream!

> Unworthily
> Your devoted Son
> S.V.

TO SHREVE C. BADGER [6]

> 1712 H Street
> Washington, D.C.
> [July] 1918

Dear Shreve:—

I hope to God you haven't accepted an election to that bastardly Elihu Club. If you have cancel it! There

5. Stephen Vincent Benét, "The Hemp," *Century,* 91 (January 1916), 342–49.

6. Badger, who died in 1956, was one of Benét's close friends at Yale. They remained friends and correspondents for the next twenty-five years; one of Benét's last letters, not included in this collection, was to Badger.

is nothing in our [Wolf's Head] customs to prevent us taking a man in Elihu Club—but he forfeits his membership in E.C. by so doing—a thing which should not cause you great sorrow!

John [F. Carter, Jr.] [7] & I sent the telegram because I visited our New York headquarters the other day & the first thing P. M. Merrill asked me was your address which I gave him—probably incorrectly. You may be interested in the lists. They run as follows—the last elections, that is.

Bones	*Keys*	*Wolf's Head*
F. D. Carter	Wood	Ross
Gaillard	Schiefflin	- - - - -
J. S. Otis	de Cernea	Griggs
McCormick	Slocum	Badger
Mallon	Dann	Avery
	G. W. Otis	B. Robinson
		Herrick

The last five on our list have just been sent elections. Ross accepted. Elihu Club has sent out 7 elections—Rodman, I suppose—Philbin, I think—don't know the rest. E. T. Smith also refused an election to Keys.

Well, I can't tell you how damn glad I will be to share all the hush stuff we have so consistently blatted upon. God, but you'll be heavy though!

7. Carter, a contemporary of Benét at Yale, was one of his two roommates during the academic year 1919–20. He and Benét were fellow members of several undergraduate organizations, and both were among the early contributors to the New Haven little magazine, *S4N*. Carter later became an economic specialist for the State Department, and subsequently enjoyed a period of national prominence as a political commentator under the by-line Jay Franklin.

I am rather in a turmoil just at present as I shall probably enlist in the Medical Corps tomorrow. Write me at The Arsenal, Augusta, Ga. George [Achelis] is in the Navy too. John [F. Carter, Jr.] sails for Italy shortly. Write me anyway—and write a pretty little "Yes" to Harry Beadleston no matter what you have to do to do it.

When we all meet after the war ......

At least I can absolutely assure you of one thing— There is *one* Senior Society which does *not* believe in Prohibition! . . .

> As ever yours
> and soon to be
> yours in—
> Steve

TO JOHN FARRAR [8]

> Department of State
> Office of the Counselor
> Washington, D.C.
> December 14, 1918

Dear Johnny:—

Of course it was entirely characteristic that the moment you left Washington I should come down to it. Undoubtedly, now that I am leaving you will be coming back. Heaven knows I had enough trouble finding you at College—but since you have left we have been the

8. Another of Benét's Yale contemporaries, Farrar remained not only his close friend but also had a continuing professional association with him as editor, collaborator, and publisher. Farrar himself has had a successful career as editor of *The Bookman* during the 1920's and as a partner in the publishing houses of Farrar and Rinehart in the 1930's and 1940's and in Farrar, Straus, and Cudahy during the post-World War II period.

Halley kind of comets that only meet once in 110 years. I wrote you a letter last July in reply to one of yours—a letter you probably never got. Then I lost your address —and since then till about a week ago I have either been working more or less like a dog in various branches of the State Department or getting rapidly discharged from the army because my eyes still refuse to read the nice little black letters on the card. Are you coming back to America? Are you ever going to revisit Yale? Why don't you write me? Are you now a major? What on earth are you going to do when you become a civilian again? What do you think of Robert Graves' poetry? What has happened to Piff Underwood? Are you married, engaged, widowed or a father? These are but a few of the questions that agitate what little is left of my mind. As soon as you send me an address where mail has any likelihood of reaching you I will forward a copy of the world's sappiest *Young Adventure* for comment, discussion and guidance as we say in official communications. I am going back to New Haven around January First. If you come there LOOK ME UP!!!! I will probably be in Connecticut [Hall]—if you don't I will officially pronounce on you the Curse of Kehama.

Too much has happened to talk about in a letter, since I last saw you. As I say, I spent three happy days in the army and the rest of the time doing confidential work in this City of the Accursed. All my lovely companions have gone to the wars—with Timmy Coward and Bill Taylor I constitute a legion of the halt, blind and heart-diseased. Mr. Tinker [9] is a captain in MID here. My

9. Chauncey Brewster Tinker, one of the celebrated lecturers in a period of overpowering public figures on the Yale faculty,

brother has been learning to fly at Bolling Field. [John] Carter was here for a month before going to Rome. [Thornton]Wilder labored on the War Industries Board and then fled to the Coast Artillery. And that is or are all the human beings I have seen in seven months. Yale has been a camp variegated by Don Campbell and one sad issue of the *Lit*. But the next six months—the special Jan to July course [at Yale]—ought to be immortal.

As for the Senior Society affair—in case you didn't get my reply to your last letter—it is perfectly all right. I am satisfied and more than that where I am—which I should not have been in [Skull and] Bones. I wanted to go there last spring because of you, because of Alfred [Bellinger],[1] because of the Lit. tradition. But the delegation from [the Class of] 1919 I should never have gotten along with—except for Bunny Campbell I haven't a friend there —the rest are the people I never ran with, whom I always more or less made fun of *causa* heaviness, for the last three years. Don't think this is mere sour grapes or spitefulness—the other wasn't my galley, that is all, and I should have seen it in time. I respect it sincerely—but the ideals and ideas of the men in it from my class are not mine. . . .

was equally distinguished as a scholar whose particular field was the eighteenth century. He retired in 1945 as Sterling Professor of English Literature. He and Benét continued and extended their friendship during the 1930's and early 1940's as fellow members of the National Institute of Arts and Letters and the American Academy of Arts and Letters.

1. A friend of Benét both as an undergraduate and during the year which Benét spent at Yale as a graduate student, Alfred Bellinger remained at Yale as a teacher of the classics. Since 1939 he has been Lampson Professor of Latin.

[John] Andrews [2] is a Pursuit Observer, still in training
—if he hasn't killed himself since I last heard from him.
My lady-love [Grace Hendrick] is still single—bless her!
The Lizzy [Elizabethan] Club has become an athlete's
paradise since Charley Seymour and Frederick Luquiens [3] ran the committee. Most of my class have mus-
taches—very weak ones. And so, for the present, I remain

as ever

SVB

P.S. Address me at The Arsenal, Augusta, Ga. as I leave
here the 21st.

TO SHREVE C. BADGER

Department of State

Office of the Counselor

Washington, D.C.

December 19, 1918

Dear Shreve:—

At present expectations I will leave this infernal town
Saturday and trot up to New Haven around the 1st of
Jan. When do you get out of your silly navy or have you
already done so? I shall expect to have a drink with you
at Mory's within at least 1 hour after arriving in New
Haven—so fail me not! Just saw —— ——, who will
do [for Wolf's Head], though heavy. Have heard from

2. John Andrews, who succeeded Benét as chairman of the *Yale
Literary Magazine,* was the son of Charles MacLean Andrews, the
distinguished historian of colonial America.

3. Charles Seymour, president of Yale from 1937 until 1950,
was at this time an assistant professor of history. Frederick B.
Luquiens, a member of the Yale faculty from 1906 until his death
in 1940, became Street Professor of Modern Languages in 1935.

George [Achelis] whom the war has made a man of. I am rooming in Connecticut [Hall]—I will be damn poor—but Lord what a six months it will be!! Whee! Kick your venereal comrades for me. Just got a letter from John [Carter] full of exquisitely dirty limericks. My own H. Alger[4] is going to be reviewed in the [Boston] *Transcript.* What price Young Sappiness now?? Hastily, yours in W.H.S.

SVB

TO GUY HOLT[5]

Elizabethan Club
New Haven, Conn.
February [10] 1920

Dear Mr. Holt:—

Sincerest thanks for the material you so kindly sent me. It is of considerable [help]—and I think I will take your suggestion and write to Mr. [James Branch] Cabell too, in proper person. I wish I knew Mediaeval French!

I notice in the leaflet that 3 of his books are out of print. Could you tell me which?

I have *Jurgen, Beyond Life, The Certain Hour, From the Hidden Way*—the New Haven (alas not the University!) library has most of the others—except *The Eagle's Shadow.*

4. Stephen Vincent Benét, *Young Adventure,* Yale University Press, 1918. This was a selection from the poetry Benét had written since 1915.

5. Guy Holt, an editor of Robert McBride and Co., was a sturdy opponent of all attempts to censor Cabell's work. He edited *Jurgen and the Law* (1923) and in 1924 published an early bibliography of Cabell. He died in 1934.

Yes, I read of Jurgen & the Tumblebug. Sanscrit will soon be the only refuge for such un-*Cosmopolitan*, un-*American* authors. It sounds like the prologue to a Dunsany story—here's hoping that a Sphinx will arise and eat Mr. [John S.] Sumner in full court! [6]

Sincerely

Stephen Benét

TO SHREVE C. BADGER

York Street

New Haven, Conn.

April 30, 1920

Dear Shreve:—

Here are all the details I know. The only newspaper accounts were the N.Y. *Sun* and *Times* last Sunday. I was in N.Y. Monday the 19th and called at Dutton's to see George [Achelis]. They said he was sick—tonsilitis—and I thought nothing of it, of course. Apparently it was scarlet fever instead and though mild at first rapidly developed to the most malignant type. On Thursday he was getting along all right—somebody in New Haven called up. Saturday afternoon his heart stopped and he died. A private funeral took place the next day, Sunday. John [Carter] and I knew nothing of this at all—didn't even know he was badly ill—till Sunday night when Lefty [Wilmarth] Lewis who had heard from the Williams[es] told us the news. I don't think anything ever made me feel so sick and sorry and rebellious. There are

6. For an account of the attack on Cabell's novel see *Jurgen and the Censor*, ed. Edward Hale Bierstadt, Barrett H. Clark, and Sidney Howard, New York, 1920.

no words for it of course—I can't believe he's dead, even now. It is a dirty piece of bad irony—he was really happy and doing so well and being so nice—for the first time. Grace [his wife], they say, is taking it wonderfully. I am sorry for her—it is brutal—but I am still sorrier for George. I wanted him to come through and be able to snot on all the _____ and _____ —we all of us did— and he would have, with decent luck. As the notice said "omit flowers" we sent none, though I got your telegram. There will be no "whereas God in his infinite mercy" in the [*Yale Daily*] *News* either if John & I can stop it— we have all kidded each other too much about that sort of thing. If I hear anything else, I will write you it— there will be a notice in the *Alumni Weekly*, I suppose.

There is nothing that can be said—as I said before— you know how I feel. I was very fond of George and keep remembering him.[7]

When are you going to be East [from Chicago] and is it in time for Reunion? I expect to sail on the 6th of July if I can get any sense out of the French Line. Bet your shirt on the [Yale] crew. Will you tell me what address you want me to wire the list to you at, Tap Day? Brace yourself and be ready for a shock when you get it—we are going to get knocked, at present. But things are started in 1922 and in 1923 we'll clean. I must stop. Answer.

As ever, yours in W.H.S.
Steve

7. Two months later, during the early summer of 1920, when Benét was preparing his second collection of verse—*Heavens and Earth*—for publication by Holt that fall, he dedicated the volume to Achelis.

TO SHREVE C. BADGER

York Street
New Haven, Conn.
June 4, 1920

Dear Shreve:—

We have finally gotten together on the question of a gift for the [Wolf's Head] Hall. Dean Worcester is to get it—triple-plated, bottled in bond, water-pitchers—solid silver & cut-glass cost too much and, as you know, we are woefully lacking in millionaires.

Will you send $10, or as much more as you can afford to Dean at 137 E. 39 St. N.Y.? . . . And write me, you fat person & say if you are coming on for Reunion. It's your only chance to see us all alive again.

Yrs. in W.H.S.
Steve

The Road to Paris: 1920

IMMEDIATELY after Commencement in June 1920, Benét settled in with his family at the Watervliet (N.Y.) Arsenal. The Colonel had returned to his former station after almost twenty years, this time as commanding officer during the last few months before retirement.

Benét brought with him to Watervliet the group of new poems which the Yale Graduate School had accepted in lieu of the conventional M.A. thesis. Now he sent them to Henry Holt and Company, who accepted them for publication that autumn under the title *Heavens and Earth.* During the summer, however, Benét laid aside poetry for the moment, grimly determined to write a novel which, he hoped, would raise an advance from Holt; he needed a supplement for his traveling fellowship to Paris. He did not get the advance before sailing time, but at the end of August he sailed anyway, an early instance of his generation's restless, eastward movement.

In Paris he stayed briefly at the right bank home of his munitions-making Uncle Larry, managing director of La Société Hotchkiss et Cie. Soon, when his friends and classmates began to arrive in Paris, Benét took a small apartment in Montparnasse with Henry Carter and Stanley Hawks. He mixed hard work with left bank gaiety.

"The early 1920s in Paris," he said nostalgically in 1940, "were something that will not happen again for a long time." By November, when he received his author's copies of *Heavens and Earth,* he had finished *The Beginning of Wisdom.*

The work of his maturity—*John Brown's Body,* "The Devil and Daniel Webster," the wartime radio scripts, *Western Star*—would identify him permanently with the rediscovery of America by her writers, but Paris was his favorite city and he would spend more than half this decade as one of her numerous American foster citizens. In 1920 and 1921 Paris became permanently memorable for him. Here began the relationship he valued above all others. In November 1920, at the apartment of his lifelong friends, Richard and Alice Lee Myers, he met Rosemary Carr of Chicago; by the end of December, as the last letter of this group indicates, she was already a recurrent figure in his letters home.

TO SHREVE C. BADGER

Watervliet Arsenal
Watervliet, N.Y.
August 2, 1920

Dear Shreve:—

. . . Written 36,000 words in the last month—a good deal of it on this novel [*The Beginning of Wisdom*]. You appear in it, by the way, a lifelike, if somewhat flattering portrait. I have had a lot of fun with the college stuff— I think it is pretty accurate stuff though somewhat local & a good deal less gaudy & Sophomore Don Juanish than F. Scott Fitz. But the three drunk scenes were a sheer pleasure to do. Don't be alarmed! I haven't blackened your character—much.

A. E. Newton's book is delightful. By the way, do you read the N.Y. *Post* Book Review. Without undue family pride in Bill, I think it's the best thing of its sort in some time.

Oh I lead such a healthy life, work, tennis, scrub baseball with the post children who think I'm fine & in a class with Ty Cobb! I'll send you "H & E" [*Heavens and Earth*] if it comes out before I leave, which it won't, or leave instructions to have one sent you with the family. Too much of this garrulity—and the end of the page—

Very best to you & all yours

As ever, yrs in W.H.S.

Steve

TO JOHN FARRAR

Watervliet Arsenal
Watervliet, N.Y.
[August] 1920

[page missing]

And what has happened to you, anyway, and have they all run out of that nice paper with worlds and farrars rampant on it that they keep in your misbegotten materialistic journalistic unstylistic cystic and phististic office? [8] Why don't you come up here for the weekend some time with Bill, it would cost you a large sum of money and you probably don't like to play tennis, but you would

8. Farrar, after being discharged from the army in 1919, was working as a reporter on the New York *World*.

have the benefit of my enchanting conversation and see
how you liked the venomous portrait of yourself I have
just stuck into Bk. II of my bunk novel? No, you are not
the Portuguese girl heroine. The damn thing marches
slowly and in as bad order as the first parade of the
Yale R.O.T.C. and I can't possibly finish it before August
28 when I sail for Foreign in the Finland or the Lapland,
and, oh lookie, if you know any dope on the I.W.W. de-
portations from Bisbee [Arizona] in 1917, book, pamphlet or newspaper account, shoot it to me that's a good
lad, I need it like hell for Bk. IV which so far exist[s]
entirely in vacuo, like one's children before one is twelve
or thirteen. I haven't written any poetry for months. But
since July 3 with interruptions I have written 26,000
words and torn up 8,000 of them. Oh well, Life is a
dream, yo ho!

. . . Did you see Masefield's letter to Archie [Mac-
Leish] re *Parabalou,* very swell indeed. Have you heard
anything from [Danford] Barney re new stuff [for *Parabalou*]? I think he is peeved at me, why I don't know
. . . It is wet here—it rains once a day but doesn't hurt
the concrete tennis-court. The abstract tennis-court on
which we play metaphysical tennis (final round All
Comers Tinker and Donne d. Mason and Plato [9] by a
neck, half-a-boat length and two syllogisms) is of course
permanently impaired by it and good lord what nonsense
I am righting (oh dear, writing, this typewriter has all of

9. Chauncey Brewster Tinker and Lawrence Mason, each a
dynamic and possessive teacher, were a pair of feuding professors
in the Department of English at Yale. Tinker, insofar as local and
departmental politics were concerned, won.

THE ROAD TO PARIS

the seven red devils that were cast out of the Gadarene swine).

Well, anyhow, come up here if you can and let me know if you can't. I am going up to a weddin' in Baa Harbor on 20th of Aug. and will go through N.Y. of a probability on the way back and so possibly see you if you wish to be seen. That sounds rather formal, doesn't it? It is the influence of Trollope on my style. Rather one trollop by the hand than two Trollopes under the eye. Oh whee, this must end. Now write me a nice long amusing letter that isn't as foolish as this.

Affectionately
marlow jr.

P.S. My regards to your mother.

TO LAURA BENÉT

Watervliet Arsenal
Watervliet, N.Y.
August 1920

Dear Girl:—

Your "Mill" [unpublished poem] received and admired. It is a powerful piece of writing—and you handle it with terseness, vigor and some admirable similes. It also has necessarily the defects of its qualities, defects which are almost unavoidable in the first draft of anything that comes from the heart.

1. Don't like the image of the Mill as a beast. True— but the beast image has been used so frequently of a modern factory that it has become worn. And the use of such large, violent & more or less well known images unavoidably leads to rhetoric. There is some rhetoric in

the piece, not much, but some, and in as short a piece as that, every sentence stands out like a capital letter.

2. Now these people. Their condition in the mill is vile but their life in the mountains—at least among a lot of the poor-white class such as we saw up by Highlands [North Carolina]—is not that of an entirely healthy hardy peasantry. Nor are all the mill-workers recruited from the mountains. You leave the impression, in my mind at least that they are.

3. First page.

"The Mill .... sprang on rich soil."
Here spring is used in one sense while right afterwards when you talk of the mill's springing not at a bound but assiduously, you seem to use it in another sense.

4. A "misplaced" Methodist church. Is it exactly "misplaced"? Isn't that just where the church ought to be?

5. Like your similes, as I say, in general very much. "Homespun" etc.—can't find place just now.

6. These criticisms, of course, are personal. But I don't want [you] to fall into rhetoric when "It Pleases Me to Remember" is so startlingly free of it. I like this. I think it's very good. I merely think it needs a little attention in spots.

I am certainly as glad as can be that you are having this time—it is the best thing in the world for you to do. Finish your novel by all means even if you have to take extra weeks to do it—the hardest thing about writing is the picking up of a loose thread. I have just got about half-way through mine, so I suppose I ought to be satisfied. At least I have written and typed 30,000 words on it since July 1st, besides writing & typing 10,000 words on other things & doing 8,000 words on it that I had to afterwards discard. If I had any idea of the magnitude of the task I would have made arrangements not to sail till October, but it is too late now to change.

I'm awfully afraid I can't get up to Peterborough [N.H.], much as I want to. You see the Albany-Boston-Bar Harbor route I have picked & the one for various reasons best for me to go by, has such beastly connections that I have to leave here at night on the 18th to be absolutely sure of getting to the wedding. And the Peterborough-Worcester connections would tangle that up inextricably. If I work here *hard* I can get five books of my novel pretty well done and in a condition perhaps to send to Holt & get a decision—and trust to the foreign Mails with as little mss. as possible. If I don't, I can't. And Lord knows I need the money. . . . Luck to you & Hilda & get her done. I love you. I have been playing baseball violently with the children.

As ever, your devoted
Steve

TO PHELPS PUTNAM [1]

Watervliet Arsenal
Watervliet, N.Y.
August 11, 1920

Dear Phelps:—

The hero of my novel [*The Beginning of Wisdom*]—who you may remember in his diaper days when he was

1. Howard Phelps Putnam, 1894–1948, a promising poet throughout his unhappy life, and a friend of Benét since their days as contributors to *Parabalou* in 1919. For a judicious summary of Putnam, see F. O. Matthiessen, "The Broken Arc," *The Responsibilities of the Critic* (New York, 1952), 256–76.

getting run through and through by a barbed & golden thought—has just passed his 40,000 word & been shipped out of Arizona in a box-car with some I.W.W.'s. Now most of my Arizona & I.W.W. stuff I have dug out of other sources, travel articles by some eyeglassed duck's egg of a man who writes for *Scribner's* & labor reports & the *Liberator* etc—but I remember 3 things, or the skeletons of them, out of your letters to Fred [Manning] that I'd like to use if it isn't poaching on your literary property & trespassers will be shot. 1. First sight of cowboy & feelings thereabout. 2. Prices in Bisbee & your remark that the I.W.W. club there had the only good library etc in town. 3. Description of Bisbee whoretown. Of course I'll put these things in my own words (a) I should scorn to plagiarize directly (b) I can't remember yours anyway. If you want these details for any work of your own, past, present & future, tell me so & I'll excise 'em—if you don't, I'd like to have 'em for it's dam hard to get the color of the ground of some place you've never been and gone to, drunk or sober. This guy's got to be chased out of Arizona to start him going again, he's a sort of human roulette-ball for 2 Books & generally lands on the double zero at that.

I'm sailing for France the 28th at present advices. I wish I could finish this novel before leaving but it isn't possible—that's all. Have you been writing any poetry? I suppose you saw Fred [Manning] safely off to connubial joys. I have lived a quiet, working, hard-eating life . . . *Parabalou* seems to have made a hit with the English Poet Laureate—I wish he would send us over his yearly cask of canary that he gets as salary. Did you ever read a book called *Birth* by Zona Gale—no, it isn't dirty—it's interesting, all about a six year old who painted God with his water-color box as a wash of pure blue. I'd like to have painted him pink. But the lad had originality all the same. My best to the Spanish mule-tender & his amorous love with the thighs or whatever they were.

Yours in the Hedge

PEDRO BENÉT

P.S. I have those copies of your poems. Do you want them?

TO ETHEL ANDREWS [2]

1 Ave. Camoens
Paris, France
[November] 1920

Dear Ethel:—

Congratulations and all my best on your engagement and marriage which I heard of a little while ago. These great events and the news of them take, of course, about as long a time in reaching us over here as the news of the War did in penetrating the back mountains of North Carolina. If you'd only gotten married over here, as every nice girl should, I would even have been able to give you a wedding present but the thought of sending one from Paris to the Tang Tze Kiang via New Haven rather staggers me. You undoubtedly wouldn't get it till you were 77 and probably some mandarin would hock it on the way as a supposititious bird's nest and served it up for soup. However as Dr. Johnson said, if the friendliest

2. Daughter of Professor Charles MacLean Andrews, the colonial historian. Benét had admired her father and taken his course at Yale, and become a close friend of both Ethel and her brother John, a member of the Class of 1920 at Yale.

wishes of a faithful heart will impress you with ever
a semblance of transitory joy—they are yours. And when
I come back I will bring a gargoyle or a concierge or
some such trifle to set up in 424 Saint Ronan St. in your
memory. New Haven will certainly not be the same place
without you and Trudy [Wells]. I've just seen the latter,
by the way, delightful and beautiful as ever, . . . Alors
or [*Chinese characters*], give my best to John [Andrews]
and tell the ungrateful child Quixote to write me. I am
well and enjoying life. Henry [Carter], Bruce Simonds,
Doug Moore, Quincy Porter etc. etc. are all here working or playing with much avidity. John [Carter] is in
Rome destroying our foreign policy and the morals of
the ambassador. Better plan to return from Wangpoo via
Paris—in a dozen years or so—and then you, who will insist on eating entirely with chopsticks and sitting on the
floor and I who will have grown fat and a beard, will
drink absinthe with the Chief of Police and talk of times
past.

> affectionately
> Steve

TO PHELPS PUTNAM

> Hotel de Blois
> rue Vasin
> Paris, France
> November [8] 1920

Dear Phelps:—

Now, as age creeps over me, I wonder did I ever answer
your last letter all about Black Pedro & your own pro-
phylactic ladies? I fear not and I should have for it

gave me absurd joy for two whole days of a hardworking summer. But now, as I sit writing & looking out at Autumn dying in her golden chair in the Luxembourg Gardens, having just had a delicious aperitif that cost me almost 7 cents in an adjoining bar, I will see if like Ariadne or was it another of those mythological guys? I can pick up the labyrinth & thread the clue.

First—Your Prostitutes

They have undergone several changes & now I hope will either appear sufficiently disguised for you to reuse them—or will not appear at all. They are merely an incident in my particular thing—taking three or four typewritten pages. Perhaps it will be better to exise them entirely. In any case I will try hard not to take advantage of a childlike & generous nature.

2. Paris

You would like this town. In fact if you ever got here it would be like rooting up the well known mandrake to get you away. It is full of liquor, amusing people & incredibly beautiful works of art. Come across if you have to crack the box (no puns intended) of the Farrell Foundry Corporation to do so. We may go through England this summer in a drygoods van as wandering Belgians who don't speak English. At least it is a thought.

3. Poe

And did you ever hear how Poe came to be damned? Well, the poor thing was sitting under an apple tree—and up comes Shelley & Marlowe & Catullus to have a talk. They passed the boozing-can around awhile as boys will & sang a few proper dirty songs & then Poe met Boueleis the Clown & went to the Devil's Sunday and—oh well, if it can be written I'll have a damn good time.

1920

Are you performing on the bitter Jewsharp at all? My
best to Alfred & Charlotte [Bellinger], Fred [Manning]
& Mrs. also if seen. Also to Sims, Bill Krieger & Don
Campbell. A sly half-arse to Professor Kent [Woolsey
Professor of Biblical Literature at Yale].

Yours in the Panpipes

SVB

TO MRS. JAMES WALKER BENÉT

American University Union
Paris, France
December 1920

Dearest Mother:—

The Christmas draft arrived—to be received with open
arms & fireworks & immense love & thanks to you all. I
am not quite sure what I will spend it on yet—probably
on keeping out of jail—but will render a lively account
to all you generous & lovely people when I do. Aunt
Margaret gave me a beautiful cane—Indian bamboo—&
Uncle Larry my grandfather's watch which the latter
had bought at Leroy's in Paris in 1854—really a price-
less gift. It was all renovated & running beautifully.
Christmas dinner there was a knockout—a perfect meal
& gorgeous wines. I took a Countess in to dinner—a
thing I shall probably never do again. . . . Also the
revillon party at Catherine's & Rosemary's was most
amusing—Doug [Moore] sang his songs & people did
stunts, drank punch & in general were amusing. . . .

By the time you get this the New Year will have come
in, 1921! the numbers get more absurd & Wellsian each
year. Well, let's hope the little ivory ball will drop into

the very right pocket for the whole Family & pay 37 to 1 —it's quite time, I think!

I am going to try & start another novel [*Jean Huguenot*]—a short one. Hope Don [Campbell] and JCF[arrar] both come up & see you—you will be charmed with them both . . . Send Phelps Put[nam] a present for me—he is a grand man—& thank you *so* for sending the other people. It was sweet & nobody but you would have thought of it. It was warm as milk here for a few days —everybody flourishing canes on the boulevards & drinking & eating on the sidewalk—now it has turned muggy.

Embrace the children for me [3]—I've seen some of the grandest toy-children in a place on the Rue St. Pères— cavaliers & Old Guard & a little leaden poilu being decorated by a stiff tin general with the Legion of Honor. I love you. I suppose the serial rights thing has blown-up by now.[4] Alas! Well I'll try to sell the next one to Hearst's itself. Love. Love.

Your devoted son
SVB

3. William Rose Benét's three children had been living with Colonel and Mrs. Benét since the death of William's wife, Teresa, in 1919.

4. *The Beginning of Wisdom* was eventually serialized in *Bookman* during the summer of 1921.

Courtship (1920-1921)

BENÉT's love for Rosemary Carr was the single most important element in his life. All the qualities which he had hitherto scattered variously through the other compartments of his young manhood—the warmth of his friendships, the serenity of his affection for his family, the intensity of his poetry, the profound convictions about America—were gathered together now in his relationship with Rosemary.

His romanticism was matured and maintained and made creatively fruitful; a love story like theirs, begun in Paris, persisting despite the obstacles of poverty and insecurity and parental opposition, consummated at the moment when editors began to buy his short stories, profoundly and continuously meaningful until the very instant when he died in her arms in 1943, was a confirmation of all his durable idealism.

His abundant fertility, which might have sputtered into prolonged preciosity, solidified instead into a purposeful and adult credo. Now there was an object adequate to his talent. "You would make an anteater burst into madrigals," he told her in one of these Paris *pneumatiques* of their courtship. And so he wrote poems to her all his life, in the letters of these first months together, on the

39

cards which accompanied the gifts by which he always celebrated the anniversaries of their engagement on St. Patrick's Day, on the backs of household lists. In 1925 he collected many of the best of them in *Tiger Joy*, but almost two decades later he was writing them yet.

Now the mind rusts into madness, the horses run without
   bit,
The paltry body is nothing but mechanics of bone and
   skin.
Nevertheless I have spoken. This nothing spoke for its
   kin
And loved one woman completely. Let her remember it.[5]

Their marriage had the luminous splendor of a fairy tale; their three children were handsome and talented and happy, and when he died so suddenly in March 1943, in the midst of his labors for his country, his wife said that her life had begun in one March, when they became engaged, and now was ended in this other March twenty-two years later. Here, in a Paris winter and spring in 1920 and 1921, is the beginning.

TO ROSEMARY CARR

Paris, France
December 20, 1920

Dear Rosemary:—

Would you like to have lunch with Henry [Carter] & myself tomorrow (Tuesday)? If so (and I may say that such is our hope) will you phone or pneumatic Henry

5. Stephen Vincent Benét, "Little Testament," *Atlantic Monthly*, 172 (October 1943), 57.

(sounds curious & like a tire advertisement but you know what I mean) at the Farmer's Loan & Trust, 41 Blvd Hausmann, saying where & when to meet you. Regards.

Stephen Benét

P.S. Have you fed the white kitten?

TO ROSEMARY CARR

Paris, France
February 14, 1921

Dear Rosemary:—

Will you have lunch with me tomorrow (Tuesday)? Will meet you Prunier's, 12.30.

Steve

TO ROSEMARY CARR

Paris, France
February 19, 1921

Dear Jane:—

Well then, what are you and Jezebel [the cat] doing Sunday. Lunch? dinner? tea? walk? swim? fence? church? movies? basketball? etc? if so—where? when?

. . . Honestly though, you have no idea what silly things may happen to me from not seeing you for 2½ days.

Lunch at the Ritz
Uncle at the Ritz
Gives very nice people extreme gastric fits.

All this sounds inane. But I have worked all day & then gone to a movie. They are bad for the mind &

handwriting. Answer. Thanks for your letter. It was nice of you to write. Doug [Moore] [6] is going to put the poem about you & the pig ["A Sad Song"] to music.

With a short blasphemous cry

SVB

TO ROSEMARY CARR

Paris, France
February 21, 1921

Dear Rosemary:—

Will you have lunch with me tomorrow (Tuesday). Prunier's. 12.30? I'll wait. If you don't arrive—I'll be sorry—Lord knows!—but understand.

Steve

TO ROSEMARY CARR

Paris, France
February 24, 1921

Dear Jane:—

It's the devil not seeing you for 2 days—but since you work, so be it. I'll work or something. I hope you weren't too tired by seeing the moon & fog so much the other night.

You are *never* boring. Simple, declarative sentence— (Example 1).

I will ask Stan [Hawkes] about Ritz but don't think

6. Douglas Moore, the distinguished American composer, had first met Benét at Yale in 1915. Their friendship became increasingly close after they returned to the United States, and included several effective collaborations on operettas during the 1930s. Moore has been MacDowell Professor of Music at Columbia since 1943.

he'll have much dope. Did you put in those Semple birds he knows?

Saw A.[lice] L.[ee Myer]s' infant. It is small, hairy, effective & intelligent. A great contrast to both lumpy ones & the *Woman's Home Companion* cover kind. A pleasing child, though, of course, as yet, immature.

You write very nice letters.

Regards
Steve

TO ROSEMARY CARR

Paris, France
February 24, 1921

A KEEPSAKE SONG [7]

The bee, he has white honey,
The Sunday child her muff,
The rich man much money
Though never quite enough.
The apple has a Springtime smell,
The starfield's silver grain,
But I have youth the cockleshell,
And the sweet laugh of Jane!

The dogs run cock-and-feather
For joy of shifting speed.
The sailor likes fine weather,
The fool likes his breed.
They grow too proud with talking loud,
Too sly with staying vain.

7. Benét published the first stanza of this poem under the title "Dulce Ridentem" in *Tiger Joy* (New York, 1925), p. 63.

43

I blow and yaw like windlestraw
And hear the laugh of Jane.

The lark's tune goes so clearly
But Jane's is clear wells,
The cookoo's voice currs cheerly
But Jane's is new bells.
Whether she chuckles like a dove
Or laughs like April rain,
It is her heart and hands and love,
The moth-wing soul of Jane.

TO ROSEMARY CARR

Paris, France
February 26, 1921

Dear Jane:—

I write such nice notes because of my worthy nature.

Your notes, though brevity itself, are quite heavenly. Still, I would rather see you, even. Curious.

Glad you liked the poem. Last 4 lines of 2nd verse weak, I think.—tend to *vers de société*. Rest as good as I can do in that line (a proud simile). Which is what I wished.

> "For what, thou painted parrot, Fame,
> —What have I taught thee but her name?"

[continued on a second *pneumatique*]

This correspondence is putting me to inordinate expense. While you have only to write ordinary letters. Unfair.

Stan has no stuff on Ritz. Too boiled or something.

Oh how laconic!

Do you believe in irony as a salvation?

I wish I were Francis Thompson. I could write you

44

better things—& you wouldn't have to look at the dictionary very often.

If the cat scratches you, I will kill it.

This sounds more and more like a Latin grammar. Balbus built a wall.
Played bridge till 3 A.M. last night. Hard on the eyes, temper, Eustachian canal.

Steve

TO SHREVE C. BADGER

Paris, France
[March] 1921

Dear Shreve:—

A letter from you would be welcome, but I suppose I owe you one & know your sense of the justice of things too well to think you would write me under such conditions. Besides you have probably heard from returning Americans that I have gone to pieces in Paris & am now head of an opium-joint, picking butterflies off the walls of Montmartre. Instead of which I am happy to say that I am well except for a bad cold, have written 4 short stories & 6 poems in the last month & only got drunk once—you see I am Trying to Conquer that Degrading Habit of putting an enemy into your mouth to steal away your brains. I won't try to make your tongue hang out with envy by describing the food, the drink, the weather, the city—their extreme excellence all round. You would love Paris & be a perfectly delightful person to show it to—I can pay you no higher compliment. I am rather broke & rather happy—rather worried over various affairs which adopting [John] Carter's mysteriousness I will not

45

commit to paper—& rather glad I'm young. Also, as an item of information, I am still a virgin to present date. Probably you are not. Chicago is a wicked city. If anything important is happening to you—marriage, syphilis, a partnership in Farwell, Knapp—write me about it—I would like to hear from you, you know. Did you ever receive the small ivory badger that my mother fell in love with in a jewelry store & bought for you—only to discover when she brought it home that it was not a badger but a beaver & hence inappropriate to send you? [John] Carter is living like God's favorite son now in Rome—he dines with Dukes & makes Thornton [Wilder] green with envy. Any dope on WHS from you would be appreciated.

. . . Dan Barney & Trudy are going to have a child. Some of my works are going to be translated into French. I don't know why those 2 sentences should go together. Heard from the statuesque [Effingham] Evarts who devoted 6 pages to cursing out the faults in my novel. A typical Evarts letter which warmed the heart to receive . . . Did you get my poems?—you were sent a copy. I must quit—I'm really working. My best to your family. Write.

As ever, yrs. in W.H.S.
Steve

TO ROSEMARY CARR

Paris, France
March 6, 1921

Sweet Creature:—

I never see you enough. It goes by too fast. There you are—a minute—and before I have time to really look at you through that minute—you're gone. No matter how long the time actually is. Now this isn't just.

Oh Jane, Jane, Jane. I love you an awful lot this morning! I get inarticulate thinking about it. It means so everything in the world to me—all heaven and humor—and to you? I want to kiss you. Send me "a constructive or mental" token of affection. I dreamt last night you had sent me the French National Library by *pneumatiques* & I was settling down to read it with a feeling of utter satisfaction when Henry [Carter] woke me. Freud, says you? I guess love came before Freud. I guess this is a lunatic pneu.—but oh, my darling I love you and so much it hurts except when I'm with you & I'm glad it hurts & I'm yours always

Steve

TO ROSEMARY CARR

Paris, France
March 18, 1921

Darling: (since I can say it now.)

I want to poke myself to make sure that I'm real. It is too incredible & wonderful.

What I want to do really is to run hotfoot to the [Chicago] *Tribune* office & take you away from your typewriter & make you come and have tea at 11 o'clock A.M. some place where I could kiss you. But c'est pas permis. Have a nice time on the Hilltop on the Marne. And think of me once in a while.

Would you prefer to have been first kissed in the little old back street in Paris outside of a bar, an Italian restaurant or a printing plant? I stood there in the rain this morning like a fool trying to decide which it was. All might be symbolical except the Italian restaurant. I don't know what that would stand for.

Henry is a sound sleeper. He merely swore mildly when I came in, started to sing & asked him to tell me a fairy story. Three cheers for his somnolence.

Dream last night. Both going to the North Pole (i.e., lack of blankets), I, peevishly "I don't mind its being so cold, Jane, but I think you might have stocked the ship with something beside hot-water bottles! What will we do when we meet the Eskimos?"

This is all very trivial & amorous & delightful & brightly contenting—to tell you all these silly things.

If you say any more about artistic careers, I will shake you. Remember. I fully intend to spoil yours.

There are too many things to say to write most of them. I love you. And I am so proud & happy that you love me —though I don't see how you can—that I feel as if I were mad or translated or something. I love you. You are so sweet & kind & humorous & true. I am not worthy of you, Jane, but I will try to be. I miss you & want you now and always. We will be jocular lovers & play tunes on irony's ancient ribs for fun—and ride comedy whenever we want to—you and I. I love you.

Steve

TO ROSEMARY CARR

Paris, France
March 19, 1921

Jane, dear:—

This is a nice & bright morning & with its face well-washed & in spite of all the funerals trailing up Montparnasse. Tried to stupify myself with tobacco, W. S. Hart & Mrs. Gaskell last night—how badly the last 2 would have got along!—but only succeeded in having a series of imaginary conversations with you, with people I wanted to describe you to, with God about you (short & irreverent), etc. etc. If you knew how everything goes back to you in my mind from any remark, contact, sight or anything else—I can think about you from any position, Greco Roman, catch as catch can, balk-line or chopstroke. The mention of tigers for instance only brings up the consideration of how singularly you differ from a tiger. Whee!

> Zenocrate, lovelier than the love of Jove,
> Brighter than is the silver Rhodope,
> Fairer than whitest snow on Scythian hills.

Now that is the way I'd like to write about you. But Marlowe had the style. Write me for Pete's sake. You don't know how rotten it is, being apart for two days. Or rather, Jane dear, I hope you do.

I don't see how you can love me. I am Lord George Hell.

And I have to rush to *Passy* & get some mail.[8]

Do you think about me at all? Or only of Loulous & typewriters and mushroom-machets?

We are going to live in Italy in a palazzo. Or in Norway in a fjord. Turn into krakens. No, you couldn't be a kraken—you can't swim.

I miss you like hell. I kiss you in my mind—but it isn't quite satisfactory. I love you. It is something deep in the heart that hurts and warms. We *will* be married in

8. Benét's mailing address in Paris at this time was his Uncle Larry's home on the Avenue de Camoens.

November. I love everything about you from the golddust in your hair to your chuckle. Darling.

Always
Steve

TO ROSEMARY CARR

Paris, France
March 19, 1921

Friday 9 P.M.

Jane dear:—

Good morning!

Steve

Note (Of course this accursed thing will probably arrive 4.30 P.M. Sat.)

TO ROSEMARY CARR

Paris, France
March 23, 1921

Jane dear:—

You *must* come to one particular spot in the Luxembourg around 5.30, when next in this quarter. I am defiling it at present with bad cigarettes—but there is grass so green it doesn't look real way across to a green brass lion, head up, howling at a pine tree. And there are decorative kids & people & 3 big trees Corot-y with green buds & a pink bush & a pigeon & the light is like melted pumpkin-pie. You ought to be here—you belong to things like that. Not pie—no, didn't mean. Maybe you will as a ghost. "Kind of mellowish, warmish feeling." And now a proud baby is coming by & there are 6 birds making remarks. "Seldom the time & the place—"

SVB who loves you

TO ROSEMARY CARR

Paris, France
March 24, 1921

Oh phantom Jane!

Thanks for the spirit-photograph. At least you died happy. Anyhow it's more fun & more characteristic to have than a beautiful blurred cabinet one would be.

I have just been having a beautiful time explaining American tailoring to a French tailor. He thinks it mad.

When am I seeing you Friday? Are you going to church or anything? Tell me.

There are too many ladies with blue dresses & large hats in Paris. I get shocks every time I see one & it always isn't you.

Now I'll go back & write you a nice poem.

Oh, Rosemary Jane!
Steve

TO ROSEMARY CARR

Paris, France
April 1, 1921

Darling:—

It makes me ill that that bland pullet should be staying at Alice Lee's! However, doubtless she is a nice athletic girl—and I got several moments of exquisite self-pity out of it later. Why haven't I got $5,000 a year?

Write me nicely, remembering when you do that I haven't had a chance to kiss you for 19 years & am a shepherd dog kind of person that needs affection.

Masefield has a nice sonnet with a line

"In the clear March of a most sacred year."

I shall appropriate. Or plagiarize.

And I didn't get a chance to give you the poem about you & your pack of hounds. Should be surreptitious & clever. Oh dear!

Don't send your letter to your family off till I have a chance to enclose my manly note in it. The last will perfectly breathe the calisthentic spirit of the YMCA. . . .

I will be so discreet at dinner with my aunt tomorrow. Discreet but with immense, internal laughter. Oh Jane, I love you, I love you, I love you.

Always
Steve

TO ROSEMARY CARR

Paris, France
April 3, 1921

July [9]

Now that the air is spice & heat,
Now there are portly moons,
Oh children, lift your voices sweet
In the high, happy times!

Let all your fledgling voices sing
Like thrushes in the corn,
In praise of her, the fairyest thing
Since all good elves were born.

9. Benét published the third stanza of this poem in *Tiger Joy*, under the title, "Chemical Analysis."

The cowslip & the cherry,
Are Summer's bread & wine,
But she's more kind & merry
But she's more salt & fine.

She's slender hands and pretty lips
And seafoam & rosemary.
Her legs are pointed at the tips,
She stayed so long in Faery.

Oh "Love's a fool!" say all the wise,
"Young man, keep cool, keep cool!"
But while such honor's in her eyes
I'll be a perfect fool.

tout forever

Some of this will have to be changed—it lurches a bit in spots, don't you think? And now for some refreshing tea!

TO ROSEMARY CARR

Paris, France
April 5, 1921

Jane dear:—

A Business

Doug & Emily [Moore] want you & Cath for dinner Thursday. Me & some other people to be there (conceited phrasing!). Em. says will you & C. pneu. her re this date. See you tomorrow—Wednesday 7.30 unless otherwise informed. Can go to movie or look at Seine or something.

Do you want to see Mistinguett in *Madame Sans Coeur* Fr. night? Tell me & I will get tickets. Or for anything else you want.

Missed you greatly at A.L.'s at tea today—what is food or drink sans Jane? However A.L. says she thinks you can keep me guessing. And this is no idea—'tis a certainty, my young divinity!

> This goddamn bureau is closing. Rats! love
> Steve

TO ROSEMARY CARR

Paris, France
April 5, 1921

And may you sleep well & may the particular angels that have charge of you look over their silly wings & be arrogant that they have such a job as that. Don't dream —particularly about me—unless you want to, now we find we both have read Freud. But I can't say all the tenderness that comes into my mind when I think of you, for fear of being sentimental before you who are not sentimental but only kind & humorous & proud and delicate & brave. I enclose some remarks about your name from your favorite paper. Everybody will be sore at me for calling you Jane when you have such a nicer name already. But then everybody never knows anything. I miss you. It will be the devil when you are in Chicago & I in N.Y. but worth it. Il faut souffrir—I suppose. Good night, dearest, dearest.

Stephen

TO ROSEMARY CARR

Paris, France
April 21, 1921

Look here now, not again for so long, *please*. Anyhow we could have lunch or tea even if you have to write letters

54

or work on anything else at night. I am *miserable* without you. Of course I missed your pneu yesterday—missed it like the devil & did little work. This novel [*Jean Huguenot*] I live in gets too much like a morbid psychological detective story without your presence. What's the matter with your family—whatever it is they shouldn't depress you too. Of course I will stop at Tronchet—Friday night. The lady who owns this hotel is Madame Cresson—write me some more—your letters are the best & nicest things in the world except you yourself. They taste like you—no that sounds too Scottfitzgeraldy & like cream puffs. I love you always & want to see you so I can't think about anything else.

TO ROSEMARY CARR

Paris, France
April 21, 1921

My Jane:—

All the little girls in the quarter have been getting confirmed at N.D. des Champs today & are now coming back, bun-eating & bridy in white dresses with proud bourgeois families beside. I sit in front of Lavenue's, drink vermouth, write you, & cast spiteful agnostic glances at them. Or not spiteful—they're too roundfaced & innocent looking. Puppies after a bath.

Wrote 2½ hours. The book goes on—pedestrianly, but still, ça marche. This part is all about ostracism and palmistry.

Been rereading your unique pneus. Always you. I miss you, alanna. Or is that an Irish battlecry? It's me that never had the Gaelic. . . . I remind myself much of your dead friend Barbellion. Introspective & always

55

doubtful of happiness. But then you come *propria persona* & everything's all right.

A delightful book—*They Went* by Norman Douglas. A tapestry out of all bounds of space & time. The kind of thing I'd like to write but haven't the stuff for yet. Ah well, I've got a poetry book in my mind that will scandalize the clean-faced some day. Please you & Fate.

I think you'd probably have a better time an I were a bad bricklayer. But probably you wouldn't like that.

. . . Reread a good deal of T. S. of P. [*This Side of Paradise*]. It seems younger somehow than last time— but on the whole, of an astonishing excellence. Oh Lord, Jane, the man can write!

I love you. Mentally I embrace you also—not wholly in a brotherly fashion. Write me, dear, & love me for my faults as Beatrix Fairfax says.

George, 13 Lord Hell Viscount Damnable. Fire Hall, Herts, Bucks, E.C.

TO ROSEMARY CARR

Paris, France
April 28, 1921

7-times respected Jane!

Everything went very nicely this afternoon—merci bien to you & M. Prunier—3 hours straight work for 2500 words & the book really beginning to have muscles & a skeleton. Never worry about work with me, it's when I can't or it goes sour that I get sad. Last summer I used to play 3 sets of tennis when I got through in the afternoon. Now I drink 2 large aperitifs. It is not half so healthy but quite as resting. . . .

TO ROSEMARY CARR

Paris, France
May 11, 1921

Dear belovedest: (Sounds a bit too much like "dearly beloved brethren," but still)

Listen! Alors! Ecoutes! And all that sort of thing.

I am now thinking with great seriousness of sailing June 7 with the Hesses—16 days but Naples, Palermo, Lisbon & a chance for 2 days in Rome & possibly a chance to really work on the boat. Probably shall if it's cheap enough.

I suppose your family wouldn't like it if you came back then—even chaperoned by Mrs. H. It would be *so* ideal—& therefore, I suppose unrealizable. Should have asked Alice Lee, our pocket guide to etiquette, about this but Frances Margaret had a pain too large for her & A.L. in consequence a bit incoherent.

Also Henry may go back then also. This is hush, by the way, this last.

. . . A.L. asks us to mind baby Thursday eve. Can you? Please, if you can! And will you pneu her about it? . . .

Good night dear
Always
Steve

Dear belovedest! (Sounds a bit too much like "dearly beloved brethren", but still)

Listen! Alors! Ecoutez! And all that sort of thing.

I am now stimulating with great seriousness of sailing June 7 with the Hesses — 16 days but Naples, Palermo & maybe ⊕ a chance for 4 days in Rome ⊕ possibly a chance to really work on the boat. Probably shall if its cheap enough.

I suppose your family wouldn't like it if you came (back) then — even chaperoned by his bf. It would be so ideal — ⊕ therefore, I suppose unrealizable. Should have asked Alice be your pocket guide to etiquette about this but Frances Margaret had a pain too large for her ⊕ A.L. in consequence a bit incoherent.

Who Henry may go back then also. This is hush by the way, this last

TO SHREVE C. BADGER

Paris, France
May 18, 1921

Dear Shreve:—

In spite of your porpoise-like indifference to the 3 letters I have written you from this side, I nevertheless set pen to paper again in order to prove to you that the thin at least are constant in both correspondence & friendship and that in the intervals of wrapping up drygoods and smoking big black cigars you might possibly find time to dash off a hasty note to an old friend on the portly stationery of one of your numerous clubs. By Bones, if you won't reply to this letter, my young Falstaff, I'll erase the ⅓ of the dedication of my first novel that goes to you & only speak to you in a whisper when I see you next!

Because I have rather important news concerning myself to communicate—news connected with a certain $50.00 bet we made some years ago. Whether I'll win the bet or you have already is still wrapped in mystery —you may have married a Farwell & had a young Rex from all I've heard of you—but as far as my side goes, I can now tell you that I have been engaged for two months to a young lady from Chicago named Rosemary Carr (*no* relative of Bill's by the way). We met over here where she is reporting on the Paris edition of the Chicago *Tribune*. You probably never met her—she went to the U. of Chicago—class of 1918. Her family knows Jake Funk, & you might perhaps get a more critical estimate of her beauty & qualities from Jake than you would from me—for to me, ever since I met her, she has been the one person in the world. This news by the way is to be kept *absolutely* secret as her family have not seen her for two years, have never of course seen me, and naturally do not approve of her being definitely engaged under such circumstances. It will be all right, I think, when we get back to the U.S.—though I am gambling horribly on my novel's being a big enough financial success for us to marry—but meanwhile this is to be mentioned to *no one*—in W.H.S. or out. I am depending on you because I know you can keep secrets. If there is anything you can do in the matter—i.e. if you should happen to ever see her family & they should mention me (a remote contingency)—use your head & do your best for me without knowing anything at all about the engagement. Or if there is any favorable propaganda you can start—do so. I don't imagine you'll be able to, but you might. Otherwise, sit tight and wish me luck, Shreve, for I'm luckier already than I ever deserved to be in a million worlds.

You will love Rosemary when you see her & she will be fond of you. I can't describe her on paper very well—except to say that she is clever, pretty, has a magnificent sense of humor, adventurous, gallant, whimsical, kind, merry, and courageous—and that all these adjectives mean very little when set down that way. As a scrap of statistics, she was Ø.B.K. & led her Prom. I don't want to give the impression that she's an Admirable Crichton—but she is so infinitely the finest & most lovely person I have ever known that I am happier than I could ever have imagined.

I am sailing around June 15. Don't write me over

here—write c/o my brother W.R., *The Literary Review*, N.Y. *Post*, 20 Vesey St., N.Y. I will undoubtedly see you during the summer—the family's moving to Scarsdale [N.Y.] by the way. It would be swell if you & I and Effy [Evarts] could get together somewhere sometime. I can't tell when we'll be married till I finish my second novel [*Jean Huguenot*], now half-done, try and sell the serial rights of it, and see if my first novel [*The Beginning of Wisdom*] goes as a book. This first novel is starting 3-part serialization in *Harper's Bazaar* with the July or August numbers. I yanked $1,000 out of them for the serial rights—which was lucky as it gave me enough to propose to Rosemary.[1]

John [Carter] intends to go into the diplomatic service permanently & may be back in America this winter. By the way, of course if we have ushers, I expect to count on you.

Got to get back to work now. Again, Shreve, luck to you & wish me luck. I see everything at present through bright pink spectacles.

yrs. in W.H.S.
Steve

TO ROSEMARY CARR

Paris, France
May 26, 1921

Darling:—

I am a wimpus not to have written you more than 1 feeble pneu yesterday but fatigue induced by trying to

1. Although *Harper's Bazaar* made a payment of $750 on *The Beginning of Wisdom*, the magazine eventually abandoned its plans for serialization.

get an intoxicated gentleman whom I had met once to leave my room into which he had strayed at 12.45 & where he stayed till 3 made me feel rather eerie all day —not to say to be in bad condition to be decadent with Douglas [Moore] this evening. I see Condé is now watching the porpoises and probably composing long steamer letters to Cath. Oh, steamer letters—the thought makes me couveler[?] steamers—and the Scarsdale garage [2] & many unpopular things. We will get married in November please & by God. Between the halves of the Yale-Harvard game in the Yale Bowl—the umpire officiating. But I must refrain from this levity like my grandpa. I love you in every way possible for us poor humans & now I've unvented myself. Sweet. Always.

Steve

TO ROSEMARY CARR

S.S. *Lorraine*
June 24, 1921

Dear, dear Jane, darling:—

It seems so funny to think you will get this after we have met in New York and then parted again and all the news in it will be old—except how much I missed you & love you—oh Heavens, now I'm throwing myself forward into the future again and have got sorry for parting from you twice when I've only done it once and—well this sentence *must* have a period or it'll go on Henry-James like for pages and pages. There!

I loved your letter. . . . And I want you. And it is hell

2. Benét was planning to spend the summer with his family in Scarsdale, N.Y. They had written him that there was a garage which he could use as a workroom.

not having you. And it was lovely yesterday—a blue glass sea and a moon at night—and all that wasted! Oh Jane, dearest. I do miss you. I do love you. I will love you always. I couldn't help loving you always if I tried. I can see you now as I write, and I would give anything in the world to have you here!

. . . Did you have another meal at Prunier's before you left? The salt smell in the air reminded me of it. That's a place to haunt, now, Jane, when we're *revenants*. The ghostly couple—nothing queer about them but the fact that they lunch till long after everyone is gone. And the money they pay with turns into sea-urchins & starts parading out after them.

. . . I dreamt about your mother last night. I don't remember quite what she looked like, but we were being very polite to each other until I said "You know, Mrs. Carr, I always call Rosemary Jane" to which she replied very firmly "I am very sorry but I cannot allow my daughter to marry any young man who calls her Jane." Absit omen.

. . . Today you must be in Cherbourg, getting fumigated and hating it, unless Dick [Myers] has discovered some way of getting out of it. Well, tomorrow, probably, we'll be sailing the same ocean and seeing the same stars at least and the same unending sea. . . . The sight of that great green goddess coming out of the waves & the whole Dunsany skyline of NY will be a vast relief. I've done *no* work on the boat at all—simply haven't felt capable of it—and now, of course, wish I'd tried anyway no matter how I felt. Heavens, I sound as if I really had things to complain about. When I'll see you in 8 or 9 days si tout va bien, my darling, my darling! Tall buildings—another background—new scenery—but what's scenery to us, who have made love with a divine irresponsibility everywhere from Versailles to—the Café de Versailles? We won't change, Jane. . . . I love you. I love you for always. I wish I could have written you a better letter. . . .

> I love you.
> Always
> Steve

The Long Summer: 1921

BENÉT and his fiancée met for a few hours in New York when Rosemary's boat docked. There then commenced a four-month separation, broken only by a brief reunion in Chicago in September, which tried them cruelly. Rosemary returned to her home. She worked that summer in the recorder's office at the University of Chicago. Benét squeezed in with his family in the stucco house the Colonel had bought in Scarsdale for his retirement. Gone now were the spacious quarters of Officers' Row. Instead they named this crowded, suburban home The Brimming Cup, somehow finding room for the Colonel and Mrs. Benét, Laura, Bill and his three children, Mrs. Benét's eighty-five year old Aunt Agnes, and now Stephen.

All summer Benét labored in the hot garage with the tin roof and the gasoline smell, driving himself to a schedule of 10,000 words of magazine fiction a week. Now, however, he worked with market-wise techniques, acquired in informal tutorials with his new literary agent, the late Carl Brandt. Their relationship was the most important and durable professional association of Benét's career, and as valued by the agent as it was in 1921 by the young poet. "He was the finest person I ever knew," Brandt said not long before his own death in 1957.

In 1921, however, the agent had more to give than the writer. Benét listened attentively and toiled courageously. All his aspiration was toward poetry, but now he painfully transformed himself into a prose writer. Fiction, he explained grimly to a friend, would keep the pot boiling. In the summer of 1921, as these letters show, he was teaching himself the method. It was the beginning of twenty years of what he called his bread-and-butter writing. The components of those twenty years—grinding labor, editorial vacillation, fatigue and strain, disappointment, delay, sudden and deceptive prosperity—are anticipated in these resilient letters that chronicle his search for his bride.

TO ROSEMARY CARR

Scarsdale, N.Y.
July 26, 1921

Darling dear:—

I sent you a foolish telegram yesterday that will probably be telephoned out to your apartment by a tittering central. But the *pneumatique* habit is still strong in me, tu sais. Please state, respected Jane, whether more or less public affection is desirable in such telegrams. This is a very serious matter and one that might Augur for our Future Future Happiness If Properly Decided.

Had lunch with JCF[arrar] yesterday who was low in his mind—I hesitate to draw inferences because he's just got back from Detroit and points west. Then he called up Carl Brandt for me and, of course, I got an appointment to see the great man at once, everything is easy if you can get your friends to roll a few logs for you. And JCF is a Roller of Yule Logs for me and always was. So went over and saw CB. As I told you he's supposed to be the best agent in NY, a very nice blond fat person looking somewhat like a plump blond sealion with a soft and pleasing voice. Well, says he, this [*Jean Huguenot*] is no serial. I'll try and sell it serially if you like but the only chance is with *Harper's, Scribner's* or *The Century* because the only thread that carries through is the change in the girl's character and that isn't strong enough to carry the reader of popular magazines through from month to month. There are several serials in the book and a number of short stories, but I have had books like this before and no matter how much I liked them they are the hardest things I get to sell serially. Well, he knows what he is talking about. But he liked the book very much indeed—said it was much better than *Moon Calf, Zell*, the last Walpole, the last McKenna, etc etc and that it had held *him* through to the end and should succeed in book form. Which cheered me quite a bit. Also he said there was no reason in the world why I couldn't write a serial that would sell anywhere without commercializing and that if I would show him the synopsis of this 50,000 word thing [*Young People's Pride*] I am going to write and a first instalment, he would do everything he could for me to show me how the thing should be constructed with big money in view. He advised very strongly against trying to commercialize in any way but said he thought I could get away with both good writing and modern serial publication if I tried. Which cheered me up considerably. He is a very nice fellow and knows the magazine game as well as anybody and better, I guess, than most. Said [Henry] Sell [editor of *Harper's*

Bazaar] wasn't the best man for advice on serials. Ray Long [*Cosmopolitan*] better or [Sewell] Haggard [*Everybody's Magazine*] or the Street and Smith man. So I am going to write an airtight plan, if possible, for this next book, write 10,000 words on it and then talk it over with him. Of course, I expect nothing from all this, and don't allow myself to build glass houses. But I am going to try like the devil to make a go of it and have an idea for this new stunt that allows for some fairly original stuff I think along various angles. Will send you a carbon of whatever I do.

And then of course I had to meet a 22 year old girl just out of Smith in John [Farrar]'s office who had sold her first novel to the *Delineator* for $4,500. She is a nice girl . . . Also John Weaver of *In American* came in,[3] he's from Chicago by the way and very amusing with one of the fastest lines I ever heard. . . . The young NY writing crowd is certainly diverting. . . .

Will you send me the size of your engagement finger by the way? This is important and I want it. I have reasons—no, I am not going to spend all the money I ought to use in coming to Chicago on one cold stupid gem—but I want the size. Now, be nice!

I hope it isn't as hot at 1400 Hyde Park Boulevard as it is in this little tin hell of a garage. I don't see how it could be. . . .

Aunt Margaret writes a grand letter and says I am very much in love with you and they were quite sure of

3. John V. A. Weaver was literary editor of the Brooklyn *Daily Eagle* at this time. Despite his early death, in 1938, Weaver was the prolific author of several volumes of verse, two novels, a play, and a number of Hollywood scenarios.

it the last time we were there to dinner because I spent the whole time positively beaming at you. Clever Aunt M!

Also says quelle chaleur in Paris and quelle drought! Which only makes me long for iced vermouth and selzer outside Lavenue's about 5 PM.

This letter seems to be mostly about me and Carl Brandt. Shall try and make the next exclusively about you and God. You first, you notice.

Good night, Titania. Good night, belovedest. Good night, my darling that I love with my whole heart.

Always
Steve

TO ROSEMARY CARR

Scarsdale, N.Y.
August 4, 1921

Jane dearest:—

Saw C.B. for an hour today—he was really quite encouraging. At least anyhow, I don't think a particularly busy person like that would sit & chat for an hour merely for the love of my brown eyes. He likes the French stories quite a lot and will send them around. *Jean Huguenot* is at *Harper's* but he doesn't think there's much show for it comme serial. Thinks Y.P.P, [*Young People's Pride*] if done right will really get away & wants to see it instalment by instalment—also gave me some very helpful ideas. Says Sell is very strong for me and anxious to push me as soon as I turn out anything that conforms in form to the usual magazine construction. So the only thing to do is to push ahead & finish Y.P.P. as soon as

possible & see how it goes. I will dig at it, believe me—
I really think it's a rather good yarn, and comes fairly
easily, thank Peter, where Jean Huguenot was driving
myself at a bar about 6 ft. too high. I've tried to put the
idea of anything really breaking for from 6 weeks to 2
months now out of my mind—it's rotten luck that it
shouldn't, but, alors, let's hope it will then. Meanwhile
I am doing my possible as hard as I can. No more air-
castles till I've earned the right to believe in 'em—but,
are we downhearted, *not* on your life.

And what did you ink over so carefully and salty at the
end of your last letter? Impudent Jane!

I'm sending you a *Parabalou* (influence of Walt
Mason [4] on prose style). . . .

Always
Steve

TO ROSEMARY CARR

Scarsdale, N.Y.
August 1921

A very peculiar Sunday

Sweet Jane:—

. . . There is no news here except meteorological facts
about the weather which has surpassed itself by com-
bining hail thunderstorm and brilliant sunshine inside of
four hours. No city editor would say that the facts that I
love you and miss you unendingly are so new as to take

4. 1862–1939.—A journalist whose daily prose poems—collected
under such titles as *Rippling Rhymes* and *Terse Verse*—were syndicated in several hundred American and Canadian newspapers.
Parabalou was the little magazine which had been founded by a
group of Yale writers.

the front page in a five-star extra—and they are the two chief facts of my present existence and the only ones worth talking about. Les'see though—news—

Murray Vickers called up from White Plains. He said he had a job in N.Y. but sounded very breezily discouraged about it. He laughed bitterly when I spoke of "congenial work."

Kathleen Anne took off her drawers publicly thrice today.

Our sixth cook has left.

I'm going to try to see Brandt Wednesday about *Young People's Pride*. The First Devoted Ten Thousand of it have marched their parasangs—enteuthen exclaunei—and now only need to be typed. Also Will and I are lunching—among those seen lunching—with Glenn Frank the Ed. of the *Century* Wednesday. He buys the lunch—let's hope he'll buy *Jean Huguenot* too. Anyhow, a lunch is a lunch.

I love you.

I miss you.

. . . Your mother wrote me a most delightful letter which I will answer tomorrow. She is really very much too nice to me—far nicer than I deserve. . . .

There is a book called *Supers and Supermen* by Philip Guedalla that you would like though it is one of those a little too monotonously clever books—nothing but rockets and rockets & not one fizzle. But he says some diverting things. As, of Frederick the Great "That young man ascended the throne with the most sinister of all reputations—a name for bad verse." Of Walker's Nicaraguan revolution "and the filibuster experiment closed after an exciting campaign over ground which is principally familar to philatelists." Also "Nothing is more humiliating to a Borgia than to figure in a collection of *Quiet Lives of the Renaissance*." That sort of thing.

I write you so much and so wordily, I suppose, because I like to pretend I'm talking to [you]—and that particular you, being invisible and inaudible, can't tell me when to stop. Forgive me if I talk too long, dear, dear, dearest, darling! It's only that it hurts so being away from you . . . I couldn't ever be even a minus poet if I didn't love you with all my heart & body and soul.

Always
Steve

TO ROSEMARY CARR

Scarsdale, N.Y.
August 6, 1921

Sweetheart:—

I think the place for us is Tierra del Fuego. The rain falls there, I understand, all but about 3 or 4 days in the year, often so violently as to permanently deafen even old inhabitants who sort of live in the mud like antique crustacea. There you would, doubtless, be almost insanely buoyant & as rain affects me with a delightful twilight-in-Notre Dame sort of painless and mellow gloom—we would be very happy indeed. I would be a rather sleepy shepherd with creaky asthmatic panpipes and a flock of very damp sheep . . . I would carve you necklets from the bones of drowned sailors in odd moments—being naturally of a mortuary turn of mind.

About the Scarborough idea—well, naturally I want you to do what you want to—I hope that doesn't sound too senile and uncleish—but I do. If you had to take it from September to June—well, to the best of my hope and probably overconfident belief that would keep us from being married before June, and I think we can be, given a few breaks. It would undoubtedly be a fine opportunity if you were going to make teaching a life work—but, as far as I know, you aren't. The offer would mean a good job for you, an easy and a lucrative one, and one where we could see each other, I imagine, very nearly as often as we wanted—which Lord knows, I should like! On the other hand, if you had to take it for the 9 months, that would simply mean that we would both have to admit we could not possibly be married before next June at the earliest. Well, what do you think? Darling, it is so hard for me to give you advice in a thing like this—I am willing enough to make bets with Luck for myself—but I can't very well for you—you're too precious to me. I hope to hear from Brandt Monday about this new thing and will write you whatever he says. He and Sell both seem to believe I can make a comfortable living easily enough if I once get the hang of what they call the "serial form"—I don't think I am overstating here. I feel confident enough myself that I can do it—sooner or later—but how much sooner is rather chancy as you know. I think this is the best way of doing it—it seems to me the only way both of us will get a number of things we want very much. The only thing that hurts is the uncertainty for you—I am used enough to my own life being uncertain but it seems pretty mean of me sometimes to be so selfish in asking you to share that uncertainty just because I love you so utterly. And then a great many people start out with a perfectly clear idea of what they want and get diverted from it—and then they age or have children and it's too late. All this is very clumsily expressed—it generally is when I really try to be serious. All I mean is that I love you and that anything you decide will suit me because I know (Stephen, Stephen, what awful conceit!) that you love me, and I somehow have an idea that you're a good deal the wiser person of the two. Only June seems to me pretty long to definitely decide to wait—especially when everything might break in our favor inside of 3 or 4 months. I hope to get something out of C.B. though next Monday, as I say.

. . . I have ⅓ the 2nd installment of Y.P.P. done. I won't send you the carbon of this bit, though, till I hear from Brandt. Felt rather low today—too few cigarettes, but much cheered later by your letter. . . . I love you dearest dear. In my mind I am holding you in my arms (bad grammar?) for always and Always and ALWAYS!

Steve

TO ROSEMARY CARR

Scarsdale, N.Y.
August 1921

Darling:—

I have done nothing at all but sneeze and typewrite all day—it seems that I *have* hay-fever, a 'touch' of it, though how anything like that can be as gentle as a 'touch' implies, I don't quite see. But cheer up! You'll get nicer letters after tomorrow, when *Young People's Pride* will be off my hands for some days at least. I started counting the words on pages for curiosity tonight and made the surprising discovery that they run from 25 to 60 more per page than I had thought—and consequently this thing will be a good deal nearer 75,000 words than 50,000—and I was wondering like a wimpus why it was taking such a time to write! Consequently, assuming I made the same error with the other 2 books —which is more than likely—the BofW will run to at least 110,000 and Jean to 90,000—and counting in the short stories that means 300,000 words in the past year— which isn't very bad for a beginner at prose. Listen, Jane, and I will tell you a dreadful secret. The reason I am as far along as I am at 23 is not due to genius or inspiration or anything one-millionth as pleasant—it all boils down to a certain fluency with language and more than that by several cubits and kilos another certain ability which I really ought to take a considerable Moral And Christian Pride in of being able to sit down and work when I don't feel like it. And that is not being modest to have you compliment me, really—that is vérité!

The doctor came in to see what was the matter with Jim who had been running a slight temperature. "Well, doctor, is there anything that can be done for hay-fever?" says I amiably. "There is nothing at all," says he. "But, mon médecin, I never had the dam thing before!" I quip and he retorts crushingly "You never lived in Scarsdale before" with a nasty smile. "Go to Cape Cod for a month" says he "Or Atlantic City—or the great green greasy Limpopo river or ride in triumph through Persepolis or any of a dozen places I can pick out if I blindfold myself and stick my finger on Mercator's projection—and, lo, your hay-fever will cease!" I love certain species of doctors—they are so Really Helpful.

There is nothing exciting to tell you—but then there never is. The only luminous moment of the day was at lunch when Ro suddenly crept up behind Aunt Agnes and roared "Under the Bridge!" in her ear and so nearly scared the poor lady into a nervous collapse—poor dear! Also a letter arrived from my aunt about Uncle Will and was read aloud with interlinear comments by Mother which were absolutely rare—it was one of those disease-catalogues, "all the skin has come off the inside of his mouth and he can take nothing but cold jellies" *you* know! But I don't know why I write you such nasty things. Oh yes, and Henry [Carter] is going to take another P.G. at Harvard next year—and I'm hoping to see him in a week or so as he is now released from diplomats. Stan has vanished into the intense inane with his smile and English suits. I must get in touch.

. . . I love you, youngest archangel. I *will* write you a decent letter b'god, as soon as this type-madness is over. I love you with all my heart and soul and mind. Think of me before you go to sleep—remember. Darling.

Toujours
Steve

TO ROSEMARY CARR

Scarsdale, N.Y.
August 1921

Most unromantically written in the middle of a stuffy afternoon, because I don't quite know when the doctor's coming around to inject the family.

Dearest:—

To answer postscript of your letter first—what do I think about your going to Paris now with Ruth—well, dear, it's up to you. What do you think, really? Of course it would be gorgeously appropriate as well as romantic to be married in Paris—but I happened to discuss the subject with Uncle Larry once and he said it took months and miles of red tape and all sorts of birth-certificates and things—that's the practical side, or part of it. Again, I should think your family would really object somewhat, though you ought to know about that a good deal better than I do. Also there is the ten day journey—uncertainty of mails—various other things. But there I'm not considering you but myself—and that isn't fair.

I know I've certainly felt ever since you went back to Chicago that it was all my fault you were there in a hot dirty city at a job you didn't like—when you might be in Paris or Paris-Plage with your friends or anywhere that was nice and in France if it hadn't been for me—and that's hurt all right, considering the fact that you are the one person I want to give most to and never have anything hurt. And these last not-quite-two-months have been the hardest time I've ever had in my life, in some ways— loving you body and mind and soul and never being able to see you or tell you anything more definite than that I was working at something that might go or might not. Because even your letters aren't like actually seeing you, and mine must be so much worse. But, Jane dear, I simply couldn't see anything else to do for either of us—and Lord knows, I may have been entirely wrong, but I really have tried to do as much as I could. No, that sounds like a little tin hero, which I'm not.

Darling, if you want to go to Paris, I want you to go. I'd so infinitely rather have you happy there than miserable in Chicago (provided you were really going to marry me in both cases, remarked the Tin Hero) that it really wouldn't matter your being so much farther and more difficultly away. Moreover, as you say, I could come over as soon—well, as soon as I could—and at least one of us would be there. The only thing about it just at present is this. After all, Jane, we've neither of us been back on this side three months—I know it seems a damn sight longer but actually that's all it is. Things are just beginning to really break for me in certain ways. My first book's coming out—Brandt is handling Y.P.P.—I haven't built air-castles in letters to you because I just can't tell you things are sure when they aren't but even the next month may make the most complete change in the whole business. Are you willing to stand things at your end for six weeks more, say, because in that time I'll certainly be able to know about both my books? The whole thing is so tantalizingly *close*—any sort of real luck would give me enough money for us and give it right away. I know how much you miss Paris—and Lord knows, I know how rotten all this waiting is—and I don't know whether I have any right to ask you to stand it any more or not. Except that, after all, we have been back such a short time in actual days, and it would be so much easier and more attractive for us to be married here and go over together if we could.

I hope the above doesn't sound too much like a dictaphone. I love you I love you, I love you—my whole heart and mind and future are bound up in our getting married—and it is perfectly devilish to me to think that you are being unhappy on account of me. I don't want you to be giving up anything in the world you want to do on account of me—I'm no Christian and I hate the idea of it. Also it is so hard explaining in letters what I could tell you in five minutes if you were here. But if you can stand the present sorry conditions for six weeks more—I really think things will come out all right in the end. But this is only, of course, if you *want* to stand them—which is wholly and completely for you to decide.

Oh and listen—what'll be the best day for me to come to Chicago when I come? You said Friday night, didn't you? Not this Friday but possibly the next and absolutely certainly the one after that. And will I be staying with you—I mean, will you have room etc for me—or shall I make hotel-reservations? Or if there's any better day than Friday, bright angel tell me which? (sounds like a minor Elizabethan carol!)

. . . So you read *Jurgen*—dear, dear! It is an amusing work—it would have been a great if indecent masterpiece if he had I don't know what—but something isn't there—gusto, perhaps. *Figures of Earth* is very good too, though the end is swiped from Frank Stockton.

I love you, my darling. And if you want to go to Paris—you *go*—though I think it might be harder on both of us than you think now. But anyhow I'll see you, D.V., in two weeks now at the most—and maybe have something definite—and anyhow we can talk the whole thing over and make some plans. I love you, dearest, dearest. You are my life, you *are*, you are all I live for and by. . . . Always

Steve

TO ROSEMARY CARR

Scarsdale, N.Y.
August 1921

Jane dearest:—

Johnny [Andrews] is nice and I'm glad he wrote such a nice letter. He is a delightfully fantastic person though like many such, what he chiefly tries to be & prides himself on being is athletically simple. I've forwarded your letter to his family address in New Haven—it's the only one I know.

(I am trying to write this letter in the dining-room while Bill, just back from his vacation is retelling the extremely intricate plot of his novel to the rest of the family just across the hall. So if I start talking about Mrs. Cole's attempted suicide or is Clara Siblay Mrs. Ventress? pay no attention.)

Called up Brandt today so of course he can't see me till tomorrow. Always the way. He said however the last instalments were "fine" but that I would "slouch with pain" when I heard what he wanted me to do with them. I await bloody but unbowed. I am willing to turn Y.P.P. & its author inside-out upside-down or any way at all & throw my immortal soul into the bargain for a sufficient amount of cash.

(I now hate every one of my family—they are all talking so loud in the next room. And I have the same sensitiveness about any interruption, intentional or unintentional while I'm writing you that I used to have about when I was writing poetry).

. . . So we are compatible even with hay-fever? Well,

1921

dear Miss Carr, I feel *sure* that such similarity in *tastes* can only result in the most *lasting* and *worthwhile* kind of happiness (which of course has nothing to do with love—love is alive.) for us *both!* But, darling, I never knew the blame thing could be so *annoying*—and I certainly hope we neither of us ever have it again.

I wish I had something shiny and interesting and amusing to tell you at this juncture. . . .

I love you, dearest, dearest. . . .

Always
Steve

TO ROSEMARY CARR

Scarsdale, N.Y.
August 1921

The Garage

Jane darling:—

I really have a chance to talk to you this evening—in my coy retreat here with a brilliant fire-new dime of a moon looking through black branches at me whenever I turn my head. The day has not been peaceful for most of the family—it has for me but then I have been typing most of the day.

In the first place my Uncle Irwin who I remember as a most gentle kind pink portly person who used to take me for walks and buy me little yellow-and-green candies when I was a little boy has just died at the ripe age of 85—and it was really a release for he had been suffering extremely—but he was Aunt A's favorite brother and one of the few links she still has with the past, and consequently she is much shaken though keeping on with wonderful courage. I really think in many ways she has more clear grit than anybody I have ever known. Then our present cook, a black frizzy Lucy has been off, probably ory-eyed for yesterday and today and between housework and the children the whole family is pretty nearly deadbeat. So I am now recuperating in my literary hutch after typing my third instalment, over a stolen cigarette you MUSTN'T tell anybody about and a letter to you.

I never told you much about Carlisle Pa., did I? Uncle Irwin's death brings it up—that sounds callous—but it was where my grandmother Rose lived and where Mother was a little girl and all of us used to visit Ammah when we were children and though we have few ties to take us back there now, Uncle Irwin was one of the last, it used to be one of the places that always meant home to us—you know. You would love it Jane—it is funny and small and quaint and hasn't really changed in the nice parts since the Civil War—it is brick paths and wide streets with big shady trees all along them, and a market in the middle of the town where the country people bring everything from fresh scrapple to big yellow pumpkins, and it is all sleepy Summer weather and has a lot of old families who are decaying like gentlemen and gentlewomen in red-brick houses with scrubbed doorsteps and little white houses covered with vines. It is the kind of place where storybook grandmothers *ought* to live. There is an ice-cream parlor there with wallpaper that has stiff scenes from Paul and Virginia on it—a Cranford kind of icecream parlor—and nobody ever seemed to be particularly rich or poor there or ever in a hurry—a spiced gingerbread cooky place, a phlox and pink garden place, a deep winter snowdrift place where you could imagine coming back to crumpets for tea and thin hot mulled wine. And it is all mixed up in my mind with being very happy at about seven years old and going to the circus and coasting down the long hill and having all the people who kept the stores saying good-morning when you went downtown. You *would* like it Jane—especially the parts that delighted me then so . . . I love you, sweeter than sweet, fairer than fair, lovelier than lovely—oh and I miss you! Beloved. Always

Steve

TO ROSEMARY CARR

Scarsdale, N.Y.
August 1921

Jane, my adored:—

I wish I had any real news but I haven't. Only that it was a fine day, thank you, and I typed and played tennis and helped wipe dishes and such, and got a letter from John [Peale] Bishop of *Vanity Fair* asking me to lunch and saying hope you won't be sore about what I said in my article on the Younger Novelists [5]—the Princeton Person, if he said anything in the least disparaging to my Superb Genius I'll crack his head like a nut—only I couldn't because he looks husky in spite of tortoise-shell-rims. Also I'm getting cartooned by Ivan Opfer Monday for the *Lit. Review*—Bill is angelical about trying to work me extra drag on that for the BofW—and seeing Brandt about the 2nd instalment and taking him the third. I

5. John Peale Bishop, "Three Brilliant Young Novelists," *Vanity Fair*, 16 (October 1921), 8–9.

should think he'd be fairly able to tell on 3 instalments if the thing was marketable or not. But mebbe he can't. Anyhow it's all on the down grade now—I wish I could only be sure I was coasting to some purpose though and not over merely imaginary snow. Ah well, when this is done, we'll try some short stories. Dum spiro spero and per aspera ad astra and tegna nina sesquipedalia and all those encouraging Latin mottoes.

The only thing that really makes me peevish is that a blonde friend of the family's is getting married here Sept. 1. I will go and scatter arsenic powder in her punch. Life is pretty blessed easy for some people though.

Most of my friends seem to think I'm dead. At least I never run into about six of them who are in N.Y. Still I don't suppose I tried very hard to see them.

. . . I love you, my dearest, my dearest. Love me. Always
Steve

TO ROSEMARY CARR

Scarsdale, N.Y.
August 22, 1921

Jane dearest:—

Yesterday after a very hot disappointed morning in N.Y. when everybody I'd wanted to see had been out of town, I decided I had to cheer up somehow—having left too early to get your sweet lovely and delicious letter—so spent a borrowed two dollars seeing the finals of the Woman's National at Forest Hills. I don't know how you feel about it—but I'd rather see first-class tennis than anything but Yale Harvard football—and this was tennis and drama and everything else. . . .

Also met a nice 1918 Bete at the tennis, with his nice and very freckle wife. They remarked calmly that they would soon celebrate their 4th anniversary and somehow it didn't seem that long. Both were having a beautiful time with each other and were very strong for marriage—the kind of young married people it does you good to see—though of course the longer I stayed with them the more jealous I got that we weren't celebrating our quatrième also—but that, they seemed to understand. I love you, Jane.

Going to be cartooned tomorrow and see Brandt. Both of which I hope will be painless.

I love you, dearest . . . wish we could live in large green forests on deer's milk and honey—sounds indigestible but charming—no sword between though, please, though doubtless romantic, but there have been quite enough of those . . .

[remainder lost]

TO ROSEMARY CARR

Scarsdale, N.Y.
September 1921

Jane dearest:—

I've decided that rest, at least under present conditions doesn't really agree with me—at least I've done nothing but it the last two days—can't see Brandt till Tuesday—and all it does is give me too much time to think about my hay fever. So I'm going to try and write a short story tomorrow—I have ideas for several and who knows, who knows? . . .

The only adventures of the day have been dish-drying

ones—we are servantless again. And the fact that a lot of our stuff from Watervliet having come, a box of the children's books was unpacked, so I have been reading *St. Nicholas* (old bound volumes) and *Gil Blas* alternately all afternoon. They were good for me, also a volume of Polish fairy tales in which I ran into a *most* satisfactory dragon. He was green, entirely implacable and had twenty-four fire-breathing heads and the only way he could die was by killing himself. For some reason, after reading and writing modern novels he appealed to me immensely. I drew a long breath when I came to him and thought—if I could ever write anything as absolutely real and good to taste as that—

Also the box had, curiously, a lot of back numbers of the *Lit.* in it from '16 to May of '18—the same old snuff-colored cover with the cut of Elihu Yale in the tremendous wig it has had since 1836—and looking them over produced a mild beautiful octogenarian melancholy in my sensitive soul. It seemed such a different and far younger world—which is absurd I suppose—but it has already, the War aiding, begun to retreat into the mists of fable, that time that was so very good, really, and I almost felt like patting my three years ago self kindly on the head. Much more so than when I really shall be an octogenarian—because we were all so sure we were going to be at least notorious in those great days—and we're [all] of us still not wholly convinced we aren't—whereas by the time I'm eighty—But the names, and seeing my name in the A.[lpha] D.[elta] list etcetera—it brought it all back very vividly—and everything we were so sure was so utterly important—well, you know. And when I was first writing poetry. It's good to look

86

back on—even when you're glad it's over—which I am. We shall have much better than that, though, dear . . .

I wish your job weren't so stupid. Oh my dear, my dear, I wish I could comfort you better and more!

I love you, darling. Darling, I love you. I love darling you.

Here sits and types the body of Stephen Vincent Benét. But his heart and soul and all the interesting parts of his mind are at present in the exclusive possession of Miss Rosemary Carr, 1400 Hyde Park Boulevard, Chicago, Illinois. . . .

Steve

TO ROSEMARY CARR

Scarsdale, N.Y.
September 1921

Dearest:—

. . . Wrote a he-and-she story yesterday—a tale about as innocuous though not as interesting as a stick of spearmint gum. But Brandt had been talking to [George Horace] Lorimer about me and if I could get the formula for the *Post* all would be shekels—it's how Harry Lewis kept alive while he was working on *Main Street.* Have several ideas for short stories but little pep—however, pep or no pep, the typewriter manages to worry along. My chief thought at present is that as soon as Farrar comes through with his last instalment [in payment for *The Bookman's* forthcoming serialization of *The Beginning of Wisdom*] I shall rush to Chicago, and then, and then. I'll probably be incoherent when I see you Jane and not get over it for weeks—I'll be so glad. . . .

Sunday—the usual rainy one.

And so yesterday I didn't write any more to you, because of many stupid and interrupting things. I've been typing my he-and-she story—my word, some of it is pretty bad! but it's an experiment to see how much I can get away with. And thinking about you. And missing you.

I shall certainly be delighted indeed to meet your friend Mr. Linn because he was so kind to you [6] . . . I know how you feel—they are divine still, aren't they, after college, though possibly not so terrifying? I know a letter from my own revered C. B. Tinker would mean a good deal more to me of commendation than from nearly all the English novelists. And I can't help still being somewhat impressed by Billy Phelps—well, he is a great teacher—and one of the kindest people in the world—if he does verge toward the bluffer. . . .

As for literary thrills—I haven't had any all summer. I'm expecting things of Masefield's *King Cole*—but that damn man—you never can tell whether he's going to put over a perfect masterpiece or something full of his worst and most obvious faults. But he continues writing masterpieces merrily after all the critics have solemnly assured us that he is dead and buried as a poet—which is one of the reasons I admire him so greatly.

The rain is coming down steadily now on my little tin roof—drumming and gurgling. I wish we were walking

6. James Weber Linn (1876–1939), for many years a teacher of composition and a popular lecturer at The University of Chicago. See, for example, James Farrell's acknowledgment of his debt to Linn in the foreword of *Studs Lonigan*.

in it along the Seine, waterproofs or no waterproofs, seeing everything black and wet and gleaming and fresh. However, we shall. In fact we will.

I love you—and "Nomenclature" came out in *Public Opinion* in England—so now they know, too. I love you. I'm making a last drive on Johnny [Farrar] to hurry up that check—Sell has apparently died on his and I can't rouse him till Brandt sees how he likes Y.P.P. Oh Lord, if he does! . . .

Always
Steve

TO ROSEMARY CARR

Scarsdale, N.Y.
September 1921

Darling:—

Finished typing my he-and-she story and began another—Red Blood and the woman this time but it should be interesting if I can only make it plausible—it has a real plot. Besides this the usual round of dishdrying, meals, etcetera, diversified by a five-mile walk with father over roads terrifyingly lined with golden rod and the discovery of a small patch of poison ivy on my arm to add to the humor of existence. . . . And all through the day, wishing for you, wishing for you, wishing for you till I nearly turned blue with wishing. Would you like me blue? It would be diverting, I should think—a pity we aren't chameleons—they are so expressive—but that way madness lies.

Oh, the poems you write of are "Poor Devil!" and "Portrait of a Boy," both in *Young Adventure.* How pleasant of them to remember! And I never gave you a copy of *Young Adventure*. Do you want one, Jane, I'd love you to have one if you do.

I am a pig to write such a short letter but my brain is addled with drowsiness. I love all yours—they are all I live for and with and by. . . .

Always
Steve

TO ROSEMARY CARR

Scarsdale, N.Y.
October 1921

Oh Blesséd Jane:—

I sent flowers instead of a telegram (sounds funereal) because it was too sort of complicated to get into a telegram . . . Well, I saw them all—Carl, Henry Sell et al—and this is what they had to say.

I've got about a week's work to do on "Y.P.P."—tailoring & carpentry. But, as I understand it from both Carl & Sell—I will be paid cash in advance! However—*not*—unfortunately—$2500. *Because* Sell, as you'll remember paid me $750 for the "B of W" and then found he couldn't use it—*so* on "Y.P.P." I am paying him back this. It is good business all right—in fact Carl told me this morning that he thought it would probably be worth 7500 or so to me later in connections & so forth—& we talked it over before he took the novel there & agreed it might be a very good thing to do though I hoped like hell I wouldn't have to do it. You see it gets me in very solid indeed with the whole Hearst crowd—which is *Cosmpolitan* also. Carl is only taking commission on

1750 which is darn decent of him but even so the net price boils to $1575 which is unfortunate. It is worth it in future business but stupid it had to happen this way just now. But Carl was intensely pleased about the whole affair—says Ray Long of *Cosmopolitan* thinks the short story he's buying ["Elementals"] is the best new thing he's seen in years—& the reception I got at *Harper's Bazaar* from Sell & Verne Porter (also a large editor) made me feel exactly as I did when first taken into A.D. with all the upperclassmen handing bouquets to me themselves & the grand old place. Carl thinks I couldn't possibly have a better start than I have—& he ought to know. Am seeing Long with him some time this week or next & also lunching with Porter, Sell & Long some time soon. So there.

Well, to seem very efficient.

1. I ought to know in a week or ten days how soon I'll get the money from Sell.

2. The same ten days ought to cover the time to rewrite the short story for Long & Y.P.P. They'll pay me at once for the short story.

3. That'll make $1845 cash.

4. Cash on hand $200 making 2050 about.

5. Advance sale of the "BofW" about 3000 copies making about $600. I should think—I really should—that it would go to 5000 anyhow. That would be $1000 more in April. Or about $3050 say for the year—as an absolute minimum.

6. Taking $100 owed you and about $600 (which might be reduced if we were good little children) for going

across, marriage etc—that would leave us an actual living minimum capital of $2300 for the 12 months after we got married.

7. This however omits the fact that I have 5 short stories out—none salable to *Cosmopolitan*—but one Carl thinks probably salable for $100–250. That *Cosmopolitan* will pay me $400 for my next short story they like & take. That I've made $2800, on paper, since July & that in the future the money will not be on paper but cash less Carl's 10% and that my price in every line will probably go up. Sell wants my next serial, for instance—and Carl will make him pay a lot more than $2500. Also, I ought easily to be able to write three or four salable short stories every 6 months.

Well, supposing all the bad luck, which isn't likely, & that I don't make a cent more than the $2300 for a year —which is blame near impossible—Jane darling, do you think we could try it on that? Personally I'd be rather surprised if we didn't pick up at least a thousand more— but there's no use supposing it when we haven't actually got it. I'm putting it in this bum adding machine way because, when all's said and done, it's asking you to take a pretty large chance. We're both of us young, healthy, capable, in love with each other (oh I know this doesn't sound like *me*) and with some practice in living economically. But it means, in a good many things, being pretty darn economical indeed. I went over on a thousand last time & spent I suppose 1600 in the 9 months—getting back thrown in—but I wasted a lot of money, especially the first two months. At least it won't be dull—it will be darn exciting. And I'm pretty sure we'll have more than that—maybe a good deal more—though I can't count on it. All I'm doing the figures out this way for is to show you exactly where we'll stand. It means 2nd class on railway trains & such & rather cheap food & few new clothes. But I think that you & myself—being us—could do it & have a gorgeous amount of fun out of it & if we just went broke over there—well, we could get jobs. Well, darling?

. . . Tell me just & absolutely what you think about the money. I'll wire just as soon as I'm sure of the definite date for it. Love to your mother & father. I wish I were kissing you.

Always

Steve

TO ROSEMARY CARR

Scarsdale, N.Y.

October 1921

Dearest:—

I sent you a night letter this afternoon because things looked so darn encouraging, so blessed encouraging. Took back the cut version of Y.P.P. today and had lunch with Johnny Farrar, Porter, and Sell. All three argued very strongly at me against going over to France for as long as a year right now. Saying thus. I'm started now —Porter says I have a wonderful start—but my position and market aren't solid yet—they've only really begun. When I'm near N.Y. Carl and all these editors can get their fingers on me when they want me, if there's anything to be changed, I can change it right away in any of my stuff, and there is always the personal contact that counts for so unbelievably much in all American business.

93

If I go away for a year, say, everything has to be done most unsatisfactorily at long distance—and there are a dozen or so of the younger bunch who write just as clever magazine stuff as I do—and well, out of sight, out of mind. Carl, for instance, simply said, "You can make at least twice as much money just by being here right now. In a year or two you can go and live anywhere you please—you'll be absolutely fixed, but we've got to nurse things along personally for at least a year more." So he suggested this—which I think is a wonderful idea. Let's get married right away *quick*—Sell is getting me his money just as soon as he can and he thinks he can do it inside a week—Porter's $270 is coming along in a couple of days. Then let's go over and spend about three months in the Italian Riviera and France and Italy— come back over here for six or eight—go over again after that—and the second time we can really stay for quite a long while because the next serial ought to be done then —I won't touch it till we get back—I am pretty darn stale and overworked on writing right now and to tell the truth pretty darn tired—the last eight months at 10,000 words a week have been somewhat of a strain. This is perfectly reasonable—we can easily do it on the money—and I don't think we'll have to worry about money when we get back. First I'm going to do a couple more stories for Long before we go—I told him three ideas the other day and he liked *all* of them. The *Metropolitan,* Carl says, is extremely interested and would make a very good subsidiary market and he expects the others to fall into line. The whole thing is a question of cumulative effect. As for Sell—well he suggested guaranteeing me an income for six months in America if I decided to stay—indefinite proposition of course, but he seemed to think he could work it—he is as anxious to get stuff from me as all that. And the whole atmosphere is simply wonderful—I wouldn't have believed [it]. I pinch myself lest it bust. Apparently, I am set—that's all—and all I'll have to do after we get back will be to sit back, take it easy, show editors that I'm a human being and be amenable to suggestions. . . . Well, that's it. And now—I'll wire you the minute the money actually comes across—I have got Carl working on it too and don't see how it will take more than two weeks more at the latest for it to come through. Sell is completely in sympathy with the whole thing—he threw up his own job to free-lance the day he was married. . . .

Well, my letters from now on may be full of boats and licenses and things. . . .

Always
Steve

TO SHREVE C. BADGER

Scarsdale, N.Y.
November 1921

Dear Shreve:—

I'm expecting you to usher Saturday November 26 at 4 P.M.—in fact to probably do a lot more than usher since my brother who will be best man will of course be utterly incompetent in that role and you will probably sort of have to be maitre d'hotel as well. The wedding will be fairly small. I don't know who the other ushers will be—I'm trying to get Henry Carter and Stan Hawks . . . Any other interesting details of the function you can get from Jane—those are all I know. I'm probably coming to Chicago around the 19th though I don't believe I'm supposed to—so I'll see you then and get other things fixed up. At present I'm trying to do about 90 things at once so am rather incoherent. Till then then.

As ever in W.H.S.
Steve

TO ROSEMARY CARR

Scarsdale, N.Y.
November 1921

Jane dearest:—

Carl called up again today and said pleasantly he'd sold the peanuts story ["Goobers à la Française"] to the *Delineator* for $200—another editor fooled—I really don't think we'll have to actually starve in Paris, my chuck! He and I had about decided the story was a bit too soppy and we would can it, too—which makes the sale even more amusing—the *Delineator* was its last chance. I finished an American-young-wife story aimed at the *Cosmopolitan*—pretty soppy too but built around an idea Long liked. I hope he takes it—he said he'd pay $400 for the next and if so I will buy you something very gaudy, useless and expensive but which will delight both our childish hearts—an immense potted calla-lilly—or a pair of gloves made out of moth's wings—or dinner at the Café de Paris. I think the last would be nicest, too.

No, don't bother about clothes. Try and fix it so you can get them in Paris . . .

Johnny F.[arrar] is giving a *Bookman* lunch tomorrow

to meet J. C. Squire [7]—more swell food and literary conversation and playing at being one of the younger intelligentsia. But it passes the time.

I want to write another short story—a real one—about a girl who had wings and her house in a pine-tree.

The book [*The Beginning of Wisdom*] has started getting reviewed—Johnny Weaver in the Brooklyn *Eagle* —Heywood Broun will in the *World*—I'll have to find out if it's selling, with, again, my usual impatience. I think it's pretty sure of 5,000 now, anyhow, from what I hear.

. . . I must write Aunt Margaret. They'll give us a dinner when we get there—hush, hush, how inordinately proper we'll have to behave!

I love you!
Always
Steve

TO ROSEMARY CARR

Scarsdale, N.Y.
November 1921

Jane dearest:—

Your heavenly letter arrived, praises be—also a delightful one from your mother which I will quote parts [of] to you later. . . . I have just taken out and looked at my check for the 7th time—it says $1794.10 and is the largest thing I ever saw in my life. That is the final, net, five star sum we have—plus $200 of mine, $100 of which

7. John C. Squire, an influential English anthologist and literary critic—he was knighted in 1933—was editor of the London *Mercury* from 1919 until 1934.

owed to you—at present. But I'm going to write that other story next week—and Carl is taking "Cockcrow" (you never saw it) over to Ray Long to see if he likes its idea enough—it will have to be largely rewritten but has the suspense in it he likes. That would mean $720 more or so if those 2 went—I will try to make them go before we sail—it would be a most welcome addition. Absurd to be getting $300 and $400 for short stories— utterly absurd! . . .

Always
Steve

TO ROSEMARY CARR

Scarsdale, N.Y.
November 17, 1921

Jane dearest:—

And this appropriately-dated missive will be the last I'll write you till sometime in that remarkably pleasing future after we're married—and how strange and gorgeous it all seems! It all comes around so nicely with a dozen pleasant coincidences—a slight shift in the scenery —from the Café de Versailles to the Versailles hotel— but much the same kind of weather—darling what has become of your large blue coat? . . .

I love you. And Sunday I'll see you—and Sunday after that we'll have been married—strange but oh how lovely . . . forever and always

Steve

The Literary Life (1922-1926)

MOST of the components of these years between 1922 and 1926, when Benét was establishing himself as a professional writer, are present even in this handful of letters from the period.

The components are screened from us, to be sure, by Benét's buoyant resiliency and by his characteristic reluctance to dwell on his personal situation. Here, nevertheless, are hints of the oppressive insecurity of a freelance writer: the speculative labor on two plays—*Nerves* and *That Awful Mrs. Eaton*—which barely missed Broadway success, the postponement of meaningful success, the necessity to compromise always with magazine formula and editorial whim. Here, too, however, are the compensating richnesses of marriage and parenthood, the ever-widening range and depth of friendship, and, as in the letter to John Drinkwater about "King David," an occasional reminder of the major poetry he was somehow able to write in the brief reprieves from hack assignments.

In 1922 he published "The Ballad of William Sycamore," and in 1923 "King David." His reputation as a robust, swinging poet in the tradition of Lindsay was further consolidated by "The Mountain Whippoorwill" in 1925. He felt that a number of the other poems in *Tiger Joy*, that same year, were an advance beyond his previous collections; the critics, who had admired the earlier work, were newly enthusiastic. In 1926 he was moderately pleased with his fourth novel, *Spanish Bayonet*, despite the misadventures of serialization which he discusses with Rosemary in the letters from the MacDowell Colony. He wrote several first-rate short stories—particularly "The Sobbin' Women"—and he began to explore American history and legend and fantasy.

On the whole, however, the period was one of professional frustration, "with," he told a friend, "the sheriff always at the door." It was not until the late spring of 1926, when he received a Guggenheim Fellowship enabling him to plan the trip he describes in the last letter of this group, that he finally felt free to ignore the market and cultivate instead the requirements of his talent.

TO ROSEMARY BENÉT [8]

Scarsdale, N.Y.
June 1922

Sweet Jane:—

Had a nice lunch with Carl today in which he told me he thought I could easily live off short-stories and certainly did *not* advise me to write a new novel purely with serialization in view. Remarked that my income for the year ought to run between $5000 and $7500—God speed the plow! Also he has for the nineteenth time nearly sold the Barefaced Saint,[9] this time to [Glenn] Frank of the *Century* but don't breathe or it will probably pop

8. The young couple had separated briefly after their European honeymoon, Rosemary traveling to Chicago, where her father was ill, Stephen returning again to his family's home in Scarsdale.

9. Stephen Vincent Benét, "The Barefoot Saint," *Saturday Review of Literature*, 5 (April 20, 1929), 906.

UNIVERSITY OF PITTSBURGH LIBRARY
AT BRADFORD

open again. That tale has won more editorial praise and less cash than anything I ever did. But Carl is the nicest fatty I know, and one of the nicest anyhow.

My next few days will probably be spent in Great Neck, Oyster Bay, Rye, Montauk Point etc etc, looking for bungalows. I have interviewed many realestate agents. They all have the darlingest little summer cottages to rent at $500 a month and all advise me to go to the beaches myself if I want to get anything done. . . .

Peter Whiffle is a delight.[1] Read it—it will make you violently homesick for the Rue Visconti inside of half-a-minute. I was happy to see that I had done practically everything on his list of what all young Americans do in Paris.

I wrote you a poem last night with a dripping slice of gold moon . . . more or less looking over my shoulder . . . It is about you, of course—like every other one of my wishes, feelings, hopes, reactions, copy-slants, dreams, yearnings, aspirations, desires, praises, prayers etc etc ever since you took that disgusting train. . . .

Always
Steve

TO ROSEMARY BENÉT

Scarsdale, N.Y.
June 1922

My Wholly Dear:—

The principal result of the trip to Philadelphia with Carl was to sell my private little receipt to you for sleeping ["In a Glass of Water before Retiring"] astonishingly to *The Ladies' Home Journal!* Carl tried them on "Chemi-

1. Carl Van Vechten, *Peter Whiffle*, New York, 1922.

cal Analysis" but they said they didn't understand it. They were all very nice and jolly and hospitable however, like most of the cur-r-sed editors I have met. The Curtis building looks rather like a small and much better-looking Biltmore—the most luxurious offices I ever saw —original Parrish paintings—reproduction of same in Tiffany glass—Chinese rugs—carved oak tables—panelled walls—the kind of chairs you sink into as into a popover etc etc. They blew us to a charming lunch and I talked my white brachet story a little to the LHJ editor and he more or less said go ahead, that I could get away with a good deal of fantasy if I had some plot as well—and also that his audience was simply dippy over dogs. Which is especially encouraging as I'm going to write the thing entirely to please myself and you without one thought as to its salability. N. C. Wyeth is doing two color illustrations to "Snake and Hawk," by the way —which makes me both joyous and very sore at myself that it isn't a better story. . . .

Always
Steve

TO ROSEMARY BENÉT

Scarsdale, N.Y.
June 1922

Mrs. Stephen (or Stevens) Bennett
1400 Hyde Park Blvd.
Chicago
Ill.

Dear Moddam:

Operative X47 reports as follows.

Rose oh so betimes and after large breakfast at Penn

Station, took train full of babies and banana peels to Red Bank, N.J. Viewed beauties of Red Bank with that homeseeking eye without result and managed via two buses to get to Sea Bright. There interviewed woman mentioned in previous report who wished to rent ½ (one-half) house at $85 per. Woman nice enough though . . . somewhat in need of shave. House furnished in best what-not, gilded rolling-pin and crayon portrait of Angel Willie style . . . Woman interviewed said lady with 3 children was to rent one floor of house for whole summer, so Operative, after consideration, retired with honors of war, saying "I will write," which he considers unnecessary. . . .

Operative would state that Darling Jane is his sole delight and that he misses her like triple hell. . . .

I send you another poem—only a little of what I feel for you— . . .

I have to stop because of the Elinor business which mother wants to talk to me about again.[2] Particulars tomorrow. . . .

Always
Steve

TO ROSEMARY BENÉT

Scarsdale, N.Y.
June 1922

Dearest:—

Today was Ocean Beach, from which I have just returned. . . .

---

2. William Rose Benét's courtship of the poetess Elinor Wylie, whom he married in 1923, so distressed Colonel Benét that he left for Europe rather than attend the wedding.

I still want to write about my little boy in the tower with the white brachet, but haven't been able to start it yet and will probably do most of it after you come back. . . .

> For always and always
> Steve

TO ROSEMARY BENÉT

> Scarsdale, N.Y.
> June 1922

Delightsome Bride:—

All yesterday was spent in the Port Monmouth Adventure— . . . The proprietor . . . was no pretty lass who dropped me a curtsey but a nice pitiful vague retired teacher named Rankin who . . . was very interesting. He had been one of a gang in London years ago whose kingpin was Arnold Bennett before A.B. was known at all—[had] known A.B. very well—said he told them once he was going to make $175,000 a year some time with a fine-pointed pen, and they had all believed him, doubting entirely his ability to write but knowing his utterly unsinkable energy. He had written himself—been in with the N.Y. art-crowd of 20–30 years ago—spoke of when they were still skying Winslow Homer and when Roger Fry came over from England to start the Burlington magazine—mentioning people all the way whom I barely knew by name, but did know that they had been among the minor gods of that rather desiccated epoch. And then—well, obviously something had happened, as he said that he had not been in touch with literature or art at all for the last ten years. One of those gentle rather broken people you run across that remind you of [Richard] Hovey's so much too truthful skit that ends "Where are all my first editions? I feel chilly and grown old." But he was so nice—I wish I could send him some bonds or make him sub-curator of the Metropolitan.

Today has been one of those perfect Scarsdale days that occur as often as once a year . . . I don't enjoy nice days without you, my dear, my darling. All I have done has been play tennis and type that story—and ache for you.

I am so glad your father seems better—and Kind Uncle James is a man after my own heart. I hope he enjoys the movies as much as my father does—I still remember how grand I used to feel when I went to the movies with him and a bag of 10-cent store candy in Augusta, for he always took me in a box which cost fully five cents extra in those simple days. . . .

> Always
> Steve

TO ROSEMARY BENÉT

> Scarsdale, N.Y.
> June 1922

Sweetheart:—

I love you, my angel, even with my mind in its present condition of tired pea-soup after tearing off 3000 words and 1000 still to do this eve, every soggy little particle in it gives you all the love there is in its tired peasoupiness—and, really, there is an extraordinary amount . . .

This damn man in my story is strapped on an operating

table, I must leap and either save or kill him. I'd much prefer the latter, but I'm afraid he's worth more money living than dead.

. . . When this story's over, I'll praise God and really write you. Till then I love you and love you past all articulation.

Always
Steve

TO ROSEMARY BENÉT

Scarsdale, N.Y.
June 1922

Darling:—

I have just put a conclusion to the troubles of my beautiful miser's daughter ["The Golden Bessie"] and feel a bit fagged in consequence—especially after a day in town where I was interviewed on the flapper and marriage by a plump lady in pince-nez who is prepared to syndicate our happy home-life all over the West. I also looked at two apartments—a bit grimy but only $75 and $85 a month, on 37th Street just off the Avenue. The owner is a neat little tailor who he informed me was a prominent member of the Dickens Society, indeed it seemed that he was once an officer therein, and much interested in literary people—especially in regard to their well known desire for a quiet life. His last tenants were actors who started hitting on all six at midnight . . .

I have been taking these last few days and the week-end off from the search for a summer-cottage as I thought I'd really better try and get some work lined up that Carl could sell before I loosed my white brachet. C. wants a love-story—modern—particularly—says Ray Long is howling for them. . . .

Always
Steve

TO EDWARD BLISS REED [3]

326 East 57th Street
New York, N.Y.
January 9, 1923

Dear Professor Reed:—

Though apparently completely forgetful of my debt to The Unknown Benefactor (to give him his proper Dickens capitals) I really haven't been as unmindful as I seemed. But getting married and other things, as well as natural laziness, have kept me from paying any of the five hundred back before now. However, here is fifty of it for a starter and I certainly hope to pay the rest of it back as soon as possible. Would you tell the Kind Gentleman, also, that it was by far the best $500 of my existence so far, as without it I wouldn't have gone to France or met my present wife? Really, I don't think anybody ever had as good a time on that amount of money! With all best wishes to yourself and the Unknown Benefactor.

Sincerely
Stephen Vincent Benét

3. 1872–1940. A member of the English Department at Yale during Benét's undergraduate period. It was he who lent the young poet $500 for his trip to Paris in 1920.

TO JOHN DRINKWATER [4]

224 East 15th Street
New York, N.Y.
[May] 1923

Dear Mr. Drinkwater:—

Thanks for your letter. I'm particularly glad you liked "King David." May I say, in return, that I read *The Pilgrim of Eternity* with the greatest interest. It seems much the clearest and fairest account of Byron's life that I know—especially as regards the extraordinary Augusta business which is unraveled as well as an incredible web of that sort could be. All the other lives of Byron I have read have been so over-heated. Thanks again.

Very sincerely
Stephen Vincent Benét

TO ETHEL [ANDREWS] MURPHY

New York, N.Y.
[August] 1923

Dear Ethel:—

. . . We're going back to the great city tomorrow and to even greater indecisiveness because all I've heard from John Farrar about the play [*Nerves*] so far has been in polite little notes that say "Dear Steve:—no definite news yet. Writing you again shortly. Affectionately, John." It may be going to be put on in the Hippodrome with a chorus of diving elephants or it may be in Lee Shubert's

4. 1882–1937. English poet and dramatist, whom Benét had met during World War I when Drinkwater lectured at Yale.

wastebasket. . . . We thought of trying to join you at one time and then people came down over the week-end to see us. Also my agent has gone on a vacation which ends Monday and when I call there—which I may say I expect to at the earliest moment to find out whether we will have to sleep in the Park this winter or not—I expect to find all approaches clogged with penniless and dying authors broken with hunger. . . . We have been leading the simple life here so intensively that we gape at an electric sign—a simple life only disturbed by incoherent telegrams from *Time*. . . .[5]

> as ever
>
> Steve

TO THOMAS AND RACHEL CARR

New York, N.Y.
January 9, 1924

Dear Mr. & Mrs. Carr:—

. . . I suppose Rosemary has told you of her job with Holt & Co. She seems to enjoy it—all except the Arabic phrases that peppered one book she was working on . . .

There is little news from Kingston [N.Y., where Benét's parents were living] except Father's return from Europe. He arrived last week, well, and adorned with a new over-coat, the gift of my uncle, having had a very interesting and amusing time. He sampled various French vintages, went to at least one ambassadorial dinner, saw Paris with a thoroughness that leaves me gasping . . .

5. During 1923 Benét wrote a series of literary columns and reviews for *Time*

The play business hitches along as usual.[6] We are hoping for a definite contract this week on this show [*That Awful Mrs. Eaton*] we are writing now but I don't know how things will turn out. I think there is a good chance of something worthwhile coming out of this particular affair—but all theatrical business is chancy & dilatory. However, we persist. The other play (the written one) [*Nerves*] is now trotting about at various managers' doors but as yet has been received with no cries of "Come to Papa!" But I'm all for 1924! . . .

Affectionately
SVB

TO ROSEMARY BENÉT

Detroit, Michigan
July 16, 1924
[Telegram]

Back Thursday afternoon. Critics favorable, audiences enthusiastic, Senator Couzens called in person with congratulations but play [*That Awful Mrs. Eaton*] needs drastic revision. Not discouraged, however. Great love from your wandering husband who is always and intensively yours. Steve

6. Benét was collaborating with John Farrar on *Nerves,* a World War I drama which Farrar had originally written for a Yale theatrical organization, and on an historical play about Andrew Jackson entitled, after its heroine, *That Awful Mrs. Eaton.* The latter—*Jackson,* as Benét several times refers to it in these letters—was produced by the celebrated William A. Brady. *Nerves* was produced by his son, William A. Brady, Jr.

TO ROSEMARY BENÉT

The Yale Club
New York, N.Y.
August 13, 1924

Jane darling:—

. . . As I surmised, my arriving Monday made *no* difference at all. But since then many remarkable things have happened, Imprimis—Winifred Lenihan is going to play the lead in *Nerves!* I hope she doesn't go around saving France all the time myself—John [Farrar] and Kenneth [MacKenna] are intensely pleased—and so am I for that matter—only I simply can't imagine her doing that sort of a part.

I spent yesterday with John and Ken—and this afternoon with J & K. Consequently, I have the following impressions on the situation

(1) *Nerves* will open Sept. 1 in a Shubert Theatre (J & K)

(2) *Nerves* can't open in a good Shubert Theatre Sept. 1—because there aren't any—and I have the pick of those there are (W.A.B.) [William A. Brady, Sr., producer of *That Awful Mrs. Eaton*].

(3) *Nerves*   entirely
        has to be partially
  Jackson   a little

          John
  rewritten by Me   before
          God
        Monday (consensus)

The Old Man [Brady senior], who is now entirely sober, and wealthier than I have ever seen him, *now* intends starting Jackson rehearsals the 25 of August and opening Sept. 15. Bill [William A. Brady, Jr.] intends starting *Nerves* rehearsals next Monday and opening Sept. 1. So—as far as I can see both plays will have to be rewritten before next Monday and when you see me again I will be wearing straw in my hair.

Also Carl called up today and wants me to write a lovely, whimsical costume Xmas story all about Xmas and a little Xtian child for the Xmas *Cosmopolitan*. Naturally, I snapped at the chance—but Judas!

Also, I have started reviewing shows for the *Bookman* and have to date seen 1 aseptic & dull musical comedy, *Marjorie,* and *Dancing Mothers* which isn't as bad as it sounds but why say any more about it? *The Werewolf* opens around Saturday after this one—and I hear it is nice. Will you go to it with me?

The house is lonely without you. I *love* you, I do. Tell me when you think it best to come back. I'll hear Thursday about the plans for Jackson . . . I could probably come up [to Peterborough, N.H.] Friday after this Friday for Sat. & Sun. Or I could come up this Sun. or Mon. to meet you at Worcester [Mass.] depending just on whatever you want to do. Or any time you wire me—I could come *right away*. I miss you like hell, but I want you and the Little Baby to enjoy the placid country and get all strong and bouncing. . . .

Always
Steve

TO ROSEMARY BENÉT

New York, N.Y.
August 14, 1924

Dear Kitty Alone:—

Torn between Brady and Brady, I feel like a stretched rubber band! Mr. B., not to be outdone by Bill is now thinking of starting rehearsing Jackson [*That Awful Mrs. Eaton*] Monday! And opening Sept. 8! But definite news will be wired to you. . . . We saw Lenihan yesterday— she isn't pretty off the stage—bad teeth—but she has a nice apartment & was pleasantly enthusiastic about the play. I was up till 3 A.M. typing but feel fine today. No— I typed in the kitchen—and the Colbys *didn't* knock on the ceiling.

How are you? HOW ARE YOU? How about dropping me a line? . . .

Steve

TO ROSEMARY BENÉT

The Yale Club
New York, N.Y.
August 16, 1924

Jane darling:—

. . . Things seem finally now to have jellied. I admit that you may have heard this statement from me before somehow—and that tomorrow you will probably hear it again with an entirely different tenor—but sufficient to the day are the Bradys thereof—and at present (1) *Nerves* opens [at] the Comedy [Theatre] Sept. 2. The

113

Comedy is the right size. It has a few disadvantages—but the terms are very favorable—we can make money there on low receipts and if it's a big hit we can move.

(2) Jackson tries out Sept. 4 in Stamford (Lord knows why!) for one night and returns to N.Y. then to be re-rehearsed and open Sept. 8.

We are rewriting the 3rd act of *Nerves* tomorrow and Sunday—and also casting Jackson tomorrow afternoon & starting *Nerves* rehearsal Sunday night. Whee! . . .

> Always
> SVB

TO ROSEMARY BENÉT

> The Yale Club
> New York, N.Y.
> August 21, 1924

Jane darling:—

. . . Since I wrote last much has happened—including a new postponement of Jackson because someone whom Mr. Brady scornfully describes as a Yiddish bootlegger put up a higher price for the National Theatre. So we now may open it the 15th or 22nd—or indeed almost any time. MacKenna commented that after each postponement of Jackson the rehearsal time grew shorter and predicts that some bright day we will be called up with the news that it is to open the following morning, with Jefferson the hero instead of Jackson. And *I* wouldn't be surprised!

Nerves is getting along finely. During the last 2 days, Lenihan has threatened to quit, Bill has threatened to quit and Johnny has left the theatre in a rage declaring he would never come back. After which—all settled down and was calm. I think we're on the right [track] and if there aren't too many temperamental explosions—the show ought to look pretty good the first night. . . .

Always
Steve

TO EDNA ST. VINCENT MILLAY

The Graduates Club
New Haven, Conn.
[October] 1924

Dear Jerry:—

This is to introduce Bus Bronson.[7] He is one of the best—pray treat him as if he belonged to the Dirty Four. Love from Rosemary, Henry [Carter] & me.

As ever
Steve

TO ROSEMARY BENÉT [8]

New York, N.Y.
May 20, 1925

Darling:—

The news that you (D.V.) will be back next Tuesday is honey and balm to my heart. I can now remark that I have simply *pined* for you all week and that if you were to be gone 2 months, say, I would simply burst into little bits with a loud report. . . .

7. Francis W. Bronson, novelist and editor.
8. Rosemary and Stephanie Jane were in Chicago, visiting the Carrs.

I'm so glad you like *Hotspur* [a novel Benét hoped to write]. I've been taking notes on it whenever I thought of anything. His full name is Thomas Clovelly Hotspur. The story is written in the first person by his friend Snipe Wigan. It won't be a pretty story but I think it has points. The one after that will be called *Apollyon* from "Apollyon straddled all across the way." "Say no more," quoth he, "for, by my infernal den, here will I spill thy soul!"

I finally decided I didn't like *The Singing Sword* for the poems, rather have it for a novel. So the poems will now be called

TIGER JOY

from this quote from Shelley's "Prometheus Unbound"

> "Oh gentle moon, thy crystal accents pierce
> The caverns of my pride's deep universe
> Charming the tiger, joy, ... "

I think this is good—at least it expresses the quality I should like to get in my poetry. I am hoping this is a year I can do some real work in and if so I intend to ride it. *Sub rosa.* I saw Lee Wilson Dodd, today [9]—his play has been tentatively taken by the [Theater] Guild —and we blew a pipe-dream together of dramatizing Conrad's *Victory* when we were both less occupied. It would make a swell play of the *Rain* type if it could be rightly done, and while our talk will probably come to nothing, I intend to keep the thought in my mind. . . .

Always
Steve

9. 1879–1933. Poet, novelist, playwright, and critic. Dodd was Henry Canby's brother-in-law.

1922–1926

TO ROSEMARY BENÉT

MacDowell Colony
Peterborough, N.H.
June 6, 1925

Darling:—

This place, in spite of Large Cool Mountains, is hot.
Not bilin', y'understand, just a-simmerin'. But nevertheless, one needs neither woodfires nor flannel nighties. I
hope this does not mean it is hot in N.Y., where you
and my heart are.

I am staying at the Men's Lodge. For studio, I have
the Wood Studio. It is covered with bark and Douglas
[Moore] was there in 1916. . . .

There are present at the Men's Lodge, M. James Rorty,
a poet, Californian, and writes review for [*New York
Herald Tribune*] *Books*. He is nice. Also M. Idon'tknow-
what Novik. A composer who wears little piqué trousers.
He is nice . . . M. Maxwell Bodenheim is expected
shortly.

Other members of the Colony include—Mr. [E. A.]
Robinson—the Heywards—a rather pretty girl named
Virginia Moore who writes poetry . . . —that Day man
we saw last summer who writes sex-plays anent the
growling of the sea—two nice artists, man and wife,
named Stonehill—and some other ladies, one of whom
is named Bates. Mrs. Anderson has not arrived—she
must be sleeping or feasting or hath taken a mate for
letters are here for her but she is not. The Louis Untermeyers are also expected. I wish you were.

I went to bed at nine-thirty and rose at seven. Am I
not a good boy?

(A strange woman in a white dress has suddenly stationed herself with an enormous black camera out in the road and is taking a picture of this studio and as far as I can see of the back of my neck. I wonder who *she* is? It is an AliceinWonderland incident—perhaps she will turn into a sheep or a chessman—I would not be surprised).

Everybody has been very nice, including the Heywards and Mr. Robinson. I am still very scairt of EAR but it may wear off. He and Mr. Rorty played pool last night. I am still very sleepy and haven't started to work yet. The quiet, of course, appals me and the birds in the morning sound louder than airplane engines. I am a city child. See-a da cockroch-a. I saw a squirrel today and Mr. Novik saw a partridge. Either he has better eyes or a weaker sense of veracity.

Darling, I miss you like hell.

Take care of yourself now, and don't try anything like getting along without maids.

. . . As I have remarked, I miss you. You are the prize sweetie of existence. Kiss yourself for me long and hard, and also Staffney. Do not kiss secondhand Rose, however —she ids too perspiry.

With the love of an aching heart,

Always
Steve

TO ROSEMARY BENÉT

MacDowell Colony
Peterborough, N.H.
June 1925

Angel of Light:—

. . . It thunderstormed yesterday afternoon quite ferociously, so today is cool and clean. Last night Mr. Day took some of us for a long ride in his bye-bye—would you had been there—the air smelt of wet pine-needles in a charming way. Being here is rather like being on a ship, because the chief interests are food and walking. Also the arrival of new colonists—one named Harris came yesterday, all the way from California in a dusty car with a blue bandana tied over one headlight. He is doing several symphonic poems and asked me if there was any rule against working before breakfast. . . .

Listen—will you look in the drawer of the desk and find a package of blank pledge-cards and send them to me? I promised [Eugene E.] Oviatt at that lunch to write letters asking for money for the *Yale Review* and now, alas, I have to do it. They have I give blank dollars for a period of blank years to the Yale Publishing Association blank blank etc. on them—you know the kind of things.

. . . Tomorrow I hope to really do some work—today I have still been acclimating and making up a form letter to send to *Yale Review* donors. . . .

Dearest, *dearest* girl! I love you like anything and everything. I would rather be with you on the hottest of

East 57 Street than walking with God and Mrs. Mac-
Dowell in the middle of these surf-sounding pines. . . .
Always
and more than always yours

TO ROSEMARY BENÉT

MacDowell Colony
Peterborough, N.H.
June 1925

Darling:—

. . . You would have loved to see us last night—everybody else had various things to do or work to finish, so I
was left alone with Mr. Robinson and talked to him behind a smoke-cloud till 10 P.M. He was very nice & kind
though tired because he had been working on a long
poem. He is evidently fond of Douglas [Moore] . . . He
astonished me by having read and liked *Wife of the
Centaur* [by Cyril Hume], grumbling that it was young,
of course, but that the young man seemed to have the
root of the matter in hand. He told me several funny
stories, though not alas, the one about the brush-broom
cocktail, and confided that he did not see how anyone
wrote when they were even slightly intoxicated—he had
never been able to. He is a grand old bird. I also like
Harris, the early-rising Californian—he impresses me as
being extremely real. I think he regards the colony a
trifle humorously. He used to run a delivery-truck for a
living & got in the habit of working early then, before

he went out on his route. He is wild, but a good sort. If the Alumni Directory has addresses in it, send it on— I will need the addresses for the damn *Yale Review* letters. I have written Carl about your friend Helen Klumpf.

Poor Staphne—I hope her vaccination doesn't hurt her too much. Kiss her for me and tell her that all doctors but her grandmother are deceptive creatures.

Last night I walked back to the Men's House late and the sky glittered like a show-window in Tiffany's. If you were here we could lie on our backs on the pine needles and look up at the stars. I wish we could.

. . . I send you a few pine-needles, a funny white flower, and all my heart,

Always

Steve

TO ROSEMARY BENÉT

MacDowell Colony
Peterborough, N.H.
June 12, 1925

Delightful Girl:—

I enclose a letter from Carl & one from a gentleman who liked "Elementals." I *knew* the last part of S.B. [*Spanish Bayonet*] would annoy them [the editors of *Pictorial Review*], but Caterina is going to stay dead by gum. The idiots! However it means I may come down. Then I will see you which will be the most pleasant and cheering thing that has happened to me since I saw you last. . . .

Last evening I went to the movies with the Heywards . . . Coming back—in M'sieu Day's car—we picked up

Mr. Robinson at Mrs. MacDowell's & I saw the latter for the first time since arriving here. She was very pleasant & hoped I was comfortable. I said I was, and felt that I should have done much more work than I have. But there is something about the quiet that I am not quite used to yet—leaving the major fact that I miss you continuously. After coming back in the car—it was a glittering night—Mr. Robinson looked up at the stars reflectively & said "There is something about those stars that mystifies and humiliates me more and more as I grow older. They keep making me suspect that it doesn't make a damn bit of difference whether I finish the poem I'm writing or not." So you see that he is human. . . .

Always
Steve

TO ROSEMARY BENÉT

MacDowell Colony
Peterborough, N.H.
June 20, 1925

Darling:—

It was a heavenly visit . . . I thought of it & you all the long hot day in the train . . .

Mrs. Anderson is here & in grand form. . . . Sara Teasdale was here last night but was called away this morning—she was very pleasant and nice. I am tinkering with *Spanish Bayonet*—some things that have to be fixed up anyhow, like the revolt which I never was crazy about—it needs thickening—and this morning sent Carl 3 alternative plans for ending the serial otherwise & keeping Caterina alive. One I wouldn't mind doing so much, but as it is the gloomiest I imagine *Pictorial* [*Review*] will choose one of the others. I am still biting my nails with fury at the whole tribe of magazine editors— but if we can get 10,000 it seems silly not to grab it if I can change it back in the book. Carl will let me know as soon as possible what price they will give & if they will be satisfied with anything less than wedding bells. . . . My darling girl, I love you with every breath I draw and if we get 10,000 we will paint the universe bright carmine & get you a 7 foot string of reed pearls from that shop at the bridge over the Arno! I love you,

> Always
> Steve

TO ROSEMARY BENÉT

> MacDowell Colony
> Peterborough, N.H.
> June 24, 1925

Darling:—

. . . I started doing a crazy story about a girl who became a swan. Lady into Fox, of course, but it amused me to work it out and I think some of it will amuse you. I will see how the first few pages look when they are typed—of course the darn thing's utterly unsalable. It should be done in verse, but I can't find the right form in verse for it.

Last night I played pool with Mr. Robinson. I asked afterwards if I played worse than Bill and he said with a dry smile, "As I remember your brother's game, I think you do!" But he is a nice fella.

. . . It was heavenly weather today, clear and fine, and

the pines rustling. It makes me sick that you are not here enjoying it . . .

. . . You are all that makes life worth living for this lonely colonist and I am never going to any colonies without you again if they gave me nine platinum studios and a jeweled typewriter. . . .

Always
Steve

TO ROSEMARY BENÉT

MacDowell Colony
Peterborough, N.H.
June 27, 1925

Darling:—

The rain is raining on the roof of the studio with such soft grey persistence that I am writing this letter by the aid of romantic firelight. Last night was supper at Hillcrest—diverted by the fact that young Richard Untermeyer removed the young lady that Maxwell Bodenheim had been devoting attention to, right from under Maxwell's nose & sat looking at the moon with her on the porch—& now Maxwell hates both the Untermeyers. Young Richard is a nice youth . . . He will enter Yale with the Class of 1929. "Ten years after your class, isn't it?" he remarked to me pleasantly & I felt senile.

He is the real younger generation & remarked to Louis "You people (meaning such hoary-headed figures as E. E. Cummings etc) of course you made a lot of *experiments* in poetry—but you really didn't have much to say." He is an amusing lad . . .

I miss you and think of you all the time and nothing
is pleasant or interesting without you to share it. . . .

Always

Steve

TO ROSEMARY BENÉT [1]

New York, N.Y.

September 26, 1925

Darling:—

The N.Y. papers fairly went into ecstasy today over
the daintiness and simplicity of Mlle. [Isabel] Rockefeller's wedding. The height of naivete was reached
when one said it was such a small house wedding that
only 16 special policemen were required to guard the
house and keep the crowds away. Darling, would [you]
have liked to marry a Rockefeller? I should not—especially after noting that young Mr. Lincoln's hair is turning prematurely grey—due doubtless to his meeting so
many wealthy in-laws at once.

. . . Saw Walter Millis in the Yale Club this evening.
He is trying to revise & cut his novel in accordance with
[Henry] Canby's suggestions & says he is having the
devil of a time.

. . . Doran is going to get out a special limited edition
of *Tiger Joy* as well as the regular one, quite doggy,
with vellum covers—but all I can think of is when I can
see my lovely girl.

I have been making notes for *Hotspur* in the interim
of S.B. [*Spanish Bayonet*]—S.B. is getting a bit melo-
dramatic, I fear—everything I think of mixes with how

1. Mrs. Benét was visiting her family in Chicago.

sweet your hands are, how Irish sea your eyes and how I should like to be a-kissing of you this very minute.

I will wire Saturday in case absolutely no news of M[innie]. She is as elusive as a flea. *Why* are servants like that? This is a silly letter but I love you and love you and love you and long for your return with all my heart, every second.

Your confused, imbecile but loving
Steve

TO ROSEMARY BENÉT [2]

The Yale Club
New York, N.Y.
May 25, 1926

Darling:—

Don't worry! I enclose herewith 2 checks for $50 apiece and will send them tonight by airplane mail. I phoned Stan [Rinehart] & he very kindly gave me $750 advance on the new *Spanish Bayonet* royalties, so you see everything is all right. S.B., by the way, has sold over 7,000 net (excluding 800 or so review or free copies) so besides *this* check we will get at least $900 more from it during the year, so that's nice, isn't it? The gross sales are over 8,000. . . .

I wrote another story yesterday and am typing it today. It is called "Bon Voyage" and is a dear little candy-

2. In Chicago briefly, before sailing for France with her husband and Stephanie Jane after the award to the former of a Guggenheim Fellowship for 1926–27.

laxative of a tale about a sweet little girl named Sally.
I do not see how it can fail to sell—it is so cheap. . . .

LOVE!

always

Steve

TO ROSEMARY BENÉT

New York, N.Y

May 26, 1926

Jane dearest:—

(I sent you $100 by air-mail yesterday. Should it not
arrive by any chance, wire me.)

It is pleasant indeed to have a little cash again. I
went & had my shoes recklessly half-soled today and
damned the expense. How pleasant it is to have money,
heigh-ho, how pleasant it is to have money!

. . . I shall meet you with a grin broader than a
Cheshire Cat's at the thought of having you back again.
I have missed you like hell. Don't go away again for at
least 25 years.

Tomorrow is Johnny [Farrar]'s bachelor dinner but I
will take precautions not [to] be carried away from it
asserting that I am a mongoose. . . .

I am going to try & write one more story, if I can, before you get back. That will make 3 in about 2 weeks,
which isn't so bad for me, if I can do it. . . .

Give my love to the Injured Warrior [Stephanie] and
to yourself the complete adoration of

Always

Steve

TO DEAN B. LYMAN, JR.[3]

224 East 15th Street
New York, N.Y.
June [10] 1926

Dear Lyman:—

Thanks a lot for your very nice article in the [*Yale Alumni*] *Weekly*, which I very much appreciated. I'd hoped to get up to New Haven some time during Commencement, but there are such a lot of things to settle up before we sail that it wasn't possible. However, if you happen to be in Europe any time during the next year, do drop in and see us, c/o Morgan-Harjes 11 Place Vendome Paris will always reach me—we have an apartment but I don't know the street address yet. As I say, your article made me feel quite a feller, though I insist that *Spanish Bayonet* is a good deal better book than *Jean* [*Huguenot*]. S.B. does what it sets out to do and I couldn't handle the other—I should have kept it much longer. And I happen to feel myself that the Golden Corpse business is the best thing in *Tiger Joy*. But your criticism was more than kind and those are the only serpent's-teeth I have to shed.

With much gratitude and all best wishes,

Sincerely
Stephen Benét

3. A member of the Class of 1918S at Yale, Lyman had known Benét both before and since the war.

John Brown's Body (1926-1929)

THIS was the single prolonged period during Benét's entire professional life—in all the twenty-three productive years from 1920 until 1943—when he was able to write without editorial restriction or financial duress. The letters reflect his serenity and concentration; in a number of them he also shows the high spirits and wit which were sometimes hidden in his public personality but always so firmly an ingredient of his friendships.

Now too, for the only time in his life, his letters were consistently concerned with his plans and progress. In part, of course, this was because he was separated from his New York literary associations; he wrote in detail what normally he would have discussed at luncheon or cocktails or over the phone. In part too, however, the fullness of professional detail is a symptom of his absorption in *John Brown's Body* and his sense of release at being temporarily free of the formula short story.

The drama of these four years is also present in the letters. It extends from the birth of his son through the enormous success of his epic poem; it includes those final months of the decade which show not only his new reluctance to publish inferior work but also the beginnings of his role as a public figure and American man of letters. These were also years of pain and tragedy, of his own first illness, of his grief for his brother when Elinor

Wylie died, and above all of the death of his father. Benét seems in retrospect to have lived the major events of most lifetimes in the months from the autumn of 1926 through the winter and spring of 1929.

TO SHREVE C. BADGER

14 bis Rue Jadin
Paris, France
October [1] 1926

Dear Shreve:—

Well, we have a son, named Thomas Carr & somewhat brunette in complexion. . . . a very nice infant. Jane is very well & the new American Hospital ideal.

When are you coming over here? We have a most charming apartment till the first of May & are living in what, for us, is great luxury. . . .

The baby weighs 3 kilo 50 grammes if that interests you—and does not look like me, which is fortunate. I am doing some work & expect to do more when Jane gets back from the hospital. Uncle Larry remembers your praise of his cocktails.

With much love & best wishes from all of us,

Hastily
Steve

TO WILLIAM ROSE BENÉT

89 Ave. de Neuilly
Neuilly, France
[January] 1927

Dear Bill:—

The profound apologies of this human earthworm and his vermicular family for not writing before, acknowledging the delightful cable . . . But really, all was not to the merry-merry during the last weeks of December, what with looking at one venomously-decorated apartment after another, moving between Christmas and New Year's and having the indispensable Françoise faint two days after we had moved . . . However, now things are more or less straightened out . . . this apartment is comfortable, large and quiet and we have just taken down the hand-painted oil picture of the assassination of St. Whoozis of Bulgaria, the alabaster bust of an unknown French lady of the presidency of Sadi-Carnot, and the two black memorial urns that erstwhile made the salon so tastefully French, the children enjoy the Bois, and we are catching our breath . . . I think the change will really be good for us all—Jane sleeps a lot better here and I have to walk at least ten blocks a day for cigarettes which enforces some exercise. My damn poem is getting ahead though every time I sit down to it I wonder if anyone else will ever be able to read it without falling asleep. So far I've only shown it to Ramon Guthrie who seemed to think there might be something in it. I shall inflict a heavy wad of it upon you sometime soon when I get together enough to really produce a comparative deadly effect.

. . . We're thinking of going to Bizy [Normandy] for the summer, if we can manage it and are going there soon with Dick [Myers] to look about a house. Of course as soon as the Guggenheim money runs out, we will be broke, but something may turn up in the meanwhile. I hear Sidney Howard's two new plays are fine—I suppose you've seen them—I wish we could. . . .

As ever
Steve

TO WILLIAM ROSE BENÉT

89 Ave. de Neuilly
Neuilly, France
March 2, 1927

Dear Bill:—

. . . The poem is getting along—I am typing the 3rd instalment—sometimes I think it is good & sometimes wonder who will read it but the typesetters—but I shall finish it or explode in loud fragments of *Battles and Leaders of the Civil War* all over my quaint little room on the 5th floor which has two quaint little porthole windows that let out all the heat of the quaint stove on one of those quaint winter days when you want to cover yourself with earmuffs & bearskins. . . .

As ever
With all our love
Steve

TO JOHN F. CARTER, JR.

89 Ave. de Neuilly
Neuilly, France
[March] 1927

Dear John:—

I have owed you a letter for far too long and now when I want to answers yours I can't find [it] under the seventeen notices from the Yale Club that I ought to pay my dues and the various appeals from stenographers who keep thinking with a pitiful faith that I wish to send my manuscripts back to America to be typed. . . . Sometime I will buy a suit without pockets and then I will be able to find letters when I want them.

There is only one thing about publishers. Whatever one you pick out will advertise less than every other publisher and will advertise every other book on their list more than yours. This is a great physical law and has something to do with the dew-point. By the way may I convey a wreath to you from Uncle Laurie, who was very much struck with *Man Is War*. He was heartily in accord with all its conclusions and thinks you a very well-informed young man—there ought to be more like you in the Republican party. So any time you want a job assembling machine-guns just come over. . . . I thought of you this morning on reading in the Paris *Herald* that President Angell [of Yale] wishes to erect a third college of somethingorother to supplement Ac and Sheff. We stopped *The Songs of Dear Old Yale* too soon. I can see a Masque—outside the door of the delivery-room—President Angell and Chorus of Millionaires:

> What is it to be,
> Oh, what is to be?
> This novel educational mule,
> Perhaps it'll be a Dental School
> Or a really bisexual most Intellectual
> College of Pharmacy.

Loud groans from the parturient Corporation.
Solo from the Ghost of The Old Yale Fence on the theme of,

> You can give your tainted billions
> To uplift the Jewish millions
> And broadcast Brooklyn babies bedtime stories,
> You can teach ten thousand Babbitts
> How to breed Bulgarian rabbits,

But for God's sake leave me something
That was Mory's.

Chorus of Economics Professors on the Better not Bigger
Yale:

Is it Better, Is it Bigger,
That depends on how you figger, etc.

Increased groans from the p.c. Chorus of Y men and
Stovers: "In the days of the Wooden Spoon."
  Magical transformations by the ghost of Mr. Sterling,
who changes Connecticut Hall to Sterling Hall, President Angell to President Sterling, and Longley's to Sterling's Lunch, shakes hands with Mr. Duke and departs.
Groans reach climax and nurse rushes in announcing
twins—a dear little taxidermy academy and a sweet little
college of sky-writing and bond-forgery. Grand finale
with red and green lights to tune of

We're coming Father Elihu,
Two hundred million more,
To put a coat of platinum
On the Spoon.

And every baby, dull or bright,
As long as he can read and write,
Is sure to be a Yale man pretty soon!

  I grieve that this did not occur while we were still in
York Street and could deal with it fittingly.
  . . . I have applied to renew my scholarship for six
months more as I don't see how I'll be able to finish this
damn poem in the required year. I hope they grant it—
I now have three parts done out of eight—sometimes

I think the thing will make a stir if I can finish it properly and sometimes that it is merely softening of the brain— probably it will sell 1500 copies and be indeterminately reviewed, that is generally the way—anyhow, it isn't quite like anything else but whether that means it is a unicorn or just a mistake I don't quite know. . . .

I have read *The Sun Also Rises*—the fiesta was fine but I got a little tired of the S bus and the woman, though doubtless reported with accuracy, doesn't get across, in spite of the underplaying. He can write though, although not for as long a distance as that, yet.

. . . With malice towards none, with charity towards all, with love to yourself, Effie and Shreve, with faith in the right as God gives us to see the right and the best wishes for a happy and profitable Easter from your old Headmaster and the boys of the crew of the *Monitor*.

As ever

Steve

TO WILLIAM ROSE BENÉT

89 Ave. de Neuilly
Neuilly, France
March [20] 1927

Dear Bill:—

Thanks a lot for selling the poem ["American Names"] —I sent it to Mr. [Ridgely] Torrence telling him to send it to you in case he didn't want it and then forgot to write you about it. I'm glad the *Yale Review* took it—I hadn't had anything there for a long time.

Wild Goslings is perfectly fine and we are simply de- lighted with it. It's a grand collection and I hope it sells like anything. I saw [Herbert] Gorman's review and your picture in the ad. and was charmed. . . .

I have grown a hay-colored moustache and am having my teeth filled by a French dentist but am still recognizable. Red Lewis passed through here a few days ago and we saw him. He wanted me particularly to tell you that he is feeling much better and is going to spend a healthy summer in the Pyrenees or the Tyrol. It was nice to see him. . . . My poem is now staggering toward the end of its fourth part—fortunately the kindly Guggenheims have renewed my scholarship for another six months at a slightly reduced figure, so I will be able to finish the damn thing sooner or later. I wish I had about a million books on the Civil War that aren't in the American Library, but then I am having trouble enough with the ones I can use—people lie so, especially when they write their reminiscences. We are eagerly waiting for Elinor [Wylie]'s arrival—is she coming here first or going to London? Give her our love—I'm awfully glad she is going to come before we go to Bizy—though Neuilly sometimes seems nearly as far when you don't catch the last bus. . . .

As ever

Steve

TO WILLIAM ROSE BENÉT

89 Ave. de Neuilly
Neuilly, France
April [25] 1927

Dear Bill:—

. . . I am simply tickled to death that you are bringing out the selected poems—it will be a marvel and there will be few books of American poetry, past or present, to touch it. I like *Madman on a Drum* as a title but not quite for that book. My vote would be for *Man Possessed* which has the same sting but sort of more amplitude and, to other heavier guns—but you get a lot better titles than I do, anyhow, so why should I put in my oar? How long will the book run and what are you putting in? I think now I'll call my thing *John Brown's Body* definitely —I am through with the fourth part and hope to see my way ahead to the finish. If I can find a cheap typist I'll have what I've done retyped & send it to you—I should do it myself but fresh groans at the thought of retyping 135 pages. I am very anxious to see what you think of it—as I say, it's a queer start & sometimes I think it will be the most colossal flop since Barlow's *Columbiad.* Needless to say I'd be very glad to have Henry [Canby] see it too and would value his opinion. Some of it could be separated & printed separately I think, though I don't know how much—maybe the invocation in the 3rd part or some of the John Brown raid in particular. But I'm afraid the effect of the thing, if any, is a mass effect. Anyhow, expect a heavy job for the short summer evenings soon. . . .

As ever
Steve

P.S. Don't leave out "Jesse James"! Gee, that will be a swell book.

TO ROBERT NATHAN [4]

89 Ave. de Neuilly
Neuilly, France
May 21, 1927

Dear Bob:—

I am at present extinguished under the tall foolscap of this long poem. Nobody will read it, nobody will buy it, and the linotypers will just shrdlu all over it. However we are having a very nice time which would be amplified by your presence . . . We all send you much love and would like to see you.

Steve

TO MRS. JAMES WALKER BENÉT

48 Rue de la Côte
Bizy, France
[June] 1927

I am very much saddened to get the enclosed in the mail this morning—the news of Bob Terrill's death [a Yale classmate and Benét's roommate during Freshman year]. I had no idea of it—though I suppose the accident was in the New York papers. It is tragic—and I feel very badly about it. We had more or less drifted apart—and it was entirely my fault that we had—but I always liked him and when I last saw him he was having a good time, very satisfied with his new job and looking forward to sailing [Terrill was drowned in a sailing accident].

4. Benét's friendship with Robert Nathan, the prolific author of a number of novels and fantasies, originated in New York in the early 1920's and remained a warm one throughout Benét's life.

He was a good person, a kind person, and one of the most loyal people I have ever known. . . . I have written his family the usual letter, saying the things one says. . . . I thought you might want to write his mother, as you knew him and liked him so—so enclose the notice with the address.

. . . The poem is now approaching Gettysburg. After that, there will be the winding up. It could go on forever as far as the information is concerned but there has to be an end to everything and I can't refight the whole war. . . . I have read *Elmer Gantry* which I liked on the whole, though not as well as *Arrowsmith*. It is hard to make a scoundrel interesting through quite so long a book—especially a rather dull scoundrel with no humor. . .

> As ever
> your devoted son
> SVB

TO JOHN FARRAR

> 48 Rue de la Côte
> Bizy, France
> June [20] 1927

Dear Johnny:—

Thanks a lot for the cable about the Lindbergh poem. I will do it if I can but it would take somebody like Kipling to get away with anything really good on the subject. However, I will see. . . .

. . . My poem is three quarters done now, thank God and ought to be finished around the first week in August. But I'll have a lot of going over it to do. . . .

We have been catching up on some of the new books . . . Why doesn't somebody write a good life of Lee, by the way. There ought to be a really first-class life of him, neither the biographical-novel kind nor the old kind—and there isn't. And now is the time when somebody could do it with a little perspective. The writers are being well taken care of but the Civil War people aren't and a lot of them were damn interesting. You could write a superb novel around Forrest—there are the Grant memoirs but there is no great life of Grant—etc etc. But Lee is a crying need. And it would take brains, for he's somewhat of an ungettable man. For that matter, Davis would be quite a stunt to exhume from his legend.

Have a nice time at Cos Cob and watch your son grow and acquire teeth and speech. It is very interesting and quite incredible. Love to you all from all of us and a lifted glass of Pederschmitt's laxative beer.

As ever
Steve

TO WILLIAM ROSE BENÉT

48 Rue de la Côte
Bizy, France
July 1927

Dear Bill:—

Thanks for your letter and for Mrs. Ward's. It was nice of her to write about the Invocation and [it] pleases me.[5] I'm glad the other people liked it. It is hard to know how a thing like that will strike. But I'm afraid Mrs. Ward if a

5. Stephen Vincent Benét, "Invocation," *Saturday Review of Literature,* 3 (June 11, 1927), 891.

friend of J.B.'s grandniece will not greatly care for what I say about the old man himself. He had his points but he was a queer proposition. . . .

. . . I just read Robinson's *Tristram*. It is certainly old Ram Dass with fire in his belly—astonishing fire of that sort from E.A.R. It is a fine thing, full of beauty and force and a curious fretting intensity. In fact it is everything but a new planet and that I don't think it is. In spite of being characteristically Robinson. But when you read "Atalanta in Calydon," for instance, for the first time there is beauty and force and then there is something else that never happened before. This hasn't that. And yet he sustains and has sustained himself marvellously, while Lindsay and Masters have trailed off. Anyhow it is a good thing and I'm glad it's had the success.

. . . Love to you all from all of us and all sorts of a good time on the trip from

As ever
Steve

TO WILLIAM ROSE BENÉT

36 Rue de Longchamp
Neuilly, France
November 1927

Dear Bill:—

I am ashamed of not having written before . . . It was so fine to see you both and the stay in the New Forest was so swell that I should have written long ago. My only excuse must be that as soon as I got back we started in on the usual parturitions of moving in from the country and getting settled here—and I was sweating at John

Brown's damn body whenever I had a minute trying to get it off.

. . . I finally expedited [the manuscript] to America and am now biting my nails while I wait to hear what they think of it. I feel somewhat as if a wardrobe-trunk had been lifted from my chest now the thing is in a way completed, and am trying to hack out some short stories in the interim for a little of that cash that we all of us need. I sent the original to Doran and a carbon to the family direct. Could you read it in mss. or would you rather wait for proof? I am very anxious to see what you think of the whole bloody thing and give me some advice on it—I am still too close to the damn thing to see the wood, if any, for the interminable array of trees. The bulk of it looks fairly impressive, just as bulk, but I dunno how it will strike for an evening's reading. Tell me which [copy] you want—I'm telling the family to send this carbon on to you, if you want. It will look cleaner in the proof but then—well, you can see that I am suffering from the usual pains of the afterbirth. . . .

As ever
Steve

TO MRS. JAMES WALKER BENÉT

36 Rue de Longchamp
Neuilly, France
November [5] 1927

Dearest Mother:—

Thanks unutterably for your very sweet and prompt letter—I was getting a little worried as I said that that copy hadn't arrived—but I got your letter the following morning and a notice about the Brandt copy, too. Glad the Gettysburg descrip. sounded all right—I have a pretty hazy recollection of the place (or was I ever there? I thought I was!)—I thought of you, when reading over the Pennsylvania part—as you may have noticed, I put in the ice-cream parlor at Carlisle! I am very glad the thing seems to carry through to you and to have a movement—that was what I was trying for and unsure of. *Please do* criticize any details and catch any errors of fact that you notice and *please do have Father do the same*. I have tried to be accurate where things were a question of fact, not of opinion, but must have committed several howlers in the nature of things. I am glad you liked the Lincoln thing—I think his soliloquy is fairly good—of course much of it is taken from his own words though not the dog idea. But I rather liked the conception of his telling God a story—he did it to everyone else whenever he was worried—and I think it is in his character. Incidentally, it was not my intention to leave the stories of Spade the negro and Jake Diefer the Pennsylvanian as much up in the air as they are now. I had planned an epilogue in which they and Benjamin were included with a final Ellyat in front of the cyclorama of the battle. But when I finished the eighth book, I saw that the poem ended there and I will have to clean up the threads some other way.

About the North and the South. Now that must be in the poem, because it seems to strike people—even Ramon Guthrie when he merely read the first book. And yet I will swear that I have been throughout more interested in Ellyat's story than in Wingate's and holding no brief for either side. The Wingate part of it is the kind of thing I can do—do easily—I had more interest in working with the other and more fun with it. Of course the lost cause is always the romantic one, and I suppose something of that gets into the verse. I can't explain it for I didn't mean it to be so. As for the politics of the time—well, I am a Union man or a Lincoln man. The more you read about him, the more genuine admiration for him you develop—perhaps that is one of the things that made me somewhat impatient with Phillips and Greeley and the rest of the rather loud-mouthed people who did their best to hinder him whenever they got a chance—oh, all with the finest and purest motives, but with so little sense or vision! Lee was a great man also, but not likewise. And Grant and Jackson had greatness in them, but for many of the others—well—

Well anyhow the thing is done, though I will have to work on it a lot still. I haven't heard about it from Johnny [Farrar] yet but expect to the end of this week. Please do tell me what you like best and also what you like least. It is a very great help to know that the thing seems to move to you. It is hard to take a year to a thing of that sort without getting criticism on it while it is in the working, but naturally I couldn't. I could have put in much more but not with keeping any sort of line. As it is, the line straggles enough at times.

I have started a third short-story and hope I can bang it out in the next few days. . . .

Thanks again and more than I can say for your letter. I wish the poem were as good as that. I'm glad you think it is. Yes I'm tired—but not so much tired as relieved at having finished it. I'd lived with it so long it was like getting rid of a serious illness to come to the end. Really.

And I certainly felt when I had finished that I never wanted to write another line as long as I lived—and yet I won't be sad to start this new novel when I do.[6] Writing is a funny thing, when you've got the habit of it.

. . . The very deepest and more grateful appreciation of your letter—if I could only have done the thing as I saw it first! but it cannot be done . . .

As ever
your devoted son
SVB

TO WILLIAM ROSE BENÉT

36 Rue de Longchamp
Neuilly, France
November 1927

Dear Bill:—

Thanks inordinately for your letter. It was swell. It was Christmas a month ahead of time. Only I wish the book were that good. But it's grand to know that you like it—because when you've been working more or less alone for a while at a thing like that you end up not knowing quite where you are.

If there are any things that you think should be omitted or changed, tell me what. I know there are lots of weak lines and will try to smooth them in the proof. But if the thing seems to you to hold—that's all I want. None of us works for very many people, in the last analysis. Well, you're one of the few this baby works for, and always

6. This novel, to which Benét had given the tentative title of *The Silver Dollar*, never got beyond the outline stage. See Benét's letter of March 15, 1928, to Bernice Baumgarten.

have been. So there aren't any words to say how deeply I appreciated your letter. . . .

Mr. Guggenheim goes out of my life January first and will be mourned with appropriate ceremonies—however I have sent off some short-stories to Carl and am starting to look up stuff on a novel. After which I hope to be able to take a vacation from American History for a while. . . .

Our best love and affection to you both from all of us . . . And more than thanks for your letter. Much more than thanks. As you know.

And as ever
Steve

TO JOHN FARRAR

36 Rue de Longchamp
Neuilly, France
December 28, 1927

Dear Johnny:—

Thanks a lot for both your letters which arrived almost together—the November 22 one two days after the other as a matter of fact. Also for the cable which I meant to acknowledge at the time but didn't, what with Stephanie's operation and other things.

. . . I am very glad indeed that you think so well of [John Brown's Body]—needless to say—and particularly glad if it seemed to you to be a whole. You lose the feel of the whole, working on a thing that size for so long, and can see nothing but the parts. But I tried to put America in it—at least some of the America I knew. If I did so, some of it should stand till a better man comes along. I feel rather curiously about it myself. I think my best work so far, perhaps, is in it and yet it is more detached from me than anything I have ever done. It seemed to me that a thing of that sort should be tried. A poet of greater faculties would have avoided my failures in it and my superficialities—and there are many of both—but what I have done, I have done to the extent of such capacities as I have. At least I hope it has in it some of the landscapes, the sights, the sounds [and] the people which are American. I tried to put them there. I am tired —not of criticism of America, for no country can be healthy without self-criticism—but of the small railers, the conventional rebels. We also have a heritage—and not all of it is wooden money.

About the publication-date—I wrote Brandt & Brandt a long letter about this when they first wrote me (not having heard from you at the time—this is the same infernal difficulty of letters taking so long to go and come) saying why I would rather have had a Spring date if possible. It seemed to me first that poetry generally sold better in the Spring, that it had less competition from novels, that there was more chance of organizations such as the Book-of-the-Month [Club] taking it up, and that, with the rather dilatory way in which poetry is reviewed, if the book came out in September the reviews might not appear till the Fall crops of novels was well under way and the thing so be swamped. If, after this, however, it still seems to you both that a Fall date is preferable to a late Spring or early Summer one, go ahead on that basis. You know the state of your lists and the various publishing conditions better than I do. I think the thing has a chance of a wider appeal than the ordinary book of separate poems generally makes and am willing, not to say most grateful, to see anything done that can help that end, if possible.

I realize the mechanical difficulties and so cabled that you could set the copy you have. But I am afraid that I shall have to see at least galley-proofs. There are a number of checks on actual fact and some revisions that nobody else could do for me. If I tried to do them now on the one old working copy I have (in which some of the corrections on yours are absent)—it would take quite as long as sending galleys over and back and probably get into an awful tangle as regards page references etc. as well. Also it will be the greatest help in the world to me to see the thing actually in type—it changes the whole appearance of the poem and makes errors stick out like sore thumbs. So, if you will, send me the galleys when you have them, and I will get them back just as soon as I possibly can. The actual revision needn't take so long—but I want a fresh eye, doing it, and proofs will help me with that enormously.

There is another thing about the Fall publication date —it shoots any novel over into the Spring of 1929 at least. Which may be an advantage in some ways and is a disadvantage in one at least—that it means I will have to live on short stories through 1928, in all probability, with no novel royalties coming in, for I certainly can't count on the poem, large Siamese child though it is.

However, as I say, if after reading all this through, you are still in favor of Autumn publication, go ahead with it. I don't want or mean to raise unnecessary objections, but simply to put the thing as clearly as I can as it seems to me.

In that case I will go ahead with the new year and start in on research for the successor to *Spanish Bayonet* which seems the next thing to do logically. It should not be a hard book to write, after the research is done. I have an idea for another and very different sort of novel [*Hotspur*?] which fascinates me—but I should have to be back in America to do it. Also one for a fairly long poem—entirely different from J.B.B.—which I have started to tinker with. But I don't know how it will go. It is the kind of thing that would almost [require] a new language to really do it—or perhaps merely more brains.

This has been an extremely long letter and entirely concerned with myself and business. But this is the difficulty when one is so far away. How are you, Margaret, the Infant Phenomenon, and the merger? . . .[7]

Alors, I suppose I must quit. Thank you again for your letter—it has made me very conceited and pleased. It is worth while working in the dark for so long to feel that you mightn't possibly have made a better plumber after all. As for genius, I don't know—but it did take persistence. Incidentally if any criticisms, either of details or of the whole, do come to you, please tell me them. When that thing was finished, I felt as if I had given birth to a grand piano. Now I am slightly more normal and can thank you properly.

With all love and best wishes from all of us, and much gratitude.

As ever
Steve

7. George H. Doran and Company, of which Farrar had been an editor since the early 1920's, was uniting with Doubleday and Company to form, briefly, the house of Doubleday, Doran.

TO PHELPS PUTNAM

36 Rue de Longchamp
Neuilly, France
January 20, 1928

Dear Phelps:—

Glad if you thought the review was all right [8]—you know how very high, wide and handsome I put your work and always have—I tried to sound judicial in the review and whenever I try that I generally sound like Official Correspondence. But I was very pleased at that to get a chance too of saying some of the things I wanted to. . . . Why don't you have a shot at resting on the bosom of Mr. Guggenheim? He has done awfully well for me through this year and a half and my only regret is that he won't support me the rest of my life. They let you alone—they don't care where you go—they have no red tape, once the preliminaries are over. I don't know if you'd consider applying for it—but it damn near saved my life—and Bill the hero is certainly as good a bet as John Brown. [9]

As for him, his body is now mouldering in the Doran office and the official interment will probably be held next Fall (no flowers by request of the New York *Times*). I wish I knew what you thought of it. I wish I knew what it was going to look like. I wish I knew a lot of things. It is about 250 pages long and even contains an Address to a Muse. There are a lot of real people in it, a lot of

8. Stephen Vincent Benét, "Two Types of Poetry," *Saturday Review of Literature, 4* (December 10, 1927), 425. A review of Putnam's *Trinc* and Donald Davidson's *The Tall Men*.

9. Phelps Putnam, *The Five Seasons,* New York, 1931.

imaginary ones, and I think it can be read. It is a little on the Tall Men line,[1] but on the whole it is more my street than that. I think it has some of my best work in it— but I know I'll have to work a lot on the proof. I wish I knew if Joel Barlow felt good after he'd finished *The Columbiad*. I guess I'm glad I don't.

We've a house here and we'll be in France till next Fall anyway—maybe longer—it all depends on the money we haven't got. You can still live cheaply over here, and I'm not going back to go crazy in New York again.

Bill's life and death and further experiences sound superb. I thought you were on to something of the sort from the parts of Bill in the book. The idea fascinates me. Luck with it. I know when it's built, it'll last. Meanwhile luck and enough money and time to do it in. . . .

As ever
SVB

TO PHELPS PUTNAM

36 Rue de Longchamp
Neuilly, France
March 7, 1928

Dear Phelps:—

I've owed this letter quite a while but I've had grippe and French dentists and other complaints. . . .

About the Guggenheim thing. It is a good graft. They are very decent. They give you $2500 in four yearly instalments and tell you to run off and roll your hoop. Then they don't bother you any more. Once you're selected you're supposed to have sense enough to know

1. Donald Davidson, *The Tall Men*, Boston, 1927.

what you want to do and how and where to do it. In the eighteen months I held the thing I got just one letter from them that wasn't an answer to one of mine—and that was to tell me not to put the money down on my income tax account. Abraham and the rest of the patriarchs could go no farther.

The man who is secretary and who attends to the actual running of the thing is named Henry Allen Moe. He is all right. He is particularly proud of doing his job with [as] little red tape as possible.

They have about three million dollars and give out around fifty scholarships a year. Three quarters of them go to the people who are investigating the habits of the evening primrose or tabulating Minoan brick-work etc. but they run quite a few musicians, painters etc and say they are anxious to get more writers.

. . . What I said in my 'plan' boiled down to this— that I was sick of writing short-stories and wanted to do a long poem on some American subject. I told them I had several ideas—including the Civil War one—but couldn't say which one I'd take—and that seemed all right with them. I should think that Bill would certainly be as good a bet as John Brown's torso any time. And, as I say, the thing is worth having a shot at. They really are very sensible and very considerate to deal with in spite of the rather awe-inspiring list of directors, etc, on the pamphlet. No expense accounts—fatherly chaperonage—no good advice. If you want to go to Europe because you can live there cheaper, they know about that. . . .

This is a lot of rather ponderous information but I

thought I might as well give you such dope as I have. If there is anything else I can do, from acting as a reference to dropping this Moe man a line to tell him you'll be in, I'd be only too glad. . . .

I don't know about this American wave, except that it has me swimming. Maybe it'll be a literature. And maybe again it will be just another Frigidaire. But I want to throw my brick with the rest of them. And I bank on Bill.

Luck—and if there's any more dope I can give you about The Guggenheims, tell me.

Steve

TO BERNICE BAUMGARTEN [2]

36 Rue de Longchamp
Neuilly, France
March 15, 1928

Dear Bernice:—

. . . About the novel. The one I have in my mind would be the successor to *Spanish Bayonet*. It would deal with the nephew of SB's hero and would take place principally in the time of the Tripoli pirates. The scene would be America, the Barbary States and possibly France. Jefferson would appear in it and possibly a glimpse of Napoleon. Dr. Gentian would reappear for a scene or two. This hero is a stronger character than his uncle and more of a maker of events. There should be something of the development of a great New York

2. A member of the editorial staff at Brandt and Brandt, and later Carl Brandt's principal assistant.

trading house and something of a young America feeling its oats and finding herself on the sea. But it isn't a sea story exactly. There should be a good deal of adventure, one incidental love affair and one love affair carrying through that comes to no fruition. But none of the principal characters are killed. The thing ends up in a knife-fight (with no result) between the hero and his dead uncle's best friend—the older man whom the hero has given a good deal of hero-worship to, quite deservedly. It should run to about 100,000. My working title is *The Silver Dollar*—an actual silver dollar plays something of a part—but I am not very satisfied with it. I have not the plot very clearly yet but see several scenes, including the first scene and the last. That is generally the way I do.

I have been hoping to finish it for around the first of next October but haven't really got into the preliminary reading yet—due to sickness, visitors, and trying to think up short stories, now Mr. Guggenheim has departed. I want to do a couple more sses before I really start work, in order to have something to fall back on. Once the preliminary spadework is done, I ought to be able to write the book fairly rapidly. I am hoping to get quite a lot of research cleared up next month.

I have ideas for two other books but one I don't want to write now and the other would need fully as much research in America and talking to various people there. Also I want to do another poem but am not up to it yet . . .

[The only text for this letter is a copy made by Miss Baumgarten & sent to Doubleday. She did not include the signature.]

TO JOHN FARRAR

36 Rue de Longchamp
Neuilly, France
March 20, 1928

Dear John:—

Thanks a lot for your cable which I am hastening to answer. It was very generous and thoughtful of you to think of such a thing and I appreciate it more than I can say. And, of course, there is nothing I should like better than a trip back to America at somebody else's expense. But, in thinking it over I seem to have run across some rather practical objections, helas, which I'm giving you for what they're worth.

In the first place, now Mr. Guggenheim has retired to his cloud, we have a rather uncertain income which is all right for over here but would hardly fit the American scale. You might bring me over and you might even possibly send me back—but I could hardly expect you to support me while I was there. America is so damn expensive—and if some or all of the money were to come off royalties (which would be the fair way of working it)—well, it would be too much of a trip to spend for my own pleasure.

Secundus, this damn illness has set me a good deal behind in my work. I feel fine now, in fact a good deal better than I have for quite a long time—but I was sicker than I thought. Which means I won't be able to start the novel for several months after I planned and I doubt if I get it finished by the time John Brown comes out. And it seems more sensible to barge straight through it once started, than to drop it and pick it up again. If

J.B. has any success I want to have another book ready as soon as possible with an eye to magazine serial rights —I have just written about this to Carl, incidentally.

And thirdly, to tell you the honest truth, I don't think my physical presence in America would do any good. There are some people whose personalities can arouse interest in their work. I am not one of them. My work is the best of me, and I would rather lie behind it, as perdu as possible. And experience has taught me that this is the best course I can follow. Writing should speak for itself—if it cannot, it is lost. And as for me—I am not even a foreign author. I do not speak Czechoslovakian, I never was bitten by a lion or caught a strange species of tortoise while flying over the North Pole. And I've lived in New York long enough for most of the professional literary gang to know who I am without wanting to know any more. You can lionize Trader Horn and introduce Leon Feuchtwanger, but you can't do much to me except to raise the remark "I didn't know he'd been away."

Please don't think I'm trying to pull a Maude Adams with all this. But it is the truth, though you may be too old a friend of mine to realize how true it is. And seriously, I'd rather let any work of mine speak for me. If the book should make any sort of success and the novel be finished —that would make a good deal of difference. But I'm sure I wouldn't help it any by being there at the send-off. Believe me, I realize the generosity and friendship that prompted your cable—but the more I think it over, the more it seems to me that way.

As for this long talked of novel—well, as I wrote Carl, I'm going to get at it soon. I think it ought to be a fairly exciting one and I do want to get it over with and get a little ahead. . . . I have written a couple of short stories and am going to write a couple more before I get to my research—the price of socks still being something, even here.

. . . Has anybody in or out of the office any criticisms or suggestions to make about John Brown and if so what? I'd be glad to know. And could you give me an idea of when I will get proof? I'd like to get the first corrections done before I get too deeply immersed in another historical period. And we both agreed that they would take time.

. . . Love to Margaret and yourself—and again thanks from us all.

As ever
Steve

TO JOHN FARRAR

36 Rue de Longchamp
Neuilly, France
April [1] 1928

Dear John:—

I am writing in haste to catch a boat so excuse the shortness. I have just heard of my father's death.[3] Now in the contract for the new novel which I am sending back signed by this mail, I see that an advance of $500 is due on signature. Will you arrange with Bill and Carl so that if there is any necessity for it Bill can take this check and use it as he sees fit? I don't imagine that such an

3. Colonel Benét died suddenly in Westtown, Pa., on March 28, 1928. He was buried in the National Cemetery at Arlington.

emergency will arise but as you know, sometimes when people die so suddenly, the estate is tied up until the will is proved, and there may be no ready money available. I don't imagine that this is the case—but on the odd chance that it should be, I want of course to do what I can. Will you get in touch with Bill about this—if he thinks the check isn't needed send it on to me here otherwise arrange so he can draw on it as he pleases. This is confidential of course and I very much appreciate your doing it.

The contract is very generous and I hope the book will live up to it. Thanks again, John. I will write at more length, later. I cannot, now.

With our best to all of you
As ever
Steve

TO JOHN FARRAR

36 Rue de Longchamp
Neuilly, France
April [27] 1928

Dear John:—

I am sending back the proof by this boat. I have altered quite a number of lines, made some cuts and additions and tried to catch all the errors. Probably some have escaped me but I have tried to work so no important corrections will be necessary in the page-proof.

I think the type-face is very good—just about the right size and legible and clear. The only thing I am wondering about is the rule that divides off the various sections in the books. When I first saw the proof it seemed to me that this rule didn't stand out enough and that the reader's eye might jump from one section to another without realizing the transition. Will you give this a thought? I know the dividing mark has to be small because of the size of the book—but does this one stand out sufficiently for the reader?

I am sending back with the proof a Dedication and a Note. Both were in the original copy I sent but don't appear in these galleys. Will you see that they get in?

I want a half-title to each part or rather I want a separate page with Book One—or whatever it is—in front of each Book. I suppose this is what they mean.

Are you carrying a running head across the top of the page?

There is just one thing that I would be very grateful if you could help me about. In Galley 31 at the very end of Book Two, I have Whitman watching the defeated troops from Bull Run pour into Washington. Now this description is taken—or adopted—from a passage in Whitman's *Specimen Days and Collect* reprinted in *Battles and Leaders of the Civil War*. And it sounds like an eyewitness account. On the other hand, I can find no mention, in any of the five lives of Whitman that I have consulted here, of Whitman's being in Washington at this time. They all say vaguely that his movements for that year were somewhat uncertain and that he went to Washington after his brother George was wounded at the battle of Fredericksburg—which happened quite a lot later. Now can you find out for me, definitely, from some Whitman expert, whether Whitman was in Washington and saw the defeated Union army come in from the first battle of Bull Run or not? There isn't a copy of *Specimen Days and Collect* anywhere around here. If he *was* there, leave the passage as it stands—it is a good passage and I don't want to lose it. If he *wasn't* put in something like "Walt Whitman etc *writes an account of* the defeated army etc." in place of "W.W. *watches* the d.a."

Thanks a lot. These little things are hell to check on and I have had a lot of grief trying to do so. As it is, I will probably be hopped on by various and sundry when the book comes out. But I want to be as accurate as possible wherever I can.

We are all well here as far as the health of it goes. For the rest of it I cannot speak—the loss is still too near.

As ever
Steve

TO JOHN FARRAR

36 Rue de Longchamp
Neuilly, France
May [6] 1928

Dear Johnny:—

Thank you very much for your letter. Of course I understand about your not writing before. It happened with such suddenness that many of our best friends did not hear till much later. I know the Washington connections were away at the time and unable even to return for the funeral.

Well, you knew my father and you knew what he was to me. It is strange that so few of my friends did know him—but it happened so. But I think that everyone who knew me at all, knew what I thought of him. I hope so.

Now that is gone. And nothing in life can ever make up for that particular relation or fill that place. He understood me completely. And he was the best man I ever knew or am likely to know. I am glad it was sudden—for him. He would have hated the slow thing so. For me —well, there is no use talking of that. But thank you for your sympathy. I know that it is genuine and deeply-felt and the sympathy of a true friend.

I sent back the proofs last week and a letter to you about various technical points. Since then I have run across a copy of the Whitman book and discover that Whitman was in Brooklyn at the time. So will you insert on galley 31

"Walt Whitman, unofficial observer to the Cosmos, reads of the defeat in a Brooklyn room. The scene rises before him, more real than the paper he stares upon. He sees the defeated army etc ....."

in place of "Walt Whitman, Government clerk, sees the defeated etc"

I want the rest of the scene, which is good, being adopted from Whitman's own words, and I think that does it. And thanks for the other kind words about J.B. I still think I am right about not coming back for the actual publication-date. I'd rather come back later if I could manage it. I'm sure it would be better. Of course all my plans are up in the air a good deal right now, as you can imagine, and depend upon news from home.

We all send you our love and my very deep thanks and gratitude for your letter.

As ever
Steve

TO MALCOLM DAVIS [4]

36 Rue de Longchamp
Neuilly, France
[June] 1928

My dear Mr. Davis:—

Thank you very much for your letter about the turning over of the remaining copies and sheets of *Young Adventure* to Doubleday Doran. I don't remember what paragraph 9 in the contract was—the book was originally published so long ago—but I'm sure that any arrangement satisfactory to you both is entirely satisfactory to me.

May I add, now that the book will no longer bear the Yale imprint, how very pleasant all my associations with that imprint have been and will continue to be? I know that, as it happened, I was looking at the thing the other night and thinking what really unusual skill and craft the Press extended on the work of a young and excessively unknown author. I only wish the same skill and craft had been extended on the poems themselves.

And may I ask you a favor? Sometime, when you're not too busy, could you simply drop me a line saying how many copies have been sold since the book was first published? I'm asking entirely for my own curiosity— of course I've had the royalty statements and equally of course I couldn't put my hand on them now to save my life. But the thing first came out in 1918—ten years ago —and your letter has given me a sort of anniversary feeling about it.

4. Editor of the Yale University Press. Davis replied, in answer to Benét's question, that about 1250 copies of *Young Adventure* had been sold by the Press.

With many thanks and all best wishes to yourself and
to the Press

> Very sincerely
> Stephen Vincent Benét

TO JOHN FARRAR

> 36 Rue de Longchamp
> Neuilly, France
> June [10] 1928

Dear Johnny:—

Thanks for the *Tiger Joy* etc. which arrived O.K. and
also for the copy of Mrs. [Dorothy Canfield] Fisher's
letter.[5] I am glad of course that she seems to like J.B.
but of course shan't count on anything from either of
the book-clubs until I read the advertisement in the
papers, if then. The ways of all committees have always
been a profound mystery to me and I have seen too
many things of that sort fail to click at the last moment.
And if I had all the money I might have made on flukes
I'd be having broiled Rolls-Royces for breakfast. There
is nothing like thirteen years of the so-called literary life
for exploding Alnaschar's castles.

However, she's a nice woman and I hope her New
Hampshire pine-forest continues to thrive. And J.B. will
go or it won't go—and by the time it comes out, I hope
I'll be too busy writing something else to worry much
about it. In ten years more I ought to be able to do
something if I have the brains. How long it takes to learn
even the A of composition let alone the B and C! But it
is worth trying.

5. Farrar had sent a set of galleys of *John Brown's Body* to Mrs.
Fisher, the New England novelist who was also one of the judges
of the Book-of-the-Month Club.

We are getting along pretty well here in spite of the rather curious weather. The children are O.K. and our healths are improved. I have been writing a slew of short stories and sold a couple to the *Ladies' Home Journal* ["Long Distance," "Fiona and the Unknown Santa Claus"]. I hope they go on buying them for they pay well. We are going to take the children to the seashore for a couple of weeks in July and I think it will do everybody good. I hope and trust the young John is flourishing like something better than a green bay tree. Thomas shows every sign of growing up handsome. Perhaps he will be the first heart-breaker in the family and what a responsibility for his parents! Especially as he has an affectionate disposition.

Will you tell me when you want a list from me of people to send J.B. to—friends and such? Also would it be possible to use a new picture with the publicity— the present one is so much the beardless boy. I could get one taken over here if necessary, and not at Pirie Macdonald prices. . . .

As ever
Steve

TO JOHN FARRAR

36 Rue de Longchamp
Neuilly, France
June [17] 1928

Dear Johnny:—

Your cable arrived early in the morning and I propped one eye open to read it. It left us quite breathless. I really did not expect such a thing, in my usual sour way, and was most pleasurably taken aback. That is swell. I know you must all have worked for it hard—you in particular—and my gratitude to you all is very genuine. I had of course envisaged the possibilities as I do of everything from sudden death to being adopted by a Rockefeller but was no less astonished for all that. Now it remains to be seen how many of these B of the Mo subscribers, with their exchange and substitution privileges, will take advantage of the glorious privilege offered them. And you can trust me not to bank on any extraordinary figures. But even if none of them took it, it would still be an unbuyable advertisement and worth it. Now couldn't you get a law passed by Congress, making the compulsory reading of JB a prerequisite to American citizenship? I wouldn't put it past you, after this. I babble. But that is because I am pleased.

To descend from the pinkcloud and get down to tacks. I am sending you herewith a list of presentation copies, critics etc. I am sorry to seem of so little help on the de luxe business, but all the people I know are either in the game themselves and get their books free or else are too poor to buy them. However if there's anything else I can do that you can think of, I'll be glad, as you know. How large will the de luxe thing be and what price are you putting it at? Also what actual publication-date will there be now—August first? and if so, and you should be unable to send me the page-proof in time, will you see to it that somebody of intelligence checks it over? The corrections I made in the galleys do seem important to me and I am nervous as a witch about them—especially the Whitman, the Dedication and the prefatory note and "Bury me where the *fences* hold the land" in John Vilas's last speech. Will you let me know about this as soon as you can? I'd be awfully obliged.

Thanks also for your letter and for the copy of the one from E.A.R.[6] The letter is very Robinsonian. Of course I agree with the dictum. Poetry should be written in bronze. And I could have taken a couple more years to JB with advantage. But not, I think, with enormous advantage. I am not built that way. As it was I did my damndest to smooth out the roughest of the verse. But ten years work could not have made some of the prosier passages less prosy. The fault there is not only in me but in the nature of both subject and medium. As it is, I am content enough that he thinks some of it good. That is much from him. If the poem is to stand eventually, in any sort of way, it will do so because of a few passages in each Book and the mass-effect of the whole. The faults are many and glaring. But I could do no better, given such brains as I had. Now it is out of me and I am anxious to do something different and more disciplined.

There are ten thousand questions I should like to ask you but I know our letters will cross so I won't. However, tell me a lot—for like Pepys I am with child to hear of this strange thing. God bless us all said Tiny Tim as he tripped up Santa Claus with his crutch in his childish way. Now I shall get this off on the first boat. Meanwhile much gratitude and many many thanks to you and to all.

Reascending the aforesaid cloud.
Steve

6. Farrar had sent a set of galleys of *John Brown's Body* to E. A. Robinson. Robinson wrote Farrar that "parts of it are very fine and parts of it are as bad as possible. 'Bad' isn't exactly the word perhaps, for Benét knows what he is doing. 'Mistaken' might be a better word."

P.S. I am enclosing the 4 slips to go in the 4 family copies. Will you see they get in?

P.P.S. I am awfully glad you are taking over *Young Adventure, Heavens and Earth,* etc. I got a very nice cite from the Yale Press about the former. I have just reread them both—and I am willing to stand by *Young Adventure* for what it was at the time it was written. But *Heavens & Earth* seems very motty to me—the Helen things are all right but I'd like to cut out at least ten of the other poems and amend and repunctuate others. It needs it badly. Some of the things there make me squirm. More of this later. There can't be many of the original sheets etc. left and when these are used up would revision be possible? Will you give it a thought?

Love
Steve

TO JOHN FARRAR

36 Rue de Longchamp
Neuilly, France
June [25] 1928

Dear Johnny:—

It was awfully kind of you to cable and I appreciate it greatly. I am sending the publicity thing over by this mail in a separate envelope. And having a picture taken. Now about the trip.

I'd like very much to come over for a short time—to see Mother first of all—and then to talk over things with you and try to make some definite plans for the future. If I do, I must go to Chicago to see Jane's mother and also try to see some people in Philadelphia—to try to get an idea of whether we want to live there when we come back definitely among other things.

I'd rather not arrive on exactly the day the book comes out if possible. It seems too pat. But that is relatively unimportant. The only way I feel about things is this. I'm anxious about Mother and want to see all of her that I can. And you know how I felt—and feel—about my father.

I'm putting this perfectly frankly because I know you will understand how I feel. In other circumstances, I should be only too glad to come back with a whoop, now the book has a chance of being talked about. I'm not so modest as all that. But this is a different situation.

Now under these circumstances, would it be worth your while to advance me passage-money out of supposed royalties, and try to get a few *small* [lecture] engagements that I could fulfill? Think it over and let me know. I couldn't explain all this in a cable which is why I am writing.

You know how much and how deeply I appreciate all you are doing for John Brown and his author. And I would be only too glad to cooperate in any way I could. But some things would be beyond me, just at present. You know what I mean.

Incidentally we are going to Cabourg [Calvados, France] the first of July. But I am arranging to have the Guaranty Trust forward cables etc.

> With love and appreciation from all of us.
> As ever
> Steve

TO JOHN FARRAR

Villa Soleil
Cabourg, France
July [10] 1928

Dear Johnny:—

Thanks a lot for your letter and for the swell quotes. More particularly for your own. They all make me feel pleasantly abashed. The [Lawrence] Stallings one is amazingly generous—it struck me particularly because for some reason I rather expected him to dislike the book and am overwhelmed by the result. I am very glad too that [James] Boyd liked it because after all it is so to speak in his field—though as it happened I hadn't read *Marching Men* when I did my thing. But I deeply appreciate his praise of a book that covers a little of the same ground. As for the rest—I can only repeat that I am both abashed and pleased.

Yes, Miss Baumgarten wrote me about the business end of things. I think—as I told her—that you have been extremely generous indeed as far as my part of it goes and needless to say I am perfectly satisfied. It seems to me that few if any publishers would have safeguarded the author so much and I should like to issue you a vote of thanks as a corporate body under the regulations of the department of Calvados. Indeed I would have been satisfied with any arrangements that you had made.

. . . You shame me by hoping the novel is coming along. I must state, embarrassedly, that so far it isn't coming along at all. As soon as I got over being sick, I started to do short stories—hence the delay—especially as I simply wasn't up to tackling the research till I felt well again. But it will come eventually. And if it isn't that novel, it will be a better one. I know what I want to do with it, if I can only get the brains.

. . . We both send you all sorts of love—and my own very deep appreciation for all you have done and are doing for John Brown's resurrected torso. Let me know if this August idea seems all right to you. It would be swell to see you again.

As ever
Steve

TO JOHN FARRAR

Villa Soleil
Cabourg, France
July 14, 1928

Dear Johnny:—

Thank you very much indeed for the cable and the letters. That is fine. I will probably come on the *Ile-de-France* then, sailing August 8th . . . And thanks a lot for sending the check. That will be swell. Brandt just sold two stories for me too—it never rains but it pours. Never did I think that I would return to New York with any money left after tipping the library-steward. But it will be a very pleasant—and novel—sensation.

. . . I was in Paris Thursday & had dinner with Mr. Drummond of your London office—a very nice young man. He seemed much impressed with your whole organization . . .

. . . I asked about the size of the edition because I didn't know how the Book-of-the-Month Club worked that sort of thing. It had just about started when I left the U.S. Heaven knows there was no thought in my mind of becoming a rarity! I am all for larger and larger editions—I have had so many of the first & only kind.

. . . 65,000! My God! What a lot of books! Who'd ever have thought it? Because I certainly wouldn't. In fact it's still pretty hard for me to realize it . . .

As ever
Steve

TO ROSEMARY BENÉT

Hotel Le Marquis
New York, N.Y.
August 1928

My dearest, dearest girl:

I am staying at this little hotel with Mother for the next week or so—it is perfectly all right and not particular[ly] expensive, though it might be cooler. But then I had forgotten the hot daytimes of August New York. In fact I'd forgotten such a lot of things—the noise—and the green greenness of the grass on Long Island with no old women out picking salads in it—lavishness—iced coffee—chocolate malteds—limp rubber roast beef—business-lunches—tall Irish cops—being called Mike by taxi-drivers—etc etc etc. But let me try to be coherent.

They got us up at 5 A.M. Tuesday—and I didn't get through customs till noon. Everything had run on greased wheels as far as the voyage was concerned up till then —then they kept us hours at Quarantine and more hours on the pier. An efficient (but very pleasant) young gentleman from DD&Co. named David Bramble came out on the cutter with a reporter in tow. He gave me cigarettes, the reporter interviewed me, then they took me up to the sun-deck of the first-class where I was photographed in every possible expression of stupid surprise by (slightly unwilling) photographers who shot first & paused to enquire what it was all about afterwards. "This is S. V. B. etc" said Mr. Bramble proudly to the *Mirror* cameraman. "Yeah?" said that worthy. "But why are we takin' pictures of him?" "Why" said Mr. Bramble "he has written J etc etc etc" for about ten minutes. The *Mirror* man breathed deeply. "Yeah, I get all that" he said. "But what's the guy *done?*" I like that man.

. . . [I] went up to Alan Rinehart's apartment where there were more reporters . . . Yesterday I was escorted out to Garden City in charge of Mr. Bramble, saw John, the gardens, the special edition, the bindery, numerous directors & everything but the Rajah's Ruby. They said my author's copies had gone on to Paris through Brandt & I immediately got one & sent it to you at once in case of *any* slipup. They were to send it by the very first boat —it has an inscription & it has every bit of the author's heart, you lamb!

Today I saw Carl—Emily Kimbrough [*Ladies' Home Journal*] is coming over from Philadelphia tomorrow & I will see her at 10 A.M. in the Brandt office. . . . The actual sales of the book so far are about 52,000 including the B of the M—that means a start of 7,000 on the normal sale—800 last week & 500 copies today. The press has really been remarkable—space everywhere & some of the praise so overdone that it makes me feel ashamed. The [Boston] *Transcript* passed on it, the *Times* &

Tribune were yes&no, the *Literary Review* of the *Post* more unfavorable than favorable. But practically everything else was favorable—& the [Sunday] *Tribune* gave it the whole front page of *Books*. I have seen Henry Canby, John Carter, Mrs. Farrar . . . John [Farrar] & I are doing a vaudeville-team act next week at a place called the Barbizon, where it will be broadcast—I am reading it over the radio a week or so later. I am having dinner with Stan Rinehart, with the Doubledays, going up to Breadloaf [Writers' Conference] with John. I can lecture if I want but I won't. I said I would like to read a detective story & Mr. Doran sent me 12. He calls me Steve in that old paternal manner & remarked that the office would get me a white elephant if I wanted one. And one of the happiest days in my life will be when I get on the boat to come back to you—and I miss you every minute with every ounce & milligram of my heart & soul and body. . . .

I found Mother & Laura better than I expected— better physically—better in every way. They both look well and they are over the first shock. But there is no need to tell you how deep that shock went. Mother has truly been heroic and she is superbly sane—and un-beaten—but, Jane, she is changed in some ways—it could not be otherwise, but it is hard. It is hard to have these blows in age. It is hard. . . . I will go to Chicago some-time in the week of September 3rd. They were all most delighted with their presents . . .

Always
Steve

TO ROSEMARY BENÉT

Windmill Cottage
Amagansett, L.I.
August 1928

Dearest:—

I am so desolated to hear about Tommy! Poor, poor
rabbit—and poor, poor Jane! I got my last letter off to
you so it would catch the *Paris,* the night before I stopped
in the Brandt office to get yours—so it will sound very
silly, being all about teas & literature, when you have
been so troubled and he so sick—damn this infernal
distance, I will *never* do it again. Give him my very
best love and tell him Papa is so sorry he has been sick
and is going to bring him back everything in New York
that would please him. And Nini too. I love you all
so much—and feel like such a bum being over here and
not able to do a damn thing to help but write and cable.
. . . Now remember—any time you say, just cable and
I'll get on the next boat. . . . I called up the hotel first
thing this morning and got your cable saying he was
better—you can imagine how it relieved me—thank you,
my darling—but I'm just counting the days till we can
be together again. Incidentally, do you need any money
—if you do, let me know, and I'll cable it at any time.
And as I say, any time that things get complicated, just
cable and I'll take the first boat I can catch. I'm going
to settle on the *Berengaria,* the 19th, as soon as this infernal Labor Day holiday is over—but *any time before,*
my dear.

. . . Always
Steve

1926–1929

Dear Tommy:—

I am so sorry to hear that you were sick—and so glad today to get the cable from Mommy saying you were better. It is miserable to be sick—and I hope by the time you get this, you will be all right again, and not even remember that you had to go to the potty so mournfully and so long. Your Papa loves you dearly and wishes so much that he were there to help comfort you. What do you want from New York to cheer you? I thought of a small gratte-ciel [skyscraper] but am afraid it wouldn't go in my bag.

With all my love and sympathy, and missing you very much

Your loving
Papa

TO SAMUEL C. SLAYMAKER [7]

Hotel Le Marquis
New York, N.Y.
August 1928

Dear Sam:—

Thanks a lot for your very nice & most flattering letter. Of course I remember you—and equally of course I shall be very glad to autograph the book when I get it. I'm glad you thought so well of it & hope the autograph won't be too illegible. Speaking of the Canterbury Pilgrims, I saw John Carter only yesterday—and am expecting to see Tim Coward & some of the others some time this week. I'm only here for a month or so—so have to try to get hold of people where & when I can find them.

7. A member of the Class of 1919S at Yale.

With all best wishes & thanks again for your letter
Sincerely
Steve Benét

TO HERVEY ALLEN [8]

36 Rue de Longchamp
Neuilly, France
[October] 1928

Dear Hervey:—

Thanks ever so much for your very swell letter and all my apologies for not answering it before. But it got forwarded to France and backwarded to America and I finally got it just before sailing.

Needless to say, I'm more than glad you think so well of John Brown—and really do appreciate, and deeply, your writing me about it.

The money, Heaven knows, is very pleasant indeed, and it is nice to know that the next winter will not be spent at Mont de Piété [pawn shop]—but, after all, the other thing is the real reward.

Heinemann is bringing it out in England some time this Fall and I shall be interested to see what happens to it there. I expect the reception, if any, will be mixed —and I can already visualize the comments on the American spelling!

Aren't you ever going to be in Paris and if so, won't

8. In 1928 Hervey Allen had just left the teaching profession— he had taught at several secondary schools and at Columbia and Vassar—and was beginning the literary career which produced his notable biography of Poe as well as a number of historical novels and the legendary *Anthony Adverse* (1933). He and Benét became acquainted in New York through their mutual friendship and professional association with John Farrar. Allen died in 1949.

you come here? The telephone actually does work and we are not as far out of the city as we sound. Straight out from the Arc de Triomphe and turn to the left just before you reach the Seine. We will break out the Napoleon brandy for you—and the cook makes good *soufflés*.

Johnny [Farrar] told me you had a new book ready but couldn't let me see sheets, though I asked, before I sailed. All sorts of luck to it—I want to see it very much —and to the new poem as well. And remember this address if and when you do come over. We are always at home—and the winter's supply of coal is arriving tomorrow afternoon.

Thanks again for your letter—and my very real gratitude. As you know, one goes blind on a thing, after it's done—and it's more enheartening than a dozen reviews, to have it seem all right then to someone whose work and opinion you respect.

As ever
Stephen Benét

TO HENRY R. HALLOWELL

36 Rue de Longchamp
Neuilly, France
October 6, 1928

Dear Henry:

Thanks a lot for writing so kindly about John Brown. I'm awfully glad you liked it—and also very glad to have news of yourself and of the class boy. So he is now entering Penn Charter. It makes me feel very old. But then we are old. I shall never forget what tottering old men the Class of 1913 seemed to me—in 1919.

Sorry not to see you while I was over—but I was in America for 5 weeks and in Philadelphia for exactly 1 day. However, we may live around there when we come back next Spring—though our plans are rather uncertain.

Anyhow, I shall hope to see you at the Decennial if not before—and in the meantime, my thanks for your letter, and my respects and salutations to Henry Jr., Dorothy and Bettina. May they and you prosper—I won't add wax but [only] because too many people I know are doing too much of that over here. Incidentally, I see that A.[lpha] D.[elta] wants a new and mammoth tomb. Didn't they tell us when we were taken in that that one was going to last forever? But that's the way it goes.

With all best wishes and many thanks

As ever
Steve

TO HENRY CANBY

36 Rue de Longchamp
Neuilly, France
October [13] 1928

Dear Henry:—

I'd like very much to thank you for your review of *John Brown's Body*. It certainly has as much praise in it as is good for any author—and of course I'm in your debt for that—but, leaving that aside, it does tell, as far as I know myself, just what I was trying to get at— and so many of the reviews, favorable or unfavorable, didn't. And particularly I'd like to thank you for what you say about the internal sympathy for the North and the reasons for choosing the symbol of John Brown. The Wingate part, metre and all, is the kind of thing I can do—in the Ellyat part, at least I tried to break new ground. And the hiders, John Brown and John Vilas seem to me the best of the book—so I am particularly glad to have you select them.

Thank you again. I mailed the review of *Giant Killer* [by Elmer Davis] by the *Mauretania* and hope it won't be too long on the way. I had rather a tough time doing it—thinking so much of the book really good and yet so much of it mistakenly planned. Incidentally, if you think another reviewer would find things in it I haven't found, don't hesitate to call on one.

As for my own thing—it is not from lack of appreciation that I do not say more about your review. But it seems to me that all an author can legitimately demand from a critic is this—an appreciation of the *kind* of thing that was intended and an understanding of the means employed toward that end. And even so, an author very seldom gets both from the same critic—the merits or demerits of the particular piece in question being outside the case. You have done both and I am very grateful.

Sincerely
SVB

TO JOHN FARRAR

36 Rue de Longchamp
Neuilly, France
November [1] 1928

Dear Johnny:—

. . . I was much impressed by the ad in the Sat. Rev. & so was everybody else, including my uncle & aunt. I thought it was very good (and why shouldn't I, for it

seemed to my jaundiced eye to take up the entire publication)—and I am very much obliged—especially because it didn't have any of the boy-hero stuff in it. I
think I shall go out and buy a new hat.

. . . I'm glad to see, according to *Variety*, J.B. still
leading the Baker & Taylor non-fiction. And *The Buck in
the Snow*. Which reminds me of 8 years ago when Millay
was living in the Hotel des St. Père's & Henry & Stanley
and I were living on Rue Vavin & we were all borrowing
money from whichever had it. I liked "Moriturus" very
much—and the Caesar poem—particularly—and the sonnets.

Our love to you and Margaret. . . .

As ever
Steve

TO HARRIET MONROE

36 Rue de Longchamp
Neuilly, France
December [3] 1928

Dear Miss Monroe:—

Thank you very much indeed for your letter and for
your good wishes about *John Brown*. I was only in
Chicago for a few days and wanted to spend all the
time I possibly could with my wife's parents—as she
wasn't able to come over herself this time.

I appreciate your asking me to come to the Arts Club
—and I'd certainly be very glad to accept—if I weren't
here! But I expect to be in Chicago some time next
year—we are coming back to America in the late Spring
or early Summer—and if you should still want me to

come at that time, I'd be very glad to do so. I don't want to disarrange your plans in any way, so I'll leave it entirely up to you.

Also, I would appreciate seeing your review, if it isn't too much trouble to send it over here. The American Library subscribes to *Poetry* but all magazines are slow in arriving here—and besides, there's generally somebody reading it, when you want it.

With thanks again and all best wishes to yourself and to *Poetry*

Sincerely
Stephen Vincent Benét

TO MILES HART

36 Rue de Longchamp
Neuilly, France
[January] 1929

Dear Mr. Hart:—

I am enclosing the slip for the book. As for the postage, for heaven's sake, don't worry about it—why should you? It is very interesting to me—and very pleasant—that the veterans to whom you showed the book should find it non-partisan. That is what I wanted to do—as far as any author can who has prejudices of his own. And as I am in receipt this morning of a letter from an irate lady who accuses me of deliberately blackening the character of General Lee—I'm glad to hear that there are others who feel differently.

With all best wishes
Sincerely
Stephen Vincent Benét

TO EDWARD BLISS REED

36 Rue de Longchamp
Neuilly, France
[January] 1929

Dear Professor Reed:—

It was a very real pleasure to me to get your letter and I want to thank you for it and tell you how much I appreciated it as promptly as possible—unfortunately not very promptly at that for mail takes such a time to get over here. But I particularly wanted you to have a copy of the book—and I was sorry that I wasn't able to write in it myself before it was sent you—and so express a little at least of the very real gratitude I feel for your helping me to France in the first place—and so to a good many things that wouldn't have happened otherwise—and again, with the Guggenheim Fellowship. I suppose I might have got the thing through somehow in New York—but it would have been breaking stones compared to the conditions I had over here. So, if you do like the book—well, you were one of its godparents in the first place—and both it and myself have every reason to feel grateful to you.

I am glad if you think it has the color of the country in it. That was what I wanted. And my own case, as well as I could put it, is put in the Invocation. It seemed to me that such a thing should be tried—if only to fertilize the ground for another planting. Of course the thing is full of faults—but I think I can honestly say that I did my best with it, given what abilities I have. And so much

182

more may be done—there are so many stories—such a rich and diverse field.

Well, that is what I wanted to do, and if the printed book really does call up for other people certain American sights, sounds, names, landscapes, men, I am very glad. And particularly if it has pleased certain people—you among them—who believed that my work had value when I had done very little to justify such a belief. The cash and the credit are both very pleasant of course—especially, I may say, the cash. But the other is what one works for, in the last analysis.

Thank you again. I am sorry to hear the news of your father's death. I had not heard of it till your letter came. My own father died last March, very suddenly. It was a great loss to me. There is nothing that one can say—but I should like to express my sympathy, now I know.

We are here for the Winter and I will probably be starting a new book of some sort soon. After all, John Brown was finished a year ago, except for certain revisions and it is time I got back to work. I think we'll be back in America in the Spring—to stay some years at least—and I'll hope to see you then. I'm hoping to do some more verse as well but not another 367 pages one very soon. Next time I'll be more laconic if I can. But it's such a large country to be laconic about!

With all thanks and best wishes

As ever
Stephen Benét

TO JOHN H. WARE [9]

36 Rue de Longchamp
Neuilly, France
[January] 1929

My dear Mr. Ware:—

Thank you very much indeed for your interesting letter. And my apologies for not answering it before. But it takes a good while to reach me here.

I am glad that anyone who has studied the Civil War as closely as yourself has only found two statements to question in *John Brown's Body*. I tried to be as accurate as I could, but it is almost impossible not to make some mistakes when dealing with so large a field. I'm very grateful to anyone who points out definite ones that I can change.

About Mr. [Jefferson] Davis's capture. I found the statement that he had picked up a cloak of his wife's—as I said, by accident—in what seemed to me good authority. But, of course, if he didn't, he didn't, and that's that. I'll try to look up the statement in his papers if they have a set of them over here. The Federal officer's affidavit should be in the Official Records, which are here, and I will look for that as well. I wanted to quash the story that he had *deliberately* disguised himself.

As regards Captain Wirz, I shall be glad to read the accounts of Andersonville that you suggest and also re-read his trial. I certainly don't wish to blacken his char-

9. Professor of Romance Languages in Shorter College, in Rome, Georgia, and author of several books on France and French literature.

acter if he wasn't guilty. My position in regard to him was simply this. Andersonville was a bad business—even for a prison camp—and even taking all the possible circumstances of the case in mind. My description of the camp itself was founded on the official report by a Southern Medical officer to the Confederate Government. And his words, none the less telling for being couched in official language, show a very bad state of affairs, to put the case with extreme mildness. They convict those responsible for this state of affairs of criminal stupidity, at the least. I saw no reason to doubt the truth of this report, as it was contemporary, written by a Southern officer, and included in the official Records. On the other hand, if Wirz was merely a scapegoat and railroaded to his death, I should like to tell the thing as it happened. I have no personal animus against him, as a human being. But—as we saw in the case of the famous Hard-Boiled Smith in the last war—this prison camp duty is apt to attract men with a rather large streak of cruelty in them or men who by reason of physical or other disabilities aren't fit for anything else. And even Channing—a singularly good and independent historian with, if anything, a Southern point of view—can find little to say for Andersonville and its keepers.

In any case, as I say, I am grateful for your criticisms and shall be glad to read the books. They are just getting out a new edition of *John Brown's Body* and I won't be able, from here, to put in any revisions before it appears. But I am hoping, sooner or later, to eliminate all the typographical and other mistakes, though it's difficult, working at long distance.

I shall certainly be glad to look for the Army of Northern Virginia in the Hugo Museum. . . .

With many thanks and all best wishes

Sincerely

Stephen Vincent Benét

TO JOHN DOLLARD [1]

36 Rue de Longchamp
Neuilly, France
[February] 1929

Dear Mr. Dollard:—

That's very kind of you. I'd be glad to come any date, say, in the last week of October that you suggest. As for how creative artists work—I don't know. They smoke cigarettes—at least most writers seem to—and finally something happens. As a matter of fact, Mr. Lowes, in *The Road to Xanadu*, said about all that anyone could say—and though the subject there is a great man, many of the things would hold good, I think, for any writing.

Sorry about the first letter. There is a rue de Longchamps in Paris, too, and they're always getting mixed up.

Sincerely

Stephen Vincent Benét

1. Mr. Dollard, later a distinguished social psychologist, was in 1929 an administrative assistant to the president of the University of Chicago. Dollard had invited Benét to lecture at the university under the auspices of the William Vaughn Moody Lecture Committee.

TO JOHN FARRAR

36 Rue de Longchamp
Neuilly, France
March [10] 1929

Dear Johnny:

Thanks for your swell letter. I've read "The Barefoot Saint"—three times, trying to see what I could do to alter it—and each time I like it less. It is a nice little story for the time when I wrote it [1921]—but it is prettyfied and it is too much like Cabell. I'd really rather you didn't do it. It seems to me too slight to deserve de luxe treatment. You need for that a story you can read in an hour but which you keep remembering for a long time. And "The Barefoot Saint" isn't that. It is just a pleasant imitative piece of colorwork.

Please don't think I am just being perverse about this. I was exceedingly fond of the story when I wrote it and mad to have it published. But I have some perspective now—and it really isn't worth it. I know you would do everything for it in the way of format—but if the stuff isn't there, the stuff isn't there. And it does seem to me important to have something for the de luxe people to work on that won't look too much like a Cinderella in its fine clothes.

I'm sorry to gum the works this way—but, really, on reading it over, I couldn't see it. I can and will do something for them that will be much better, I promise. I wish I could think up a sort of Rip Van Winkle theme—maybe that will come. I know you'll appreciate how I feel about this—as I say, it isn't really perversity, or even mock-modesty. I just can't see it as a book. . . .

> As ever,
> Steve

TO ROBERT GRANT [2]

> 36 Rue de Longchamp
> Neuilly, France
> March 20, 1929

Dear Mr. Grant:—

That's very kind of you indeed. And, if I'm alive next Autumn, I shall certainly be very glad to accept, no matter in which of the United States I am.

> With thanks again
> Sincerely
> Stephen Vincent Benét

TO HENRY CANBY

> 36 Rue de Longchamp
> Neuilly, France
> March [20] 1929

Dear Henry:—

Your copy of "The Barefoot Saint" just reached me this Monday and it seems to me to need a lot of revision, so I am going to send it back to you on the *Paris*—which reaches New York April 2nd. I will put it on the boat-train myself so there won't be any slip up—and you said

2. The Boston novelist, a senior figure in conservative American letters, had invited Benét to deliver the Phi Beta Kappa poem at the meeting of the Harvard chapter.

you weren't sending it to the printers till the 13th of April. I'm sorry to hold it over a mail, but I really do want to rewrite and alter it a great deal if you are going to use it, and take out some of the chichi in it. And I will clear up the ambiguity about the mother. Also I will remove the sacristan and change the name of the town— I cannot have old sacristans at my time of life.

I was just going to write you in answer to your other letter when "The Barefoot Saint" arrived. You know so much more about that sort of thing than I do that I appreciate very much indeed your kindness in speaking to Mr. Doubleday and the other people. I should think the way you suggest would certainly be better—and I don't see why Doubleday, Doran should object, as after all, they do very little textbook work. Of course I shan't mention your name in the matter but will try to handle the thing through Brandt & Brandt, who make all my contracts. It makes me feel rather queer to think of an actual school edition [of *John Brown's Body*], not to speak of a college one. . . .

As ever

Stephen Benét

TO JOHN FARRAR

36 Rue de Longchamp
Neuilly, France
March [25] 1929

Dear Johnny:—

I am sending by this mail the revision of "The Barefoot Saint." I have gone over it pretty thoroughly, rewritten quite a bit, and I think, taken out a lot of the chichi in it. I still think it a very slight thing for de luxe publication but of course if they will be really disappointed not to do it, I withdraw my objections, as long as they'll do it as you suggest in your cable. I'm sorry to have seemed perverse about this, if I have, but I know you'll understand my feeling about it. I wrote that tale in 1921—and now it's 1929—and that's the whole trouble. . . .

As ever,
Steve

Return to America (1929-1932)

B ENÉT's letters during this period tell their own story; the chronicle of personal and professional duress needs little editorial comment. To a substantial degree the Benét story is also a miniature of the national experience during these years. Thus the narrative begins with twelve weeks as a script writer in Hollywood at $1000 a week in 1929; it ends in 1932 with a pile of unpaid bills.

For Benét the story of 1929–1932 also included months of extremely painful arthritis, the loss of most of his *John Brown's Body* royalties in the stock market, and the bitterness of an enforced return to the bondage of magazine fiction. Gradually, too, during these three years, Benét found increasing burdens as a public literary man. In the letters to college professors and lady editors one senses the transformation of his rather prickly resentment of invasions of his privacy into a good-tempered acceptance of the inevitable public role and a sturdy assumption of additional responsibilities.

TO ROSEMARY BENÉT

Hotel Ambassador
Los Angeles, California
December 1929

My darling:—

Well, here I am! [3] We got in last night & today I have eaten an orange, walked under palm trees, gone out to the studio, met dozens of people whose names I will never remember, been photographed with Mr. [D. W.] Griffith, dictated a lot of hooey to a stenographer, seen & heard screen-tests of various Lincolns and Ann Rutledges etc. The sun is actually out, the roses & poinsettias in bloom in the lush hotel garden . . . It is all quite mad. And everything has gone well so far. And I am lonelier than I can think about and miss you more than any words can say. *Gee!* Only—at the worst 83 days more. And by the time this gets to you it will be less. I don't mean to crab and I'll try not to. I like Griffith—he's a human being—and he certainly has been extremely decent to me. He is kiddable—which I didn't expect—and really laid himself out to be pleasant. We worked all the way out in the train and cut the thing about a third. Of course I imagine the final version—if there ever is one—will be entirely different. That seems to be the method. At present I am giving my celebrated imitation of a piece

3. Benét had been brought to Hollywood by D. W. Griffith to work on the script of *Abraham Lincoln*. For an account of the episode see Charles A. Fenton, *Stephen Vincent Benét: The Life and Times of an American Man of Letters, 1898–1943* (New Haven, 1958), pp. 231–40.

of furniture. I don't know why anything happens and I don't try to find out. Tomorrow I am to be given an office—why? I don't know. And I am also apparently going down with Griffith for the weekend to visit some millionaires named Sprechels. I don't know why I am doing that, either. Apparently, at the moment, Griffith likes to have me around as a sort of mascot. Things happen with sequence or consequence and I take them as they come. Tell Phil [Barry] he really must see it. But not alone.

. . . I'll wire you my change of address as soon as I make it. You can always get me c/o D. W. Griffith, United Artists Studio in case of need but I think it would be better to send most things to my private address, when I have one. We're going to get a nice house out of this— concentrate on the house—I am. Kiss the children for me. I miss them. Love to Mother, Laura & Bill. My darling, my darling, I love you more than anything that ever was!

Always
Steve

TO ROSEMARY BENÉT

Feature Productions, Inc.
Hollywood, California
December 1929

Darling, darling:—

Your grand letter just came and I am answering it with what promptness! . .

The children sound simply grand. So do you. So you

are. I wish I'd been at the Zoo. I wish I'd been everywhere. You would make even Sid Grauman's Chinese-
Theatre a palace for heroes—and, darling, it would take
somebody to do that.

This is Wednesday. Let me recount a little about this
madhouse. In the first place Hollywood—Los Angeles,
Glendale, Pasadena etc etc—is one loud, struggling Main-
Street, low-roofed, mainly unskyscrapered town that
straggles along for twenty-five miles or so, full of stop
& go lights, automobiles, palm-trees, Spanishy—& God
knows what all houses—orange-drink stands with real
orange juice—studios—movie-theatres—everything but
bookstores. I am the only person in the entire 25 miles
who walks more than 4 blocks, except along Hollywood
Boulevard in the evening. There are some swell hotels—
up in the hills or between L.A. & Hollywood—& a few
night-clubs. But in general, everything is dead, deserted
at 11.30 P.M. There is the continual sunlight—the ad-
vertised palms—coolness the minute the sun sets—and
plenty of people with colds. The boys go around without
hats. They look like prize ears of corn. The girls, ditto.

As for the studio—it's like any office—where I am.
People sit around—gossip—smoke—waste time. Outside,
of course are the stages & the sets—a perfect reproduction of one corner of a French street—and half of a
German castle elsewhere. Occasionally, in the corridors,
somebody is wandering dressed as a *gendarme* or an
Arab or something. But only occasionally. There isn't
much being "shot" at present.

I get to the office about 10—work till about 1—either
with Griffith or without him—lunch—work from about 2
to 6—or not but anyhow am around the office—walk

back here—eat—if there's nothing else—a movie—letters —read—bed. A chaste & sober life.

Last Monday, however, was D. W. Griffith night at the Roosevelt. I sat at the stag table with Griffith & a lot of the men who have at one time worked with him—and was included by the worried announcer in the list of those discovered by D.W.G., though nobody cared. But I stood up with the rest, had a spotlight played on me, and felt silly. . . .

The place was packed & everybody talked about when they wanted to fire Mary Pickford from Biograph because she wasn't pretty enough & when Chaplin got $5 a week—until I felt I had been there too.

The previous weekend—or rather Sunday—I went up to Palo Alto—it's a 450 mile trip, I discovered to my surprise—to see the Norrises & the children [of William Rose Benét]. The children look simply fine and are really perfectly charming. . . . I felt shy with them, of course —but saw something of Rosemary, not so much of Jim & Kay—but they all were nice—and very happy where they are—though looking forward a great deal to coming East. . . .

The work goes on. I think we're about through & then Mr. Griffith has a new idea. The trouble is—he's generally perfectly right. I continue to like him—and really to think a lot of him, in many ways. He's all right. And he can produce loyalty.

. . . Saturday I may go over [to Pasadena] to spend the weekend with the McClures.[4] And then—Lord—it will be Christmas. I shall go out & look sad-eyedly at all

4. Robert McClure, novelist and editor, and a contemporary of Benét at Yale.

the Christmas trees on Hollywood Boulevard. My Lord, how I miss you. Oh Eastern wind, when wilt thou blow?

Thank Stephanie for the letter. Tell her it's beautiful & she's a darling. And tell Thomas he's my favorite *fils* and his papa [is] very devoted to him. I look at all your pictures. Lordy, when will this be over?

Have a good time in Richmond & remember me to your aunt. I wrote the Kinsolving woman I might be able to come [to lecture] in March & the Vassar woman that I would come in April. I haven't heard from Miss Pinckney about Charleston, though I wrote her.

. . . Always
Steve

You will get sapphires, too!

S.

TO FRIEDA LUBELLE [5]

Feature Productions, Inc.
Hollywood, California
December 1929

Dear Miss Lubelle:—

I enclose $200 representing your commission on my first 2 weeks salary ($2000). The 3rd week won't be paid till January first so I'm sending this along now to make the books straight for the year—& the income tax.

This is a madhouse but I don't mind.

Best to everybody—and, by the way, Merry Christmas & Happy New Year. One forgets such things out here.

Stephen Benét

5. A member of the staff of Brandt and Brandt.

TO ROSEMARY BENÉT

Feature Productions, Inc.
Hollywood, California
December 1929

Darling, darling; darling, darling:—

I got your lovely telegram and your last two letters. They make all life to me.

I can't tell you how inexpressibly I missed you—Christmas and now. I spent it with the McClures who were most kind . . . But I missed & thought of you and the children all day.

. . . Pasadena is very wealthy and full of beautiful houses, all brand new. They're the kind of home we'd like to live in *if*—just a little different country and other people. It is still unreal, unreal, unreal.

Sid Howard walked into my office today,[6] I'm happy to say. He sat down, grinned & remarked "God, how I hate this place." He is fine. He said he'd seen you in New York.

. . . The work goes on and for the last few days I've had a secretary—Miss Neville. She's intelligent, thank God, & knows lots more about pictures than I do. We will complete tomorrow a new version that has every historical character & incident in it except Millard Fillmore repairing the White House plumbing & is about 60 pages too long. Then we'll start the dear old job of cutting it again. If you could run it for four hours, it would be

6. Sidney Howard and Benét had first met in Paris, in 1920. It was Howard who urged Benét to talk with Carl Brandt about the prospects for his fiction. Howard's very productive career as a playwright was cut short by his premature death in 1939.

a good picture the way it stands. But apparently, you can't.

My rays of hope are there. Huston—he's now definitely going to play Lincoln—arrives here January 11th & they'll probably want to start rehearsing some of his stuff as soon as he gets here. And general rehearsals are now scheduled for the first of February. That means they won't actually start shooting before March first & as I can't possibly stay through the shooting, I don't see why I should have to stay for any of it. And, in a talkie, you cannot rewrite during production—it costs too much money.

Anyhow—it's like this. I only have to stay till around the first week in February—which would make about 8 weeks since I got out here. But I'm damned if I see why I should have to stay any longer. Griffith has been talking of another picture he wants to do after this—a sort of "Remember the Alamo" one—and how if certain things work out he wants me to write the script for it for large sums & perhaps a percent of the profits. But I've been extremely non-committal. I've worked on this one & I think they'll get their money's worth. I wouldn't sign a new contract for sums untold. Not without you, dearie. Life simply isn't worth it.

This Saturday will finish up the 3rd official week here— plus 2 days—for Uncle Tom. We get paid the following Wednesday—and that's a bright spot. It will be $3000 in the bank next week. Every now and then I look at that bank book—and at my return ticket.

I enclose a very nice letter from Uncle Larry. And also their Christmas check to us. Will you cash it & buy something for us all—or deposit it to the children's savings accounts—whatever you think. And would you write Uncle L & Aunt M?

Do you need any money? I can send you any you want. I hope you took drawing rooms to Richmond & back. Spend anything to be comfortable. I want you to take care of yourself & be happy, that is all I want.

. . . I'm tired. Worked till 6 or so this evening writing a goddamn anthem for a choir to sing in the finale. The boys in blue and grey are not at present dissolving into the boys in khaki, but negroes are dissolving into American flags all over the end of the picture. I wish I could do a lap dissolve—into your beddy-bye. I kiss you anyhow, across 3000 miles & a great deal more of snow. I do all the same.

Mr. Griffith is known as D.W. I am not yet known as S.V.

. . . My script is full of things like "Camera trucks, shooting from reverse angle." They sound fine, but I don't know what any of them mean.

Goodnight, lamb. I love you forever.

Always
Steve

TO WILLIAM ROSE BENÉT

Feature Productions, Inc.
Hollywood, California
January 1930

Dear Bill:—

Thanks a lot for Mr. [Robert] Graves's autobiography which I'm reading a little of each night and which is good, if cocky like all young English intellectuals. And merry Christmas and happy New Year and I don't know whether to wish you happy Lincoln's Birthday or not but considering my present state of mind on the Great Emancipator,

I should say not because I don't want to put a curse on you. Well some lecture & some write for the movies and I say it's spinach anyhow, no matter how it's boiled. This is a mad place of which I am seeing the tamest side but it's mad for all that from screenart to the climate. . . .

I saw Thornton Wilder out here—lecturing—having just finished *The Woman of Andros* and sent the last misc. pages by air mail to his publishers—and Louis Bromfield is expected hourly, in any number of special trains. As for me, I hope to be back soon, as I'm just completing the 49th version of Lincoln. Next week I'll start the 50th, I suppose. But all the same, I hope to get through by the first of February, if I have to shoot somebody. At the moment, Mr. Griffith is sick in bed with a cold, which makes things even more complicated than they usually are—but, my God, this Penelope's web will have to be finished sometime!

I sent Mother a check for $2000 which I want her to keep & use—Lord knows, I'm making enough. Give everybody my love and tell them I'm well and sassy, even on this rice-plantation. Say a prayer for Uncle Tom. Much love to you.

As ever
Steve

TO CARL BRANDT

Feature Productions, Inc.
Hollywood, California
January [23] 1930

Dear Carl:—

The next time you sign me up on a 12 week contract to come out here for any amount of money, there is going to be a good deal of blood flowing around the Brandt office. Happy Lincoln's Birthday and so's your old man!

Of all the Christbitten places and business[es] on the two hemispheres this one is the last curly kink on the pig's tail. And that's without prejudice to D. W. Griffith. I like him and think he's good. But, Jesus, the movies!

I don't know which makes me vomit worst—the horned toads from the cloak and suit trade, the shanty Irish, or the gentlemen who talk of Screen Art. . . .

I have worked in advertisting and with W. A. Brady Sr. But nowhere have I seen such shining waste, stupidity and conceit as in the business and managing end of this industry. Whoopee!

Since arriving, I have written 4 versions of *Abraham Lincoln,* including a good one, playable in their required time. That, of course, is out. Seven people, including myself, are now working in conferences on the 5th one which promises hopefully to be the worst yet. If I don't get out of here soon I am going crazy. Perhaps I am crazy now. I wouldn't be surprised.

At any rate, don't be surprised if you get a wire from me that I have broken my contract, bombed the studio, or been arrested for public gibbering. Don't be surprised at all.

I enclose a check, due you, for 400 more drops of Uncle Tom's blood. Don't waste it on riotous living. I worked for it.

I am going to try to get out of this place before March 1 at any rate—this Saturday ending my 7th week of occupation. I will count on your assistance if necessary.

Love and kisses to the office
As ever
Steve Benét

TO ROSEMARY BENÉT

Feature Productions, Inc.
Hollywood, California
January 23, 1930

Darling:—

I have just written a long covering letter to Carl telling him just what I think of the movies. So that's that, and I can sit down and talk to you.

But really! The laughter lies too deep for tears.

All *this* week we have been working on what-I-hope-will-be-the-last-but-which-undoubtedly-won't ver-sion. With some of the money boys, including my friend Mr. ———. I said he was a Yale man. Add to that the simple words "son of a bitch"—and, I think, you have him. All we need now is Mr. Schenck—old black Joe himself—to make things a real family party.

There is a tragedy going on here which I will tell you later—D.W.G.'s. And there is comedy. Lord, what comedy! If it didn't make you so mad.

Arthur Hammerstein, whom I think I mentioned when I first came out here (those 15 years ago) as not knowing quite what it was all about, is now slowly and harmoni-ously going crazy over *his* contract. Griffith said with his usual politeness today "Well, how are you Mr. Hammerstein?" "I am just ready to jump in the river," said Mr. H. This will give you a rough sketch of his—and my—state of mind.

I'm sorry to bawl out all this to you. But it vexes me to see bad work done. It vexes me to see ignorance and stupidity and arrogance enthroned and time and talent wasted. . . .

Take care of yourself—and Nini & Tommy. Good God, how I want to see them—and you. I am bending every effort to get away as soon as I can but this damn thing seems endless. There is no system & no sense—just a rat-run of politics. I'll stick it out if I have to—for the cash —and this is the end of the seventh week, when this will get to you. But how I hate it, how I miss you, how I want to get back! . . . The one thing that consoles me at all, is the time we can have with the money. We will do that. . . .

> from
> homesick
> Steve

TO CARL BRANDT

> Hollywood, California
> February 3, 1930
> [Telegram]

Please see story in January Twenty Ninth issue of *Variety*, page eleven, headed Considine's changes on two UA films upset studio. This story must be retracted at once or I will sue. Please get busy on this immediately. Get in touch with Authors League. Stephen Vincent Benét.

TO CARL BRANDT

> Hollywood, California
> February 5, 1930
> [Telegram]

Considine has telegraphed denial *Variety*. All serene. Drop matter.

> Stephen Benét

TO NANNINE JOSEPH [7]

> 60 East 93rd Street
> New York, N.Y.
> February [20] 1930

Dear Miss Joseph:—

Thanks for the suggestion but I don't think it would be good policy for me to do an article on Hollywood. I'd rather be the person who went there and didn't.

> With all best wishes
> Stephen Benét

TO WILBUR L. CROSS [8]

> 60 East 93rd Street
> New York, N.Y.
> March [5] 1930

Dear Dean Cross:—

It's kind of you to think of me—but I'm afraid an article on the talkies [for the *Yale Review*] is beyond my powers. It's always very difficult for me to write articles in the first place—and Hollywood is such an indescribable place in the second. Besides I was only

7. An employee of Brandt and Brandt.

8. Wilbur L. Cross was a member of the Yale faculty from 1894 until 1930, when he launched a new and equally notable career as Governor of Connecticut for four successive terms. Cross had been dean of the Yale Graduate School when Benét was a student there; he was editor of the *Yale Review* and sympathetic to Benét's literary ambitions.

there for ten weeks and know very little about the technical side, which is the interesting one. Sorry.

> With all best wishes
> Sincerely
> Stephen Vincent Benét

TO FREDERICA FIELD [9]

> 60 East 93rd Street
> New York, N.Y.
> [April] 1930

My dear Mrs. Fields [sic]:—

I wrote "Elementals" in a tin garage at Scarsdale, N.Y. It was very hot and I had just been shot for typhoid. As for why it was written—it was written in the hope of making some money. After the story appeared I had quite a few letters from people who wanted to take the neck-or-nothing side of the bet on which the plot depends —it seemed a pity not to be able to oblige them.

> Sincerely
> Stephen Vincent Benét

TO CARL BRANDT

> Peace Dale, R.I.
> August [10] 1930

Dear Carl:—

Thanks for your letter. I will be coming up for the opening [of *Abraham Lincoln*] as I have to see my doctor anyway. Besides, it ought to be amusing. I hope the thing

9. Literary Editor of *Golden Book Magazine,* which reprinted "Elementals" in its May and June issues in 1930.

goes over. Don't speed up the publicity *too* hard—you know what a shrinking plant I am.

I'm much healthier though still a barren stock as far as work is concerned. However, I'll try to have some puppies soon.

As ever
SVB

TO PAGE COOPER [10]

Peace Dale, R.I.
September 13, 1930

Dear Miss Cooper:—

Thanks a lot for thinking of me in connection with the Barbizon—but I'm afraid I'm not yet up to facing an audience. I'm a lot better but still seem to get unduly tired for the silliest reasons. So may I beg off this time?

With all best wishes

Sincerely
Stephen Vincent Benét

TO CARL BRANDT

Peace Dale, R.I.
October 7, 1930

Dear Carl:—

Will you, like an angel, get somebody to send the State of New York all this [income tax] information? They are always writing me about something and I have never tried to cheat them yet.

10. Miss Cooper was a member of the promotion department at Doubleday, Doran.

It is beautiful weather down here. I am trying to get to work.

As ever

SVB

TO HARRY E. MAULE [1]

Peace Dale, R.I.

October 29, 1930

Dear Mr. Maule:

I've been thinking over your suggestion of either *American Ballads and Poems* or *American Names* ever since I got your letter, and hope you won't think me pigheaded for not wanting to use the word American with this particular book. It's hard to explain, but, in the last analysis, the book *is* a compilation, a great number of poems in it are not American in subject, and I simply don't feel, after a good deal of consideration, that that particular adjective belongs on the title-page. I know *Ballads and Poems* has no particular kick in it but damn if I can find anything else that does seem to fit the book. Titles either come easy or hard, and most of mine have come easy, but not this one. But I don't think American belongs on it—too many Greek girls and knights. Sorry.

I'm glad if you liked "The Island and the Fire." I tinkered with it a lot and it ought to be better than it is, but one can't rework forever. Of course, if you want to

1. A former editor of Doubleday, Page, and Co., Maule became a vice president of Doubleday, Doran. He is now associated with Random House.

issue a limited edition, I'd be glad to have you do so, and sign sheets or anything else.

With all best wishes
Sincerely
Stephen Vincent Benét

TO DANIEL LONGWELL [2]

27 East 95th Street
New York, N.Y.
November 18, 1930

Dear Longwell:—

Thanks very much for your suggestion about the map. It would really be an enormous help to me if such a thing could be made. What I want particularly is the main routes Westward, showing the flow of settlement, Boone's Wilderness Road, the Nollichucky Trace, Delaware Water Gap, the Natchez Trace, the route or main route North through the Five Nations and Sir William Johnson's country, then the Oregon Trail, the Santa Fe Trail, the line of the Southern Pacific and Union Pacific, the Chisholm Trail, and finally the Lincoln Highway indicated. The explorations, DeSoto, LaSalle etc I don't need so much and I think would just clutter things up. It would be nice to have some of the forts in, Fort Bridger etc in the Indian Country, also Boonesborough and a couple of things like that. But what I principally want it for is to

2. Promotion Manager of Doubleday, Doran and, with John Farrar, one of the men most responsible for the effective promotion of *John Brown's Body*. During the 1930's the friendship between Longwell and Benét became a close one.

get a clear idea of the big roads, with the principal mountains and rivers they crossed.

Incidentally, I should think a map of this sort, rather more pictorial than I should need, might be a good thing for children, high schools, etc., if your Junior Book department ever does maps.

We've been running around, seeing people off to France and getting settled ourselves. Hope to be calmer soon.

With all best wishes and many thanks,
Stephen Benét

TO ROY W. COWDEN [3]

27 East 95th Street
New York, N.Y.
April 30, 1931

Dear Professor Cowden:—

I have received the manuscripts for the Hopwood Award and am reading them. As you were kind enough to say that I could ask for further information in regard to the contest if necessary, might I bother you with a few questions?

I gather that the minor award is open only to undergraduates, but that undergraduates are eligible for the major award as well. If so, who else is eligible for the major award?

Are the bequests to be given every year?

3. Associate professor of English at the University of Michigan, and assistant Director of the then recently established Avery Hopwood Awards in creative writing.

Are there three prizes of $2500 in the major awards? Or only one?

In case no manuscript seems sufficiently striking for a major award, what happens?

I hope this doesn't seem unduly inquisitive on my part, but as you undoubtedly realize, it isn't the easiest task in the world to judge young work, and I'm anxious to do it to the best of my ability. Of course, if any of these questions seem unnecessary to you—just don't answer them.

Very sincerely yours,
Stephen Vincent Benét

TO CARL BRANDT

Peace Dale, R.I.
June 9, 1931

Dear Carl:—

Here's some light summer reading for the chewing-gum trade. Try and get it swallowed by some large editor.

With all best wishes
SVB

TO ERD N. BRANDT [4]

Peace Dale, R.I.
June 11, 1931

Dear Erd:—

Glad you liked the story. Raise the price if you can— I want to buy some things—about $5000 worth of things.

4. Carl Brandt's younger brother, a partner in Brandt and Brandt until his resignation to become an associate editor of the *Saturday Evening Post*.

Emily Wrench [Kimbrough] would have bought this kind of story immediately for the [*Ladies' Home*] *Journal,* if she were still extant—I mean if she were still editing.

I'll do some more work.

Regards
SVB

P.S. Couldn't "American Honeymoon" be resold to *Harper's,* now Wells, who didn't like the end, has gone.

S.

TO ERD N. BRANDT

Peace Dale, R.I.
June 26, 1931

Dear Erd:—

Sorry—I have tried to make Mr. Washington come down off his monument but with no success.[5] If you don't hear from me by Monday, you will know the attempt is a failure.

> It's easier to lie on the
>   beach & burn your belly in the sun
> Than to write a thousand poetic
>   words about George Washington.

I have started work, however, with the coughs and sputters of a Model T crossing the Great Smokies. But maybe something will come of it.

Regards
SVB

5. *Country Gentleman* had asked Benét to write a poem about Washington.

TO CARL BRANDT

Peace Dale, R.I.
August 2, 1931

Dear Carl:—

I've been meaning to write you—and I'm delighted about the sales. But I've been trying to finish the first section of this poem [*Western Star*]—so not much time for letters.

I have several ideas for stories but want to get this first part done before I try one. Best wishes to you all. Do not weary in well doing.

As ever
Steve

P.S. If Bob McClure should come into your office, treat him well for me.

S.

TO CARL BRANDT

220 East 69th Street
New York, N.Y.
December 18, 1931

Dear Carl:—

I have cut about 800 words of this story and that is all I can or will do. If [Lee] Hartman [of *Harper's*] isn't satisfied with that, tell him to send it back. There has to be a certain development and progression in fiction whether editors like it or not. The last story they almost took they thought was too short. In fact, they're all crazy.

SVB

1929-1932

TO CARL BRANDT

220 East 69th Street
New York, N.Y.
December 20, 1931

Dear Carl:—

I enclose a new Oldest Inhabitant story—"The Yankee Fox." I think this is one of the best of this type of story that I have done—a remark always calculated to make one's agent sigh "Oh yeah?". But, seriously, I should like you to think over the possibility of getting a new market for this variety of story—since the *Country Gentleman* seems about washed up on them. It is much more my kind of thing than a story like "Serenade," and, if it were possible to make some sort of profitable connection, I could do a series on the line of an American "Puck of Pook's Hill"—though, hardly, as you will agree, with the same ability. Nevertheless, it seems to me that a series of rather simple, romantic stories, American in background, with a certain fairytale quality might have a chance of appealing to the larger market in this particular time when nobody very much wants to read about the depression any more. Would the *Post,* with its new color-work, be interested in such a series? And will you devote a few minutes to thinking the possibilities over?

If anything came of it, I should be glad to do as good work on the stories as I can—and, incidentally, to supply a new frame, in case you think the Oldest Inhabitant, as recounter, is getting a little shopworn.

With all best wishes of the season—I haven't done *my* Christmas shopping yet either—

SVB

P.S. Do you suppose the *Country Gentleman* has a file of previous Oldest Inhabitant stories? I'd like to look them all over some time and am not sure that I have all of them

S.

TO CARL BRANDT

220 East 69th Street
New York, N.Y.
January 3, 1932

Dear Carl:—

Thank you for the comment from the *Post* [about "The Yankee Fox"]. I certainly don't care whether the story is told in dialect or not—all I want is some sort of frame to put that story in—and would be perfectly willing to suppress the oldest inhabitant entirely.

The other comment seems to me a little foolish. I have already specifically stated that it was the sort of country where people went out with their hounds whatever errand they happened to be doing. Naturally they'd take the hounds with them, when they went on a lynching-party. And, in this case, they'd certainly take them, not because they didn't know where the hero was—but specifically to humiliate him by chasing him out of his house with the descendants of the hounds his grandfather had brought from England. Hasn't anybody on the *Post* ever seen a Southern possum hunt or a Southern mob? What a lot they've missed.

A very happy new year
from
SVB

TO BENNETT WEAVER [6]

220 East 69th Street
New York, N.Y.
February 12, 1932

My dear Mr. Weaver:—

I'd be glad to judge the Hopwood awards again—
unless they are to be awarded by a numerical averaging
of the ratings of the three judges. That particular system
seems to me to make for mediocrity—I'd rather have anybody's first choice than two or three people's second
choice. So, if that particular system is to be adopted,
I think I had better step out. Otherwise, I would be glad
to serve.

With many apologies for the delay in answering your
invitation.

Stephen Vincent Benét

TO ALICE LEE MYERS

220 East 69th Street
New York, N.Y.
[February] 1932

Dear Alice Lee:—

Some of the books (fiction) about American history
that a boy might like reading are,

Arundel and *Rabble in Arms* by Kenneth Roberts. Pre-
American Revolution and Revolution. Exciting and pretty
accurate. Maine background in *Arundel*.

6. Assistant professor of English at the University of Michigan
in 1932, and Director of the Avery Hopwood Awards.

Drums by James Boyd. Revolution. Also *Marching On*—Civil War—and *Long Hunt,* pioneer.

To Have and To Hold by Mary Johnston. Colonial Virginia. *The Long Roll* and *Cease Firing* by Mary Johnston —Civil War.

Richard Carvell by Winston Churchill. *The Crossing* by Winston Churchill (Lewis and Clark).

The Covered Wagon and in general the Western stories of Emerson Hough.

The Long Rifle and its successors by Stewart Edward White. Pioneering all the way West. White is a gun-crank and knows his stuff on guns etc.

Cardigan, by Robert W. Chambers. Chambers, oddly enough, knew a great deal about early NY history. This is a good romantic novel with excellent stuff on the Long House and Sir William Johnson. Lots of Indians and fighting.

God's Angry Man by Leonard Ehrlich. By far the best semi-fictional account of John Brown.

America has so far unfortunately produced no Dumas and no one historical novel of the past as good as *Henry Esmond.* Of course Mark Twain gives you the Mississippi and the West and Hawthorne's short stories (if they haven't been spoiled for you in class) give you a good deal of the Puritan and New England.

I don't happen to know of any one-volume history of the USA that would make really good reading for a boy. Adams's *Epic of America* is popular enough in key for professional historians to regard it with suspicion and it is copiously illustrated. It is probably the most modern of the popular histories though a somewhat hasty job.

The buff-and-blue source books I speak of were to me fascinating—I wish to God I could remember their names.[7] They had things like the Pope's bull dividing the New World up—some of Smith, Bradford, Raleigh, early voyagers etc. I'll try to look these up. The first part of Mark Van Doren's *Anthology of American Literature???* again I'm shaky on names has some of this material. *American Poetry and Prose,* edited by Norman Foerster, gives a little of the same thing.

Sandburg's *Lincoln: The Prairie Years* is a swell book and I think there is an abridgment of the boyhood and youth called *Abe Lincoln Grows Up.* If so, worth looking up. Marquis James's *The Raven* on Sam Houston is a good biography. I know of no really good life of Washington, and of no good short life of Washington.

The DAR book I spoke of is called *Colonial Captivities, Marches and Journeys* (Macmillan) and you would like it yourself.

Then there are books like Edward Eggleston's *A Hoosier Schoolmaster,* Hamlin Garland's *A Son of the Middle Border,* Herbert Quick's *Vandemark's Folly.* All Middle West, the first two fiction strongly founded on fact, the third autobiography.

The thing, of course, is to make the people come alive. They do, if you can dig them out of the dust. The Puritans, as everyone knows, were a stern, hardhearted people, without human emotions. So when John Winthrop writes his wife, "oh. how it refresheth my heart to think that I shall yet again see thy sweet face in the land of the living!—that lovely countenance that I have so much

7. Benét was probably referring to *Source-Book of American History,* ed. Albert Bushnell Hart, New York, 1899.

delighted in and beheld with such great content!" it may change your ideas about one particular Puritan. "Be sure to be warm clothed and to have store of fresh provisions, meal, eggs put up in salt ..... a large frying pan, a small stewing pan and a case to boil a pudding in ..... I kiss and embrace thee, my dear wife."

And she wrote back in one letter. "P.S. I have not yet received the box, but I will send for it. I send up a turkey and some cheese ... I did dine at Groton Hall yesterday: they are in good health and remember their love. We did wish you were there, but that would not bring you, and I could not be merry without thee. Mr. Lee and his wife were there: they remember their love. Our neighbor Cole and goodman Newton have been sick ... I fear thy cheese will not prove so good as thou didst expect. I have sent it all for we could not cut it."

Human beings?

. . . you shouldn't have got me started. I'll send Dickie one of the Roberts books and see how he likes it. And we'll hope to see you soon.

Affectionately
Stephen

TO RICHARD MYERS

220 East 69th Street
New York, N.Y.
February 21, 1932

Dear Dick:—

. . . We continue to exist, one jump ahead of the sheriff—the children well, thank God, and very interesting and pleasant—the house satisfactory—Rosemary at the moment translating a French detective-story which has the charming title *Six Hommes Morts* and scares her when she's alone in the house with it—and me writing short stories to run between the fashion-drawings and the article on . . . the smart way to cook bullock's-heart for a formal Valentine dinner, in the better women's magazines. So far I haven't had my price cut though the *Post* tried to so I just turned around and sold the story to the *Delineator* instead. It is strong, grim-minded men like that who are needed in this time of depression and soul-searching. Needed, I should say, in Guam.

. . . I am being mildly approached by the movies at the moment but I fear their intentions are dishonorable. In fact I know they're not honorable but I fear they rate the price of dishonor too low. I won't be seduced on a park bench—it's a suite at the Ritz or nothing, screamed the pure young girl. But it was entrancing to get back, even for a moment, into that protoplasmic atmosphere. There is nothing like the movies, except soap sculpture and zymotic diseases.

. . . Write us how you are and how Paris is and everything and sundry. And our dear love to you all.

As ever
Steve

TO CARL BRANDT

220 East 69th Street
New York, N.Y.
March 31, 1932

Dear Carl:—

I don't know much about this story but I've cut around 7000 words out of it, which is something. Let me know how you feel on it.

I will try to think of a serial idea over the weekend.

I don't think $500 and *College Humor* is entirely worth while. A place like *Harper's* with a low price means a little something. But C.H. at that price strikes me as rather betwixt and between, except for a commercial story that can't sell anywhere else.

> God be with you.
> SVB

TO CARL BRANDT

> 220 East 69th Street
> New York, N.Y.
> May 16, 1932

Dear Carl:—

Here's a vapid little short short story ["Transit of Venus"] you might be able to work off. I have been trying to work a long one but it hasn't quite jelled.

> With all the best to yourself,
> SVB

TO CARL BRANDT

> 220 East 69th Street
> New York, N.Y.
> July 12, 1932

Dear Carl:—

This is merely to let you know that I am not dead and have been working on the long story ["Princess Pauper"]. It's taken more time than I expected for I rewrote the second section completely and, I think, improved it a good deal. I think I have something, if I can get it the way I want, and do it right. At least I feel I want to more or less shoot at the moon with it, and that takes time. I'm in the third section now. It will certainly run 30,000 words, maybe 40,000 words. If I could, I'd get it about the size of Willa Cather's *The Professor's House*. But I don't know whether that will be feasible.

. . . When I finish the first draft of the thing I want you to see it and talk it over with you. Meanwhile—ahem —any sales of any sort would be appreciated, as you know.

With all best wishes
SVB

TO WILLIAM ROSE BENÉT

220 East 69th Street
New York, N.Y.
September 14, 1932

Dear Bill:—

I wish to God I could! Maybe some money will turn up in the next week or so and if it does, I'll ship some along. But just at the moment I'm stony, with a $260 insurance premium to pay and the children's school bill ahead, if we send them back, not to speak of the rent and the coal. Things are bound to turn and I'm trying to get this novelette through in hopes Carl will do something with it—but I've only sold one story in the last four months. Lord knows, if I had the cash, you should have it too—and it seems perfectly ridiculous that I shouldn't —but we are strapped. . . . I think we had as inexpensive a summer as we could, with no visitors and a nominal rent, but I begrudged the 96 cents it took to bring the dog back on the train. Well, this is all perfectly mad and I have faith in the United States and art, but if present conditions keep on, I'm afraid I'm going to be in a hole. I should say a rather long one, too. Anyhow, if any rain falls before the first, you shall have some of it—and let's meet and pool our tears in the near future. I'm sunk not to be immediately helpful—and God knows I wish I could be. But I just haven't got it—and if I don't get some soon myself, we'll probably be out in the Park.

With love and sadness
Steve

TO CARL BRANDT

220 East 69th Street
New York, N.Y.
December 20, 1932

Dear Carl:—

Here is a story with, at least, a worthy moral. See what you make of it.

Is *Harper's Bazaar* dead or what? I don't like to nag but they ought to know their minds by this time.

Best to you all.
SVB

Man of Letters (1933-1940)

DURING the 1930s, though he was regularly in servitude as a skillful hack for the movies and the circulation magazines, Benét slowly consolidated too the massive and decent popularity which had begun with *John Brown's Body* and the ballads of the 1920's. Gradually he developed a short story technique which enabled him to sell to the *Saturday Evening Post* not only fantasy and folk tales but also the antifascist short stories which grew from his new political maturity. "He was the only one of us," said his fellow craftsman John Marquand many years later, "who could write a story for the *Saturday Evening Post* and make it read like literature." His series of nightmare poems in the *New Yorker,* and such savage political verse as "Litany for Dictatorships," brought him grudging respect from those who did not read his fiction but assumed it was a stereotype. Through his lectures and reviews, through his editorship of the Yale Series of Younger Poets and, for Farrar and Rinehart, the Rivers of America series, and above all through his generous support of young writers, he assumed a role of private and official leadership which no American writer had exercised so fully since the nineteenth century. He had become, with all the costs and compensations which accompany leadership, a revered and honored man of letters. He was, as these letters show, serious but not solemn as he conscientiously dispatched his duties; in the warm circle of his old friendships he referred to himself ironically as "the good grey poet."

TO DANIEL LONGWELL

220 East 69th Street
New York, N.Y.
May 25, 1933

Dear Dan:—

. . . The novel [*James Shore's Daughter*] has stuck and unstuck and stuck again but I hope to finish it relatively soon after I get up to the country. As Bernice [Baumgarten] has probably told you, I am going in with Rosemary on the child's book [*A Book of Americans*] for Johnny, as it struck me as an amusing proposition, but I don't think it will take time away from the novel—the two things are so different. I want very much to get your opinion on the novel as soon as it gets back into recognizable shape. I'm thinking of it at present as *James Shore's Daughter* but am not wild about that title if I can get a better one.

I'd love to have some books for the summer. And let us know any time you can come around.

As ever
SVB

TO GEORGE PARMLY DAY [8]

220 East 69th Street
New York, N.Y.
June 14, 1933

Dear Mr. Day:—

I'd be glad to act as Editor of the Yale Series of Younger Poets and resume a connection with the Yale Press to which I still owe gratitude for *Young Adventure*. I'm going to be here in New York till the first of July and if either Mr. Davidson or Mr. Donaldson [of the Yale University Press] should happen to be in town during the next couple of weeks, I'd be very glad indeed to talk over details with them. The series has always been an interesting one and most certainly deserves carrying on, especially in these times, when it's harder than ever for young writers to get their work in print. And, if I can do anything to help it, I'll consider it a privilege. . . .

With all good wishes to yourself and the Press
Sincerely
Stephen Vincent Benét

TO GEORGE PARMLY DAY

220 East 69th Street
New York, N.Y.
June 18, 1933

Dear Mr. Day:—

Thank you for your letter. Mr. Davidson writes that he [will] see me Monday, which will be very pleasant.

7. Founder and president of the Yale University Press, and, in 1933, treasurer of both the University and the Press.

I think the public—or rather the very small poetry-reading public—is or can be interested in young unknown writers. But it takes a little advertising.

As regards the fee, I think I'd like it paid by check in one instalment. This is, of course, only in case that Governor [Wilbur] Cross does not intend to strike coinage of the Free State of Connecticut which I would greatly prefer. A very nice design could be made—by Dwiggins perhaps.

> With all good wishes
> Stephen Vincent Benét

TO EUGENE DAVIDSON

> Peace Dale, R.I.
> July 4, 1933

Dear Mr. Davidson:—

I have prayerfully read the fifteen mss. submitted in the Yale Series of Younger Poets and have finally decided on *Girl in the Mirror* [retitled *Dark Hills Under*] by Shirley Barker as the best candidate. It's the most ambitious book of the lot and the best unified—and she has narrative ability and a very good feel for New England. Also, as she seems to be a junior at New Hampshire, considering what her age must be, the book really shows promise, though, like all beginning writers, she is influenced. I somewhat regret *The Gardener Mind* by Laura Haley, but that particular kind of metaphysical poetry has to be nearly as good as Donne to be good at all, and she doesn't quite measure up to that, and, occasionally, falls flat on her face in a bog of words.

I enclose a letter to Miss Barker . . . I have written all the other people whose manuscripts you sent me and have returned their mss. to them. Or rather I will return it tomorrow. Incidentally, I am leaving tomorrow for the above address.

It has been an interesting thing to do and I think Miss Barker's work has youth, freshness and distinct potentialities. What will become of her eventually only God can tell, but she may turn into somebody important.

Sincerely
Stephen Vincent Benét

TO SHIRLEY BARKER

Peace Dale, R.I.
July 4, 1933

My dear Miss Barker:—

It gives me great pleasure to notify you that your manuscript, *Girl in the Mirror,* has been selected for publication as the next volume in the Yale Series of Younger Poets.

It's a pleasure to find anyone of college-age with such decided narrative ability and such a strong feeling for the native scene. And your book has a unity, both of scene and feeling, which seems to me quite remarkable.

Now, may I make a few suggestions? Editors always do.

In the first place, *Girl in the Mirror,* while a pleasant title, doesn't, to me, suggest the book. The book itself is very New England, even in the sonnets—indeed, one of the things which helps the last nine sonnets to rise so well toward their climax (and they lift beautifully) is the sense of New England landscape behind the story. Now *Girl in the Mirror,* as a title, might be any girl in any mirror, anywhere. Can't you think of something more suggestive of the countryside and spirit behind the work? I don't suggest you call it *Puritan Bones* or *Plymouth Passions,* in the Hollywood manner. But, something a little more distinctive and evocative would help.

In the second place, reviewers are both busy and lackadaisical persons. They're apt to pick up a book of poems, look at the first few, look in the middle, then at the end. Now, *Girl in the Mirror* is a good poem, but the little lyric that begins it is, perhaps, the weakest thing in it, especially the first four lines. I wonder if it might not be a good thing to begin the book with a couple of shorter poems, such as "Question" and "Old Voices." And, if you could possibly strengthen the beginning of "Girl in the Mirror," it might be to the poem's advantage.

I am saying this, because you have great facility—and it is an admirable quality—but it occasionally leads you into writing at too great length. Concision is also a virtue—and a hard but valuable thing to practice.

I should appreciate a better last couplet to "Lover's Meeting" and you cannot, you must not rhyme "dawn" and "warn" in the last sonnet of your sequence. It is a fine sonnet and the end is splendid, and therefore all the more reason why it should not be flawed by a bad rhyme.

Now that is all I have to offer, definitely, in the way of criticism—oh yes, one more and very minor thing—do *not* say, "Meet, Ben, young William Browne of Tavistock." Say, "His name's young William Browne of

Tavistock" if you can think of nothing better but "Meet, Ben" is a little incongruous—a sort of "Shake hands with Mr. Jonson," coming in the middle of a good poem.

Also, as I am supposed to write a foreword to the book, I wonder if you could write me a letter telling something about yourself—age, family, education, habitat, etc. You see I know nothing about you but your work and your signature!

Meanwhile, again, my very good wishes and congratulations. If possible, I should like to look over the manuscript again, before it is put into proof, for the changes I suggest, if they appeal to you, and for any others that may occur to you—especially in the way of concision and mending the very few relatively unmusical lines which occur here and there.

And I hope you won't find this letter either too critical or too long. Such criticism as there is springs from a very real interest—and a considerable astonishment that you haven't appeared in magazines before!

Very sincerely yours,
Stephen Vincent Benét

TO CARL BRANDT

Peace Dale, R.I.
July 9, 1933

Dear Carl:—

Thanks for your nice letter and also for the good news about "The Bagpipes of Spring." Why does the *Post* always fuss about prices so—however, you're perfectly right and I'll be glad to have the money. Can you get it for me as soon as possible as I have to pay the rent. I usually have to pay the rent about the time somebody gives me a medal or a testimonial.[9] This is not biting gift-horses in the teeth—merely a coincidence that I have remarked before.

It is lovely down here and I am trying to labor industriously. I want to finish the child's book as soon as possible and also clean up the novel. Happy new apartment to you and many thanks again.

As ever
Steve

TO PAUL ENGLE [1]

Peace Dale, R.I.
July [30] 1933

Dear Paul:—

I meant to write before and should have, but, what with one thing and another, times have been a little jammed. Also, it always takes about two weeks to straighten out, when you get down here from the city and get used to birds instead of Elevateds. However, the summer is now well under way . . .

I thought you'd probably like the MacLeish [*Conquistador?*]—I did; and some new things he's done which will be in the Selected Poems [*Poems 1924–1933*] and made me very excited, as I have not been in a long

9. Benét had just been awarded the Roosevelt Medal for distinguished American poetry.

1. Benét had met this young Iowa poet in 1932, and was one of Engle's sponsors in his successful application for a Rhodes Scholarship.

time. He seems to me right now to be going about as well as a man can go.

Rosemary and I are getting ahead with our child's-book on the line of *Kings and Queens* and expect to have it ready for Fall. Charles Child is doing us some superb pictures. Also I hope to finish this dragging novel. We'll be back in New York around the middle of September as far as I know, so we'll maybe see you if you pass through. How's your appendix?

Since I began this letter, the weather has changed, boiled and now become beautiful. There is an intense clarity about the light today, and, two nights ago, the Wakefield Band played on the village-green beneath an almost full moon. As a matter of fact, they played too dam loud, because I was trying to write something and they nearly drove me crazy—the applause was given by auto horns, too—but the idea was a pleasant one.

. . . I just met a man named Veiller (son of [the author of] *Within the Law,* I think) who was out at Iowa City this Spring—working, I think, with the Drama Department—and thinks it the most interesting University in the country. So we exchanged reminiscences. It—the whole country as well as the University—sounds very fine from your description. I'd like to see it that way, some time. And you must see this small, independent and curiously warm corner of New England. It has a great deal of hardness and grace. All our best to yourself and a good August with very large moons. Cats are witches in Rhode Island.

As ever
SVB

P.S. Rosemary says they're nice witches.

TO BASIL DAVENPORT [2]

Peace Dale, R.I.
July 31, 1933

Dear Basil:—

Thanks a lot for your very pleasant letter. The runner reached me at the Falls of the M'Bwuinga, where there is a very nice bit of shooting, chiefly ostrich and leopard (Chitty's lesser leopard, of course). We are being a little bothered by gorilla, who are remarkably enterprising at this season, and have eaten three of our bearers, cracking the bones of the last one as my dear grandfather used to crack his after-dinner walnuts, between thumb and forefinger, disdaining the use of all artificial appliances and lived and died a true-hearted English gentleman with no damn Methodism about him, he would as soon have shot a fox, but otherwise we are all quite fit.

I don't quite know what you do with a medal except carry it around in your upper breast-pocket and hire somebody to shoot you in it, so you can say afterwards that it saved your life—but it is very nice of them and I am pleased to get it. We've had rather rainy weather up till now and a couple of three-day Northeasters, but yesterday & today were perfect & I hope the next weeks will improve.

Rosemary and I are trying to finish up our American *Kings & Queens* [*A Book of Americans*] for fall publication—and I've got to the novel, too—so we've been busy.

2. Anthologist and editor—including a two-volume edition of Benét's prose and poetry—and today one of the judges of the Book-of-the-Month Club. He had written to congratulate Benét on the award to him of the Roosevelt Medal for poetry for 1933.

The children are fine and Jinny finds many new and attractive scents, though not so far, thank God, a skunk.

All our best to you and much appreciation of a delightful letter,

As ever

Steve

TO CARL BRANDT

220 East 69th Street
New York, N.Y.
September 24, 1933

Dear Carl:—

This is a somewhat ground-out story, I fear, but maybe you can do something with it. I'm getting back to the novel and hope for results shortly. The kid's book is all done and in the works.

Much love to you all and I'll be in, one of these days —I hope with a large wad of mss.

As ever

Steve

TO CARL BRANDT

220 East 69th Street
New York, N.Y.
October 2, 1933

Dear Carl:—

I am enclosing the first two parts of *James Shore's Daughter* and hope to have the third by the beginning of next week. After that is done, there shouldn't be much trouble, though it will all have to be retyped. I changed the first two parts a lot more, originally, and have gradually come back somewhat toward the original version, as it's the third part where the trouble lies. However, I will get it all through by the 15th or bust. Will you get three copies typed? Thanks a lot.

Can I have the *Delineator* check by the 4th or 5th? It's the usual insurance difficulty which seems to be chronic with me. When I get it paid up finally, the insurance cos. will probably all go bust. But what the hell.

It was marvelous to get "The Main Street Camel" sold so rapidly and I'll do another as soon as I'm through with this.

Love and pretzels
SVB

TO VALENTINE MITCHELL GAMMELL [3]

220 East 69th Street
New York, N.Y.
November 22, 1933

Dear Valentine:—

I have been trying to look up prizes for you but they seem few and far between. I don't think you'd be interested in a prize of $82 offered for the best short poem expressing the ideas behind the poetry of Edwin Markham—said poem to be presented to Mr. M. on his 82nd birthday by a committee (the ideas include the Brotherhood of Man)—and that seems to be the largest going around at the moment. However, if you have any Brotherhoods of Man up your sleeve, the person to send them

3. Mrs. Gammell, a daughter of the Philadelphia man of letters S. Weir Mitchell, was a summer neighbor of the Benéts in Rhode Island.

to is Mrs. Ida Bentley Judd, 415 Central Park West—and
after all $82 is $82. *Bozart and Contemporary Verse,*
Oglethorpe University Press, Oglethorpe University,
Georgia, offers a prize of $25 for the best poem in each
issue. This magazine is edited by Ernest Hartsock, believe it or not, but has managed to remain in the land
of the living for several years, which must show something. *Poetry,* of course, is continuing both its existence
and its yearly prizes which are large and worthwhile.
Have you tried the *New Yorker* recently? They wrote me
a while ago and said they were anxious to get more
serious verse—and they pay very well. The University
of Virginia Quarterly [*Virginia Quarterly Review*] is
more hospitable to long poems than most and just printed
an extremely interesting bunch of sonnets by somebody
called Jesse Stuart—I liked them.

Any more prizes that I hear of, I will pass along to
you—but there seems to be a dearth, just at present, due,
I fear, to those same old economic reasons. Love to Bill
and you from us all—we have had a rather animated
time since coming back, with my uncle's illness and other
things, but are hoping for something of a respite now . . .

As ever
SVB

TO JOHN WINCHESTER DANA

220 East 69th Street
New York, N.Y.
[December] 1933

My dear Mr. Dana:—

Storer Lunt [of W. W. Norton and Co., Inc.] was kind
enough to show me your copy of *John Brown's Body* and

I have been more than interested in seeing the comments and notes you have made—and also the extremely interesting letter from John Brown, Jr. It is a great thing for any author to have such a faithful and courteous reader. I have taken the liberty of changing your notes in two places—"lackeyes" in Pennsylvania are horse-chestnuts not walnuts—2nd, no Pennsylvanian would be really satisfied by your coldly referring to scrapple as "pork-scrap." That is like calling pumpkin-pie "boiled pumpkin cooked in dough." The description is truthful —but it doesn't go far enough.

With all good wishes and my genuine appreciation of your interest in the book.

Sincerely
Stephen Vincent Benét

TO PAUL ENGLE

220 East 69th Street
New York, N.Y.
January 1934

Dear Paul:—

I should have written you long ago and would have but for two things (a) a spurt of work and (b) a hope that I'd be able to give you some good news about *American Song.* . . . And now, when I am writing, it's, alas, without any more definite news on the book. John Farrar kept [it] a long while and was very much interested in it but finally decided they couldn't do it—I then took it to Dan Longwell of Doubleday who was ditto and is writing you a letter but unfortunately didn't see his way clear either. It really has been a bad year to get books accepted, especially poetry—most of the publishers have been cutting down their lists, and poetry, of course, is one of the first things they cut. However, both Doubleday and Farrar & Rinehart are really interested in you as a writer . . .

. . . As for here, this large, spectacular and crazy country has been spinning so fast since you left that you feel as if you were living in the middle of a kaleidoscope. Great issues surge up and bellow and are frantically discussed—and then, all of a sudden, evaporate, like drops of water on a hot stove. People write articles for magazines on the crucial events of last week and before the articles can be published everybody has forgotten that last week existed. The midwestern governors go to see the President and practically issue an ultimatum —which the President rejects—will there be a revolution? —no, everybody is seeing *The Three Little Pigs* and Mae West—everybody is singing "The Last Round-Up" and "Have You Ever Seen a Dream Walking?"—the Bourbons are gloomy about inflation but the inflation doesn't inflate the way they prophesied and all of a sudden the inflationists say they're for sound money—Tammany can't be beaten but Tammany is overwhelmed—before leaving the city, Tammany puts through one of the biggest pension grabs in history—the N.R.A. is a failure—the N.R.A. is a success—the N.R.A. is to be continued forever and to be abolished next week. . . . I know one thing—the dead weight, the black chill of last winter, that lay on the spirit like frozen blood, is gone. Things are popping and boiling, things are happening, there's a different smell in the weather. How much of it is Mr. Franklin Delano Roosevelt, I do not know—I think a good deal. I'm for him, for one. . . .

Before the beginning and the end of this letter, I called

up Dan Longwell who said he wanted one or two more days on the manuscript and if times were different—there was something in your work that interested him very much. So I'll wait—though I'm afraid it's definite that he's going to return it. But I'll try to be more speedy with the next publishers. The whole family sends you a very Happy New Year and much affection. And next time, I'll try to write a somewhat saner letter—but the last three months have been exciting to say the least . . . We miss your visits here and Tom would love to tell you about his school. Let me know if you want any American books or if there's anything else I can do for you on this side. And, always, a great deal of friendship and good wishes from the Benéts.

As ever
SVB

TO DANIEL LONGWELL

220 East 69th Street
New York, N.Y.
January 28, 1934

Dear Dan:—

Would there be anything in the Doubleday Doran bookshops for a girl of twenty-eight or so who's passed all the highest normal school and teacher's exams., taught for several years in the West, and knows enough about books to write one? She was married to a Communist poet who has deserted her and is trying to support a crippled child by working in a steam-laundry. Macy's book-store wouldn't take her on, apparently, because she was under-nourished—which is a sort of circle, when you come to think about it.

1933–1940

I haven't met the girl myself, but Archie MacLeish and his wife have been trying to do something for her and asked me if there was anything I could suggest. So I know it is entirely bona-fide and would be very grateful if you could possibly suggest anything.

As ever
SVB

TO ANDREW D. TALBOT JONES [4]

220 East 69th Street
New York, N.Y.
February 15, 1934

Dear Andrew:—

I am taking the liberty of sending you, under separate cover as all good businessmen say, the galley proofs of my new novel, *James Shore's Daughter*. It's rather an imposition to ask anyone to read galley proof but I thought you might be interested in this and, for selfish reasons, I am anxious to know what you think of it. Do not bother about most of the French as I am putting a good deal of it back into English, but if I've made any notable slips in conversation, costume or period, I'd be very grateful indeed if you'd tell me so. I'd very much appreciate any criticism you cared to make as you know I value your judgment and your taste. The book is coming out in April with Doubleday and I have sweat[ed] so much on it that I simply don't know what it's like any more or how it would strike a reader.

4. A cousin by marriage of Benét, on his mother's side, who had lived abroad a great deal and known the atmosphere Benét was attempting in *James Shore's Daughter*.

. . . There are floods of new books but not as many good ones as there might be. I want to get Maurice Baring's life of Sarah Bernhardt, if I can, and I was a good deal interested in a book called *The Unforgotten Prisoner* by R. C. Hutchinson. It's too long and not very well constructed but the man can write. It gives a fearful picture of Germany just after the war. Try it, if it comes your way. I was much interested in what you had to say about the Jules Romains. I was impressed by it, too, and as far as I'm concerned he can go on writing it for the next eighteen or twenty volumes—I'll read 'em . . .

The world seems in a parlous state and you will be sorry to hear that the stars promise very little relief for the next few months. I have taken up astrology again, as a hobby, and have been casting various horoscopes of family and friends. Send me the day and hour of your birth and I will do one for you. I haven't a stuffed crocodile yet or a witch's peaked hat but I am saving up the money to buy them.

> . . . With much love from all of us
> As ever
> Stephen

TO DANIEL LONGWELL

220 East 69th Street
New York, N.Y.
February 23, 1934

Dear Dan:—

Herewith the proof [of *James Shore's Daughter*]. I have put back a good deal of the French into English and added here and there, principally for clarification. Rudolph still remains unexplained but I have cleared up the first mention of Guido, a little, and added a few lines about the Grants and the Antwerps in Uncle Roger's visit. I am also sending a dedication and a note. I don't know if there is—or was—an American Copper Company but I suppose I had better state that mine is fictitious. Anderesplatz can be Andreasplatz if you or the printers prefer—I don't care—maybe the latter sounds less made up.

My uncle . . . read it and said he thought there was a little too much French in parts of the plot for the average reader. He also said, dryly, that while there were scenes in Rome and Switzerland I did not employ either Italian or German to any extent. So I guess that is right. He made no objection to the atmosphere being too twentieth-century in 1900 and seemed to think the Paris atmosphere OK except for the private telegraph line, which couldn't be done.

I am grateful to whoever made the notations on the manuscript—they're very good and I've accepted most of them.

I like the type very much and the dingus on the title page.

Probably when I see it in pages, I'll see holes I ought to have plugged in the first draft. But I'm blind on it now, from the point of view of any radical revision. Anyway, I've been over it as I'll never go over anything again.

The editorial from the Richmond paper is swell. Thank God, the Confederacy still holds its own.

As ever
SVB

TO PAUL ENGLE

220 East 69th Street
New York, N.Y.
February [26] 1934

Dear Paul:—

The new mss. has arrived and I've sent it on to Doubleday and am going to see Dan Longwell sometime within
the week to find out just what his plans are about publication—dates etc. I think you've improved it a great
deal and have a note from him this morning to the same
effect. Hal Smith and Morrow both called up about it
and were interested—but, after all, Doubleday is about
the largest firm in the business and has one of the best
sales-forces. Also, Dan Longwell himself is particularly
interested in exactly the kind of American thing and flavor
that both you and myself are trying to get at. He collects
the names of queer postoffices and knows what buffalo
grass looks like and the names of the clubs in the Three
I League and is, I imagine, one of the few publishers
who knows how to call a square dance. I think you'd
like him very much as a person and he's a good publisher. It's a big shop and you sometimes get the impression that your book has dropped into it as a stone
drops into a well—then, suddenly, you find out that
somebody has been working quite hard on it though you
haven't known it, and there is a complete program
mapped out. I'm telling you this because I think it's
always hard having a book published when you're out of
the country and you're apt to feel—I know I did—that
it's a sort of orphan . . .

Thanks a lot for sending me Spender—I like him. I was interested in the *New Voices* also, but that is rather harder to tell about. I'll try to dig up some new poetry for you . . .

. . . I'll write you more at length in a few days but I wanted to get this off so you'd know the mss. was safe in hand.

As ever
SVB

TO EUGENE DAVIDSON

220 East 69th Street
New York, N.Y.
May [7] 1934

Dear Davidson:—

Thanks for your letter. Don't worry about overworking me—I'd be glad to read 50 manuscripts in the hope of getting a good one. The obviously illiterate and crippled, of course, there's not much point in my seeing—but I feel a certain responsibility about the thing and would be glad to do all I could. By the way, when you send me the mss., will you send me some more stationery etc? I used up all I had last year—I think I wrote letters to a dozen or so of the contestants.

With good wishes
S. V. Benét

TO EUGENE DAVIDSON

220 East 69th Street
New York, N.Y.
June 9, 1934

Dear Davidson:—

I have been thinking about the Yale Series of Younger Poets—to this effect. It seems rather disproportionate to pay me $250 for reading the mss. when the lucky boy or girl who wins the competition can only make, at the most, $100 if he completely sells out the 500 copies of his book. I therefore suggest that you pay me $150 and pay the winner of the competition the other $100 as an outright prize, exclusive of any royalties his book may earn in addition. After all, I'm old and tough.

I have narrowed the mss. down to about 5 and will report shortly.

Sincerely
Stephen Benét

TO MURIEL RUKEYSER

220 East 69th Street
New York, N.Y.
June 21, 1934

Dear Miss Rukeyser:—

I am not accepting *Theory of Flight* for the Yale Series of Younger Poets. But it interested me so much and seemed to me to show so much promise that I thought I'd like to show it to at least one other publisher before sending it back to you. Of course I won't do so if you

have any objection—but it occurred to me that somebody like Random House, say, or possibly Farrar &
Rinehart, might, perhaps, be interested in it. If you have
other plans in mind, however, you have only to write me.
I might add that my only interest in the matter is an
interest in seeing that good new work gets shown to somebody who might like it.

Very sincerely yours
Stephen Vincent Benét

TO EUGENE DAVIDSON

220 East 69th Street
New York, N.Y.
June 22, 1934

Dear Davidson:—

I am sending under separate cover by mail the mss.
of [James] Agee's book which he wishes to call *Permit
Me Voyage.* Also he is writing you today giving some
publicity information about himself etc. I think the long
poems show extraordinary promise, especially the Dedication one. I'm sorry to have taken so long over it, but
the level of work was a good deal higher than last year's
and made decision more difficult.

I'm also writing Archie MacLeish to see if he will do
the preface for this particular book. If he consents, I'll
pay him for it—and it seems to me it would be pleasant
to get a little variety in the prefaces, now and then. In
this case, particularly—as MacLeish knows Agee while
I've just met him.

I suppose I might as well send the rejected mss. back
to their owners themselves this year—as I discover I've

already written short personal notes to all but 15 of the 42 you sent me.

This has been a lot of fun and I think you may be able to get somewhere with Agee—possibly even some attention from the daily reviewers. You never call tell, of course. But the Dedication thing in particular might hit people like [William] Soskin and [Lewis] Gannett, if they got a squint at it.

I hope the Press is agreeable to paying me $150 and Agee the other $100, exclusive of royalties.

With all good wishes
Stephen Benét

TO EUGENE DAVIDSON

220 East 69th Street
New York, N.Y.
June 26, 1934

Dear Davidson:—

Thanks for your letter. I'm glad you like Agee's work —I think he has real ability. Archie writes me that he is willing to do the preface so that's all right. I'd be glad, of course, to do some small note or blurb if Donaldson thinks it valuable. My point simply is that any series tends to a certain amount of monotony—and that any little diversity we can get into it, the better. Most of the time, I'd probably rather do the introduction myself, and will. But I should like to feel free, now and then, to ask people of importance to introduce work they have a genuine interest in. It seems to me a valuable thing for the books. And, naturally, I'll pay them out of what the Yale Press pays me.

246

I don't want to seem to be poking my fingers into some-body else's pie—but I was wondering if possibly the "wolfer night" poem or "The Happy Hen," sent out as cheaply as possible to a select list of booksellers and critics two weeks before publication, mightn't stimulate interest in the book? To be followed, say, just before publication with a fragment of "Dedication"? I don't know anything about publicity or costs, so I may be en-tirely crazy on this—but I am sending it along because it occurred to me. I would like to see some of the daily-paper boys get on to this—and they're hard to reach with verse. Also the collector's booksellers like [Louis] Cohn —though I suppose you take care of those.

All this merely arises from my genuine interest in the series, so you must excuse me if I run on. . . .

With all good wishes
SVB

TO MURIEL RUKEYSER

220 East 69th Street
New York, N.Y.
June 29, 1934

Dear Miss Rukeyser:—

I've sent *Theory of Flight* to Donald Klopfer of Ran-dom House but haven't yet heard what he thinks of it. So I expect I won't before I leave town—we're going to Rhode Island Saturday.

If he should happen to return the mss. to you, you might send it to John Farrar of Farrar & Rinehart and I will write him a note about it. If he returns it to me or writes me about it, I'll let you know at once.

My summer address will be The Homestead, Peace Dale, Rhode Island. Nobody can ever tell about getting a book published—but I hope they will do something with yours.

Sincerely
Stephen Benét

TO EUGENE DAVIDSON

Peace Dale, R.I.
July 3, 1934

Dear Davidson:—

Thanks a lot. That's fine. Only don't call it the Benét prize—call it the Yale Prize or the College Plan prize or anything else you like—*please*. If you call it the Benét prize, I'll feel as if I ought to have ivy planted on me. . . . However, I don't see why, eventually, the series shouldn't be something in which all the budding Spenders & Audens would want to publish *first*.

With all good wishes
As ever
Stephen Benét

TO MURIEL RUKEYSER

Peace Dale, R.I.
July 6, 1934

Dear Miss Rukeyser:—

I haven't heard anything from Random House but I *think* the copy I sent them had both your addresses on it. It didn't strike me as being a particularly bad copy —at least I read it without any difficulty—but, if you want to send them another one, go ahead. It would probably be easier to send it direct to them as I'm down here for the summer now and don't get up to New York much. If they've sent it back to you, let me know, and I will write a note to Farrar & Rinehart.

If it would interest you, now you're back in New York, to see Bernice Baumgarten, of Brandt & Brandt, the literary agents, I'd be glad to give you a note to her. She handles the book-rights for the agency and is a very intelligent girl. Agencies, as a rule, don't do very much with poetry—the financial returns being small—but if you had any prose in mind, it might be worth having a talk with her.

Sincerely

Stephen Benét

TO MISS LILLA WORTHINGTON [5]

Peace Dale, R.I.

July 11, 1934

Dear Lilla:—

I'd be glad to adapt *Dotty Dimple* or the works of the Marquis de Sade for $1250 a week. So don't hesitate.

By the way, now the clean boys are up in arms, couldn't you get the movies to buy that wonderful clean-cut epic of American life, *John Brown's Body*—just to show the League of Decency that their hearts are in the right place after all?

As ever

Steve

5 A member of the staff of Brandt and Brandt.

TO EUGENE DAVIDSON

Peace Dale, R.I.
July 14, 1934

Dear Davidson:—

I wonder if the Yale Press could send me a check for the $150. I hate to bother you but it would be convenient at the moment.

I've had some very amusing and pleasant letters from people who missed out in the competition—sometime I'll show them to you.

With all good wishes
Stephen Benét

TO HERVEY ALLEN

Peace Dale, R.I.
[July] 1934

Dear Hervey:—

I am having Doubleday send you a copy of Paul Engle's *American Song*. He's a young Iowan now at Oxford —and I think he's going places in American verse. If you like the book and don't mind being quoted, I wish you'd drop them a line—it's not so hot living right now on poetry and a Rhodes Scholarship, even for young Iowans—and I believe in the boy.

With all good wishes from Rosemary and myself,
As ever
Stephen Benét

TO WILLIAM LYON PHELPS [6]

Peace Dale, R.I.
[July] 1934

Dear Billy:—

I am having Doubleday send you a copy of Paul Engle's *American Song* because it seems to me the sort of thing you'd be particularly interested in. He's a young Iowan, now at Merton, on a Rhodes—and he is the first voice in poetry that I know of that represents the new, young generation just out of college—and it seems to me good speech. It's authentic Americana, and it has a queer new idealism that ought to surprise a good many people—though not yourself, after the years at Yale. But I think you'll like it—and if you can do anything for it, that would be simply swell. You know what a row most young poets have to hoe—and this is a real one.

Thank you very much indeed, by the way, for what you said of *James Shore's Daughter*. I appreciated it greatly. And am deeply regretful that I wasn't in the audience that saw one of the best-deserved honorary degrees ever conferred.

With all good wishes
Steve Benét

6. Phelps, like Chauncey Brewster Tinker, was one of the Yale English Department's eloquent lecturers, though he differed from the others in the extraordinary career he had simultaneously as a national maker of literary taste. He was a member of the Yale faculty from 1892 until his retirement in 1933. He died in 1943.

TO PAUL ENGLE

Peace Dale, R.I.
July 25, 1934

Dear Paul:—

You are going to be pretty celebrated. It's a long time since a poet had the front page of the N. Y. *Times* book review all to himself. I hope this will be the first one to reach you. And, believe me, you deserve it all. It is a fine book, beautifully tempered, and Rosemary and I feel deeply honored by the dedication. I wanted to write you about that at once—but I also wanted to be able to give you some news of the book when I wrote—and now I am glad I did. Because there could hardly be a better or more appreciative start for a book of poems than this particular review placed where it is. There will be others—indeed I think there will be all you could wish for in the way of praise. And every bit of it will be true. It is a heartening thing to see fine work received as it should be, and not always is—and it gives me the deepest sort of personal satisfaction to see yours acknowledged. I didn't want to say too much about it in advance—and so, probably sounded rather bleak and discouraging often enough. Anyone who has been through the mill is apt to. But, for once, the work and reception have met—and I am throwing hats in the air—with a little, "Told you so," . . .

. . . You will doubtless be attacked by the Communists as a fascist and by the Silver Shirts as I don't know what—but that is all good clean fun and part of the game. And you can sit in the middle of the Black Forest and laugh at them both.

. . . I've been writing some short stories to boil the pot but hope to get out of it shortly. . . . Our best to France, if you get there and cordial regards to the Black Forest, which I haven't seen but would like to. And our congratulations to you—and our deep gratitude that you should have dedicated so fine a book to us. May you always go on—it is the real work and we are more delighted than we can say!

As ever
Steve

TO MURIEL RUKEYSER

Peace Dale, R.I.
August 6, 1934

Dear Miss Rukeyser:—

I'm sorry to hear that Random House has turned down the book. The mss. hasn't reached me yet—could they have sent it to my N.Y. address? I thought I gave them this one but may not have.

I don't know the Macmillan people, unfortunately, though I know they're a good firm, of course. But you're at perfect liberty to tell them that I'm interested in the book and think well of it. Meanwhile, I am enclosing 3 letters that you can use if you see fit and want to—to John Farrar, of Farrar & Rinehart, Tim Coward, of Coward McCann, and Bernice Baumgarten. Tim Coward happens to be my near neighbor down here and I have mentioned your name to him.

Macmillan is an excellent firm and generally do well with verse. So I hope it clicks with them. If it doesn't, you might try some of these others.

With all good wishes
Stephen Benét

TO LILLA WORTHINGTON

Peace Dale, R.I.
September 3, 1934

Dear Lilla:—

Thanks for your letter—and for all you did in regard to the movie thing. A prospect of a possible fifteen months seemed a little long on that sort of contract—and I gathered from your telegram that you and Carl thought so, too. But heaven knows, I'd be glad to go out on a one-picture contract, any time—and would be glad to discuss any reasonable offer anyway, as they say in the real-estate business. So, if you hear of anything else, keep me in mind.

With thanks again
SVB

TO WILLIAM ROSE BENÉT

Peace Dale, R.I.
September 4, 1934

Dear Bill:—

Thanks for your letter. You are a great sport to be so nice about the criticisms. I don't know a thing about writing a play, as you know, and was just getting down what struck me. But I did find out from dire experience, in that awful awful play, *That Awful Mrs. Eaton,* that you can put in too much local color, especially when you get interested in the time. Also that people will accept a situation, if you tell them it's a situation, but they get confused with historical intricacies. And the clash must be onstage, not off. So [John] Drinkwater, for instance, puts in the entirely imaginary Burnet Hook [in *Abraham Lincoln*] to focus all the enmity against Lincoln. And theatrically for his purposes, he's right. It always seemed to me that one of the finest pieces of historical juggling extant is the English part of *Twenty Years After*. For there the situation starts with an irresistible force meeting an immovable object. King Charles must get his head cut off because you know it happened. But the musketeers must save him because the musketeers are invincible. And Dumas is such a superb stage-manager that by the time the tale is well along, you read breathlessly, perfectly convinced that the King *will* be saved any minute and end up convinced that only the worst sort of luck prevented it. Which is the Indian rope-trick, in fiction, nothing less. And the whole darn thing goes so fast that you haven't time to see any flaws in the narrative, though there are precious few, if any. And Scott could also do it, in *Redgauntlet* and the *Monastery*, for instance. The incidents are invented, but the historical character acts so characteristically that you believe in the incident because of the characterization. (That last "characteristically" was the straw that broke the camel's back.[7] It caused my faithful typewriter to burst into a loud whirring in a vital part, thus scaring me horribly— I am writing at night in the Stepping Stones [a studio], with hoot-owls and crickets about. Within the past three

7. The remainder of the letter is handwritten.

days, the car's battery has gone dead & I have swallowed my front porcelain-inlay at a clambake. Probably before I finish this letter, my fountain-pen will explode in my eye or a hoot-owl swallow the paper. Well, well, some weeks are like that.)

Pardon this digression on How To Write History By One Who Knows. I don't. But the subject interests me. I'm sure Rupert will be a swell play. And I will be cheering, the first night and the hundredth. . . . You [and Lora Benét] both shame me—now it's time to pack up and go [back to New York], I've only done 3 short stories and the beginning of a novelette. But the stars, or something—very probably me—were against good work this summer, somehow.

Also, I'm a little bored with financial difficulties, which seem to be persistent. However, that's that. . . . Hollywood fiddled around with me again but nothing came of it in the end—which generally happens. Sometime when I don't want to go and it's even more inconvenient than the present, it will probably come through. . . .

This is the sleepiest country I ever was in—it is very nice but not sophoric. I think next year we'll have to go to the mountains, if we can. However, I shall miss the clams—clams are delightful. It is almost impossible to eat too many—one can eat too many for comfort but not for the spirit.

Bless you and keep you—I'm very interested to hear what Lora [Baxter, an actress, William Rose Benét's third wife] thinks of Rupert, and to talk about it some more. I haven't sent you back the carbon copy but will do so at once. I don't know about "Honi Soit Qui Mal y pense" —I think I'm agin it—things like that have to be said just right by the actor & so few actors can. Ahoy, ahoy check—and much love from all of us, including your nieces & nephews, who are all lengthening out like brown string beans.

As ever
Steve

TO DOUGLAS S. FREEMAN [8]

220 East 69th Street
New York, N.Y.
September [25] 1934

Dear Dr. Freeman:—

I have just finished writing some 2500 words about your superb *Lee* for the *Herald-Tribune*—and, while that ought to be enough, I cannot resist the opportunity of sending my personal congratulations as well as my official ones. It is the best life of Lee that has ever been written and one of the finest American biographies we have ever had. And my hat is off to your patience, your thoroughness, your splendid sense of proportion, your extraordinary readability—and a dozen other qualities which are going to make and keep this book a classic.

I hope you will like the review—there were a great many things I would have liked to say and just didn't have room for. I could have written one three times as long with no difficulty at all.

With congratulations again
Stephen Vincent Benét

8. Benét was an admirer of all the work by the southern historian whose four-volume *R. E. Lee* was only one of several massive undertakings. Freeman, who was also editor of the Richmond *News Leader* from 1915 until 1949, died in 1953.

TO CARL BRANDT

220 East 69th Street
New York, N.Y.
November 14, 1934

Dear Carl:—

Thanks for your note. I have been meaning to go right ahead with the "Three Fates" [short story] thing but got switched off writing some lyrics for music. But I'll try to get right back at it the end of the week.

Also [thanks] for the *Cosmopolitan* comment. Of course it's Wodehouse—but it's fairly good Wodehouse for less money. If only Emily Kimbrough were still editing—it's just the kind of thing she liked.

I wish you could sell a story this month because I'd like to finish up "The Three Fates" without having to write another short-story in the meanwhile.

By the way—Kenneth Roberts oughtn't to write another book like *Captain Caution.* You know me—I'm an original *Arundel* fan. I picked it up in a drugstore— *Arundel,* I mean—and told everybody I knew about it. But this book. It should have been twice as long and twice as solid. It has no weight in it. It repeats situations and characterizations. It reads like a badly cut movie— you feel there are great blocks left out. Even the hero's nickname is dragged in by the heels toward the close of the story. And both Corunna and Marvin are repeats of earlier characters. And the prison stuff he has used before.

The trouble is that Roberts has now developed an audience that is going to notice things like that. It's none of my business, God knows—and I don't usually run around giving unpleasant free advice to other craftsmen. But I happened to feel this so strongly in reading the book that, for the first time in my life, I am going to pass it on to you.

> With apologies
> SVB

TO EGBERT S. OLIVER [9]

> 220 East 69th Street
> New York, N.Y.
> January 1935

Dear Mr. Oliver:—

In reply to your questions.

Individual members of the [Yale] English Department did encourage me while I was in college. And helped to get a scholarship or so for me afterwards. They didn't aid me in the sense of criticizing or pointing out merits or demerits in my verse. But then I never asked them to do so.

I took a course in Creative Composition with Henry Canby—a prose course. It was a good course because he was a good critic and spent a lot of personal time and attention on the individuals. But the virtue was in the man, not in the system or scheme of the course.

The whole thing is in the man. You cannot devise any course to teach people to write. If you have the right sort of man, however, he can teach something about

9. Professor Oliver was a member of the faculty at Willamette University in Oregon. He was investigating the role of undergraduate courses in creative writing. He is now professor of English at Portland State College.

writing to most people. Even he, to my mind, cannot teach an original creator of the first or second rank, though he might help him to avoid certain mistakes. I can teach anybody with a moderate literary bent how to write a sonnet that scans or a short story that might sell. But I couldn't teach anybody to write "Responsibilities" or "The Killers" because I don't know myself.

As far as I know, one of the few courses in writing that is worth anything is given by the Breadloaf School of English, Breadloaf, Vermont. You might write them and ask them what they do.

I think the colleges—or the ones I know—are probably doing as much about writing as they can. You cannot force writers like early peas. And then: writing is about life. And all life can't be in a college.

Sincerely
Stephen Vincent Benét

TO FLORENCE LOCKE [10]

220 East 69th Street
New York, N.Y.
January 10, 1935

Ladies:—

My task of introduction, this afternoon, is a remarkably easy one. Because, usually, you see, in introducing a program of this sort, you have to pay some attention to the author. He or one of his relatives is apt to be lurking in the audience—and, if he's a normal author, he prob-

10. A well-known monologuist of the period, who had asked Benét for permission to recite from *John Brown's Body*. She also requested this introduction to the evening's reading.

ably has his little pencil out, ready to take notes on what you say about him. And, if you don't say enough—well, authors are like elephants—they never forget. But, fortunately, this afternoon, we're not going to have any trouble of this sort. My disinterest in the author of the work you are going to hear is complete and I can devote my entire attention to Miss Locke.

A great many people write poetry—very few can read it or speak it well. And that is a pity. For poetry is not something to be read with the eye alone, it is something to be heard with the ear as well. When you read words on a page—unless you hear them sing in your mind as well—you have only grasped half the intent of poetry. But where this is generally recognized where the kindred art of music is concerned, it is not so generally recognized with verse. It has always been my thought that we needed great speakers and sayers of verse, exactly as we need great interpretative musicians—to give us not only the words but the music behind the words. Nor should these speakers and readers be necessarily poets themselves—any more than an interpretative musician should be per se a composer.

For some years now, Miss Florence Locke has been doing exactly this—and a very interesting and salient thing it is. She has been presenting, both in this country and in England, programs of poetry—poetry as a living thing to be spoken aloud. To this task she has brought, not only the gifts of trained voice and presence but a spirit of genuine interpretation which is a rare thing. A difficult thing, as well. You have all heard musicians who played every note correctly and yet gave you very little of the real music. That is not the case with Miss Locke.

She brings both technical skill and inner comprehension to the work.

I think that is a fine thing to do—and that is the reason I am here today—not because she has selected a portion of my own work to give you this particular afternoon. It seems to me that to create a living interest in poetry by speaking it finely, is to be very much of a poet. I shall therefore introduce her to you, not as a reciter—that's a very dreary word—nor even as an actress—but as a true and creative interpreter in the field of poetry. It gives me great pleasure to introduce Miss Florence Locke.

Stephen Vincent Benét

TO VALENTINE MITCHELL GAMMELL

220 East 69th Street
New York, N.Y.
April 1, 1935

Dear Valentine:—

For goodness sake, if you want to do a poem on Columbus, don't let any thought of me stand in your way! As a matter of fact, I probably have all the stuff on Columbus written that I shall use [in *Western Star*]. I am using the man himself, a rather detailed account of the first voyage and possibly a soliloquy from jail or the deathbed. That's all, and he will appear only in the first of either 8 or 12 books or parts (depending on how long the poem runs). I don't see why there shouldn't be at least as many works on Columbus as on Oedipus—and I shall expect you to do a very good one.

. . . As ever
SVB

TO CARL BRANDT

220 East 69th Street
New York, N.Y.
March 4, 1935

Dear Carl:—

Here is a new Oldest Inhabitant story ["Silver Jemmy"]. I wonder if the *Post* might not take a look at it for a change. I am devoted to the *Country Gentleman* but I would like to get a wider audience for these stories if I could—and also would like to do a series of them using certain real American historical characters and going into the history more carefully than I have done in the past—a sort of *Puck of Pook's Hill,* done rather differently. I wish to goodness I could get an order for half-a-dozen of them—they are so much more interesting to me than he-and-she contemporary stuff. The Oldest Inhabitant frame in this, for that matter, could be dropped out with no injury to the story. I used it because I wanted to get back in time—and also bring up vaguely, in the reader's mind, a Huey Long comparison for Burr.

Let me know what you think about this, will you?

As ever
SVB

TO PAUL ENGLE

220 East 69th Street
New York, N.Y.
May 1, 1935

Dear Paul:—

I just got back from Iowa yesterday and I must say it looked pretty good. Spring's a little late this year everywhere but Spring was there—and the ebb and flow of the land was striped brown and black and green—the big horses out with the plow—you could hear the harness jingle as they turned. . . .

The occasion was another literary conference—I took the opportunity, by the way, to read "The Last Whiskey Cup" at a round table in the Senate Chamber—it reads dam well, incidentally. I was talking about Spender, Auden and Lewis, yourself, Agee and a girl named Rukeyser who has been doing what seems to me good work. And, everywhere I went people came up to me and asked about you . . .

They have built an Art building, broken ground for a University Theatre—Virgil Geddes is out there as guest playwright—*American Prefaces* is going to start in the Fall. A lot of interest in painting. . . . And [Norman] Foerster is going ahead with his School of Letters. He interests me very much. I'm not a humanist in any shape or form and many of our ideas on life are entirely dissimilar. But, in spite of his frame of humanism, he does seem to me vitally interested in getting the live thing instead of the dead in education. And he's willing to take a chance—a remarkable gift.

As always, traveling those miles, I was impressed once more. My God, the cows, the chickens, the fruit-trees, the ploughland, the abundance, depression or no depression! It is just so completely different from any European scene. And the Mississippi . . . The enormous backlog of energy and possibility, in spite of any number of mistakes and a lot of crooks.

I sent off the books you asked for—glad you liked *Of Time and the River*. . . .

I'm sending you a long poem I did about Walt Whitman for the Sat. Rev. ["Ode to Walt Whitman"]. I want to do some more and make a book for Fall [*Burning City*], if I can. I liked the extract from yours that you sent in the magazine and am looking forward to seeing the whole thing. I'm not very sold on Marxism as a doctrine—they have built it into too cast-iron a theory and life seems to take pleasure in fooling cast-iron theories. Also, the leading professors over here are a little too witch-burning to suit me. However, we'll see what we'll see in the next twenty years—and that will undoubtedly be a bellyfull. You will find some changes, when you come back. I think most of the ordinary people here now look at Europe with puzzled wonder—as they would at somebody deliberately committing suicide. And if there is a strong feeling, it is that we should keep out of the suicide. That feeling, of course, can be changed. But I'd say it was the way they felt now. . . .

Much love to you from all of us—and looking forward to seeing you.

As ever

SVB

TO CARL BRANDT

220 East 69th Street
New York, N.Y.
May 24, 1935

Dear Carl:—

I enclose a revised version of "Silver Jemmy." I have rewritten the first part twice and am afraid I can't do any more with it. I could see no way to get the girl on the island—any time I tried it it just went into Robert W. Chambers. But I have brought Burr into the foreground and tried to keep the girl more in view and to tie up some loose ends. It still seems to me a good story and if [George Horace] Lorimer himself has not seen it, I'd like him to. I have pondered the Cosmo's criticism of its being intellectual—and don't quite agree. If patriotism is intellectual, so is the banking system—and Father Coughlin can fill Madison Square Garden by talking about the banking system, not about cuties. In other words, this happens to be a time when people are interested in things which might have been considered intellectual in '28. And any editor with brains can tie this story into the present with a ten word blurb. Doesn't the Cosmo think that a few men might like to read the magazine once in a while? This is a man's story, as I see it— but I'm damned if I think that's a defect, in principle.

Well, well, pardon my grunting to myself and tell me what you think of this.

As ever

SVB

TO MRS. JAMES WALKER BENÉT

220 East 69th Street
New York, N. Y.
June [20] 1935

Dearest Mother:—

I have just made out a chart for your friend Catherine's baby and will write an analysis as soon as I get time.[11] If the date you give is correct—12 noon April 16,

11. Benét's interest in astrology as a hobby was constantly tapped by his relatives and friends, who sought—and invariably

1935, everything is very favorable—Leo is rising, the
ruling planet the Sun in mid-heaven, and nearly all
planets in good aspect. The health is strong, the native
will rise in the world. I say, if the date is correct, because
you say both April 16th and the day after Palm Sunday,
while April 16th is Tuesday. If it is April 15th, this will
make a slight difference in the chart. I have also erected
it for the latitude of Philadelphia as you don't give the
place—but I suppose it was either in Philadelphia or
near it. This all sounds very pedantic—but a day is supposed to make quite a bit of difference, according to the
rules. Let us hope it is April 16th, in which case the
native, now in a crib, will be very fortunate.

I took my long story down to Carl last Monday and
since then have been reading mss. for the Yale Series of
Younger Poets—trying to write a little verse myself—
and doing several odd jobs. The musical-comedy [*You've
Got to Be Rich*, with Richard Myers and Christopher
LaFarge] came back from Mr. Wilk [Warner Brothers]
and we will try it somewhere else. I think I have sold a
short-story to *Cosmopolitan* but won't be sure till
Wednesday as they want some revision on it. . . .

I have been reading many books but few of much
account. My young poets for the Yale Series are promising but *so* serious and intellectual—it's all "the grim
geometry of loins" and "vaguely the spirals of the mind
recede"—and so forth. All very worthy—but the one with
the clearest emotion is a 17 year old boy, and he isn't
mature enough to be given the award, though I'd like

received from him—detailed horoscopes. Twenty-five years later,
when they re-examined the horoscopes, many of the recipients
were startled by the accuracy of Benét's predictions.

to encourage him. Intellect is fine, God knows—but you do like a little jam on the cracker. . . .

> As ever
>
> your devoted son
>
> SVB

This is Tommy's poem

The Wind

Is it a cobweb blowing across my face?
Or is it the lady queen's lace?
What can it be?
What terrible thing has happened to me?
Whatever can the matter be?
Whoever is lying to me?
My kite is gone. What is wrong?
I must find the one who stole it.
Why, it's you, the wind. I forgive you.

> Thomas Benét, Junior I

TO CHRISTOPHER LAFARGE [1]

> 220 East 69th Street
> New York, N.Y.
> June [20] 1935

Dear Kipper:—

Dick [Myers] and I showed the musical comedy to Delos Chappell last week. He thought it was perfectly charming, extremely witty, delightfully new, the character of Pepsogate splendid etc etc. He laughed, chuckled, etc etc. Nevertheless, in spite of his rapture, he

1. 1897–1956. LaFarge, member of a notable American family of artists, was a poet and short story writer who at various times was a neighbor of Benét both in Rhode Island and Manhattan.

couldn't possibly do it—he didn't know how to do a musical comedy—he wouldn't think of trying—in fact he wouldn't do *Pinafore* with the original cast. Or so, at least, I gathered. He then sailed for Europe. I think we ought to go live on a boat. Ho-hum.

The script is now with Brock Pemberton and Max Gordon. I am also going to see Harold Friedman [of Brandt and Brandt] about it as I now feel a little confused and am beginning to have noises in my head.

Do not take this too seriously—I just thought you would like to know. I am now wondering which is better—the dead-pan or the rapturous smile. Probably neither.

With the best to you and Louisa
SVB

TO EUGENE DAVIDSON

220 East 69th Street
New York, N.Y.
July [6] 1935

Dear Davidson:—

Sorry to hold up the Yale Series so long but I am now trying to get back a book [Muriel Rukeyser, *Theory of Flight*] that was submitted last year. I don't know if that is quite cricket but the trouble is that last year I had three outstanding people and this year I have eight or ten perfectly competent ones. So I am going to try to get the girl whom I thought of as second last year to put her book in again.

Thanks for the check.

As ever
SVB

TO EUGENE DAVIDSON

220 East 69th Street
New York, N.Y.
July 14, 1935

Dear Davidson:—

I am selecting Miss Muriel Rukeyser's *Theory of Flight* for the Yale Series this year. She is the girl I told you about who was my second choice last year—she's 22 and I really think she has lots of stuff. She has appeared a lot in Left Wing magazines, in the *New Republic* etc. and strikes me as being a really talented gal . . . I had yearnings for my 17 year old schoolboy but hope I have put him away in a cellar to ripen—he ought to be lots better at 20 and I'll hope to snap him then. Miss [Margaret] Haley I am attempting to place with somebody else.

After all, as you or Nig [Donaldson] remarked, the point of the Series is to encourage real promise and Rukeyser to my mind is head-and-shoulders above anybody else this year. I hope you will agree with me when you see the mss.—I am sending it on as soon as I've written the preface, which will be in a couple of days, unless you want it before. It consists of a long poem with some pretty exciting spots in it, and two sections of shorter poems. The 70 odd unsuccessful contestants weigh heavily upon my soul as always . . . However, hope springs eternal in the poet's breast, and I'll probably have them all back again, sooner or later. But my heart goes out to the gentleman who is writing about his soul in the University of Notre Dame.

With all good wishes
Stephen Benét

TO WILLIAM ROSE BENÉT

220 East 69th Street
New York, N.Y.
[July 15] 1935

Dear Bill:—

Thanks a lot for "American Laughter." [2] It's really a very curious piece. I have stolen shirts in my time myself—but I *did* try to erase the original laundry-mark. It always seems so funny not to. And yet I've got one mss. in the Yale Press Series which is really a very excellent imitation of Archie [MacLeish]—so faithful that you wonder that anyone with the brains to do it wouldn't have the brains to work out something of his own. Mr. Robinson's effort made me feel very odd—kind of as if somebody had presented me with an illegitimate baby I had begotten in my sleep.

With much love—we have been having some slight financial difficulties but are now (D.V.) creeping out of them.

As ever
Steve

TO CARL BRANDT

220 East 69th Street
New York, N.Y.
July 18, 1935

Dear Carl:—

I'm delighted about the Napoleon story ["The Curfew Tolls"]. I thought you would probably have to part with

2. Kenneth Allan Robinson, "American Laughter," *Scribner's*, *98* (July 1935), [41].

that for $50 to the *American Historical Journal*—and you certainly did a very swell and surprising piece of work with it.

If they [*Saturday Evening Post*] illustrate it at all, the artist will have to be awfully cagy. There are some pictures of N.[apoleon] at Longwood in a straw hat, however, which differ a good deal from the conventional portraits—and it might be worth his while to look those up. Erd [Brandt] probably knows of them. Maybe no illustration at all would be better. I want a nice tombstone, though, if they'll do it.

> With much pleasure
> SVB

TO MRS. JAMES WALKER BENÉT

> 220 East 69th Street
> New York, N.Y.
> July 30, 1935

Dearest Mother:—

We will be leaving for Peacedale on Friday, my business here being finally settled. Paramount bought the picture-rights of a short story of mine called "Mystery Train" for $2500 and this will pay up our bills and give us some money ahead—quite a relief! Also the "Miracle" thing [a movie treatment] will probably come through which will also be a help. And I have some more short stories going the rounds.

. . . I've been writing quite a bit of verse and while I won't have a book in shape for the Fall, I hope to have one [*Burning City*] shortly afterward. And that pleases me. The musical-comedy is still kicking around—but

August is the month when people go away, so we don't expect to hear much about it till after Labor Day.

I'm glad this thing with Paramount came through when it did for August is always a slack month.

> . . . As ever
>
> Your devoted son
>
> SVB

TO SHREVE C. BADGER

> Peace Dale, R.I.
>
> August 27, 1935

Dear Shreve:—

I am very sorry to hear about your father and you have all our sympathy. I know how much I miss mine. He meant a great deal to me and died while I was in France, so I could not even get back for the funeral—not that funerals matter much. I always remember his saying "When we are young, we are apt to consider our parents immortal. Unfortunately, they are not." Well, as you grow older, you realize that, too—and yet it does not help the break.

We heard of you from Tim Coward, who was spending a couple of nights with us and were sorry not to have been in New York and caught a glimpse of you. As a matter of fact, due to the strained condition of the Benét finances, we didn't get away from the city till about the first of August. However, since then, finances have improved and everything is now much cheerier. It was the simplest thing in the world. Five years ago, the time you were so surprised to find me in lonely splendor in a drawing room in the Wolverine, we acquired a nurse for the children—and a very good nurse she was. In fact, so good a nurse that the only reason she had left her previous jobs—two or three—was because her employers had lost their money and were no longer able to afford her. Well, I do not suggest that she was a Typhoid Mary—all I know is that she stayed with us five years and we constantly grew poorer and poorer. Till finally, and regretfully, we let her go on the first of June. Since her departure, I have sold four short stories to magazines, one to the movies, changed my publisher [to the new firm of Farrar and Rinehart, now that Dan Longwell had left Doubleday for *Life*], paid all the back bills and bought a new seersucker suit. I now want to hire her to one of the Rockefellers and see what happens to them.

I meant to send you a series of angry telegrams last June, when you did not come to Reunion. God knows why you should have come—but I carefully engaged a room in a dormitory for you and myself . . . I also engaged in a Virginia Reel led by ——— ———, who fell out of the window of headquarters two days later thus effectively putting a damper on the proceedings. I did not have the interesting conversations with previously unknown members of the Class who have since become prominent inventors or sculptors which one is supposed to have . . . And when I got home, I went to bed at 9. I guess my arteries are weakening.

. . . I'm feeling better than I have in a long time, and more like writing verse. I want to get [a] book out next Spring (it's announced for Fall but won't be ready) and another one two years from then. If I can do that, I won't be satisfied, but I'll be pleased. Rosemary isn't working on anything at the moment except the children

—and God knows that's work enough—but sometime we hope to get out another book of Americans together. I do not think that any of the children are going to be poets, but I'm afraid my nephew [James Walker Benét, II] is going to be a playwright, hard as his father and I have tried to dissuade him from a literary life. Personally, I think it's time some of the Benéts went back to making guns.

I don't know why we live in New York—inertia and friends seem to be the principal reasons. I suppose we'll move out, eventually—but the trouble is I would like a small section of France with the 1927 prices somewhere in America with excellent American schools of both sexes with the Congressional Library within easy reach. As this seems a little hard to find, we will probably be in 69th Street till Mr. Rockefeller decides to build another Radio City on our block. Meanwhile we have a pretty good time, in spite of noise, soot and Republicans.

. . . As ever, affectionately,

Steve

TO COLLIER YOUNG [3]

Peace Dale, R.I.
August 26, 1935

Dear Collier:—

This is the Xmas story ["Christmas City"] to Mr. [Valdemar] Vetluguin's specifications for *Redbook*. If he likes it, stick him for it.

As ever
Stephen Benét

3. A member of the staff of Brandt and Brandt.

TO CARL BRANDT

Peace Dale, R.I.
August 29, 1935

Dear Carl:—

With a few deft touches, I have changed the opening of this ["Mystery Train"] to October and the end to March. Is this OK? At present, it opens in summer and ends in October. I would be glad to change it in any other way that is necessary. But this will give them a chance to illustrate the first part with an Autumn scene if they want—and you said time was important.

. . . With all the best
SVB

If they don't like the end being March, they can change it to December and put in a couple of allusions to snow. It's all right with me.

TO LILLA WORTHINGTON

Peace Dale, R.I.
August 29, 1935

Dear Lilla:—

I have your letter about the change in the Paramount contracts and entirely agree with you. The altered proposition is ridiculous. If they are considering making this in the way [Arthur] Hornblow talked—or indeed if they're going to make it at all—they'll have to pay money to whoever does the job. I see no point in giving ideas without money in advance—and I certainly wouldn't do a 20–30 page story outline for less than an assured $2500. A short story only runs 15 pages and you have the magazine rights of a short-story as well.

In case they should want me to adapt either one of the Wells books or Buck Rogers, that is a scenario proposition and somewhat different. But I certainly won't produce an original for $1000. Nor would anybody else!

As ever

SVB

TO CARL BRANDT

Peace Dale, R.I.
September 2, 1935

Dear Carl:—

I think that is a little whimsical on Mr. [Edwin] Balmer's part [editor of *Redbook*]. The wild party idea is certainly old—the point of the yarn, if any, is that the hero and the gal have no longer anything in common or anything to talk about. They have to be alone together to find this out—if she takes him along to a party, they aren't going to be alone, and he's apt to think it would have been all right if they could only have had a good long talk together. Unless you want to have a blight of the city idea and the girl having gone to the dogs, which seems to me entirely conventional and uninteresting. I enclose Vetluguin's letter in which nothing of the sort was suggested.

Vetluguin is a good egg, I'd like to please him, and if you consider it absolutely necessary, I'll make the revision. But I would like to point out to him or to Mr. Balmer, that I have to have a little fun writing a story of this sort or it isn't going to be any good. I'm perfectly willing to work to any sort of specifications, but I think I ought to be allowed to put in my own doors and windows. If you revise and revise, and put in this and take out that, it gets to be like the movies and the thing goes dead and flat. There's no use their pretending that I'm a Royal Brown or Rex Beach—when I try to do that kind of stuff, I'm lousy. Therefore, if there's any chance of selling the thing elsewhere, I'd consider it seriously. If there isn't, I'll do the revision, as I hate to waste the time. But I'll probably do a bad job on it, and serve them right.

> . . . With all good wishes as ever
> Steve Benét

TO CARL BRANDT

Peace Dale, R.I.
September 9, 1935

Dear Carl:—

I return herewith "Princess Pauper," with the new ending suggested by Cosmo. I have also toned down the other scene objected to so now it merely, I hope, suggests that She Is Falling Under The Blight of Her Old Life But Will Make a Brave Fight Against It.

I have tried to do as good a job as possible—yet somehow, I fear the first fine careless rapture has gone. In fact, on rereading this little gem, it seemed to me one of the biggest pieces of tripe I ever saw. It really astonishes me that I should have been able to heave such a shovel-load. However, this is merely for your private ear—and I hope you will be able to dish it up to Cosmo à la mode de Caen. If you can't, God knows the last person to blame you will be SVB. Really, one or two of my little touches are pretty itsy-bitsy.

I will now devote myself to inserting Mr. Balmer's wild party into "Xmas City." Maybe I'll have people break red balloons with cigarettes.

With much love to yourself and the Brandt office— we'll be back in NY around the 15th—

As ever
Steve Benét

TO PAUL ENGLE

220 East 69th Street
New York, N.Y.
October 4, 1935

Dear Paul:—

. . . I'm glad you like the Whitman piece ["Ode to Walt Whitman"] and hope you will like the other one ["Litany for Dictatorships"] I sent you. I'm anxious to see the poem when you finish it. To reply to what you said two letters back—if any of the reviewers think it's like me, I'll feel flattered—but I'll think them a little stupid as well. You have your own way of saying things and it is getting to be more and more your own. I once made a list of all the people reviewers said had influenced me—I think there were something like seventeen of them. Yet none of them caught the derivation from William Morris whom I read and reread in my youth. It doesn't matter very much. If you feel certain things about the country you are bound to say them—all we can do is say them as best we can. This spring a reviewer in the Herald-Trib called a gentleman named [Thomas Hornsby] Ferril to account for writing like me. After which I got a perfectly charming letter from Ferril who said he knew I was a good poet but he was a research-chemist and had to spend all his spare time in *writing* poetry, so did I mind very much his admitting he'd read practically nothing of mine, and probably wouldn't have time to until he was old and gray.

. . . As for politics, there is a great deal of hullabaloo but really things are marking time. It's bound to be so until the Supreme Court decisions on the AAA, TVA etc. If they throw them all out, then the issue will be perfectly clear. But probably they won't—[they'll] accept some and reject others. Meanwhile, the Republicans are working hard. They have an idea they may be able to beat Roosevelt now—and that is about the only idea they have. I listened to two of them—both locally prominent—talking in Rhode Island. They agreed that something must be done for the farmers. Not, of course, the AAA, but something must be done. Maybe buying up the surplus and holding it (till it rotted) instead of paying people for not planting. But something must be done for the farmers. They couldn't quite think what. Only it didn't matter very much as long as Republicans were doing it. Meanwhile they breed bitterness and lies. It is horrible to see—the nervous violence of the comfortable once they get the idea that one cent of their precious money is being touched. It makes you feel degraded. The patriots and lovers of America who put their money in Newfoundland holding companies—the descendants of Signers who talk about the people on relief as if they were an inferior breed of dog. What a sorry class of rich we have here—their only redeeming feature is their stupidity.

1933–1940

. . . We have some more money and I hope to get my book [*Burning City*] through in time for February or so. Then I will start going West with the pioneers. That is always at the back of my mind, and now, I think, I'll have some time.

With many friendly waves from the Benét family,

As ever
Steve

TO CHRISTOPHER LAFARGE

220 East 69th Street
New York, N.Y.
October 9, 1935

Dear Kipper:—

I am writing because it is easier for me to think on paper than just with the old head.

I think the trouble with this is the end, which seems to me grandiose and conventional. You have been giving me an interesting and sharp series of pictures—first your detailed, small landscape—then flashes of other places. Then at the end, you clear your throat, step aside and deliver a generalized dictum in indefinite terms—"golden promise"—"all mystery," etc. And I feel rather as if you had been talking to me very interestingly and definitely about a specific people and then wound up with, "But honesty is the best policy and it's a small world after all"—or words to that effect.

Of course I know you want to make the point. But I don't think you've made it poetically—or in key with your first part. "It's not in the grand style, then; you love inch by inch"—fine, apt, well-said, grainy like wood. But

"What need of more when feet on the earth can touch
The source of grandeur ... "

well, say that over to yourself and see if you can help
intoning. There are two people speaking here and the
first one is the good one. The second has someone else's
shirt on.

My only objection is to page 2. Page 1, I like very much.
Thanks for letting me see it.

As ever
SVB

TO CARL BRANDT

220 East 69th Street
New York, N.Y.
December 12, 1935

Dear Carl:—

Sure—put "There Is a Tide" [short story] aside. It has
an unhappy ending and is pretty jammed up anyway.
Maybe some new thought or new editor will pop up
next year.

All the best
SVB

TO CARL BRANDT

220 East 69th Street
New York, N.Y.
March 10, 1936

Dear Carl:—

I hope this ["The Minister's Books"] will give you a
slight shiver—though I'm sure I'm giving you a problem

from the point of view of sales. I can plead no excuse for writing it—except that I've always wanted to write a ghost-story, and the idea came to my mind.

As ever
SVB

TO CARL BRANDT

220 East 69th Street
New York, N.Y.
March 23, 1936

Dear Carl:—

I will try and write Oscar [Graeve, editor of *Delineator*] a couplet. Sure he can take our picture. I will get my suit pressed.

As ever
SVB

TO KATHERINE S. WHITE [4]

220 East 69th Street
New York, N.Y.
April 1936

Dear Mrs. White:—

Thanks for the clippings. I had seen them, as it happened, but I'm glad to have extra ones and will send these on to my mother. Carl Sandburg wrote me a very nice note about the piece ["Notes to Be Left in a Cornerstone"].

I don't mind Old Man H. ["Old Man Hoppergrass"]'s being in the back of the book. Maybe he'd like it better.

4. An editor of the *New Yorker;* wife of the essayist E. B. White.

Anyhow, the *New Yorker* has been so very considerate and receptive about my works that you could print some of them upside down if you wanted.

> With good wishes
> Stephen Benét

TO ANDREW D. TALBOT JONES

> 220 East 69th Street
> New York, N.Y.
> April 22, 1936

Dear Andrew:—

Some books will go to you shortly—rather a mixed lot, I fear, but I have been doing most of my reading through Womrath. However, I've been asked to review a couple of novels which sound fairly interesting and when I've done so, I'll pass 'em on. The Spender is interesting—William Empson is a young English poet supposed to be pretty hot stuff in Bloomsbury, though not by me. I haven't got the Rebecca West—but it's worth reading though on the superficial side. . . .

I've finished up my own book of poems [*Burning City*] and sent it to the publisher—it was a choice between getting it out and sitting around biting my thumbs hoping I'd write two or three more poems for it when as and if they flew in through the window—and as some of the completed work is rather timely, I finally decided to shoot it along as it stood. Also, and thank God, we sold the movie-rights of a perfectly fearful little story of mine called "Princess Pauper"—to a British movie-company, so now we'll be able to pay off all our bills and buy some spinach. . . .

1933–1940

. . . We have been living in a quiet way, broken by occasional sallies forth into the larger world, in one of which I got into a heated argument over the legal aspects of the New Deal with a gent, whom I later discovered was the counsel for the Stock Exchange. However, I succeeded in irritating him, which was something, even if my legal points left much to be desired. . . .

Saturday, we take the children up to West Point to christen them all in a row—I hope Rachel will not ask embarrassing questions in the middle of the service. I do not know what the embarrassing questions would be, but you can trust Rachel. Ever since we took her to the movies and when the Metro-Goldwyn-Mayer lion roared from the screen, she remarked "Stop it!" in a loud firm voice, I think she has realized her powers.

. . . Affectionately, and with love to you all

As ever

Steve

TO CARL BRANDT

220 East 69th Street

New York, N.Y.

June [26] 1936

Dear Carl:—

Thank you for sending me a copy of the letter from Eric Pinker [Benét's English agent] on the "Princess Pauper" matter. I am grateful to him and you for his frank explanation of the circumstances involved. Nevertheless, the hard fact remains that the deal was closed on April 15th and that its terms have not been carried out. Under the circumstances, I cannot but feel that

Pinker and Morrison are both legally and ethically responsible for the payment of the sum under discussion—and I would appreciate your making my position plain to them. As you know, I have dealt with agents for a good many years, and, frankly, I do not see how the agency-business is to be carried on if a buy is not a buy but merely a form of words that may mean something or nothing according to the whim of one of the principals involved. As it stands, the affair means a serious financial loss to me. It also means the disruption of my working-plans for the year and the very decided impairment of a valuable property for any other possible future sale. I appreciate, as I say, both Mr. Pinker's candor and his words of sympathy—but I still fail to see why I should be the goat for the transaction—and as a mere matter of protection for other working-authors, I cannot see that the matter should be allowed to rest in its present state.[5]

As ever

Stephen Vincent Benét

TO MARGARET MITCHELL

220 East 69th Street
New York, N.Y.
July 1936

Dear Miss (Mrs?) Mitchell:—

It's a pleasure to hear from you and I'm glad you liked the review. As you may have gathered from it, I liked *Gone With the Wind*. I wish I had more space to say some more things about it—particularly on the very skilful and admirable way you handled the code and con-

5. The outcome of this disagreement is unknown.

ventions of the time (it's such a temptation to sort of
point a finger and say "Look—aren't they funny, wearing hoopskirts—and, would you believe it, they won't go
out without an escort!"—and you never did that for a
minute) making them entirely real *to* the characters
which is the hard part—and also on the entire episode
of Scarlett's second marriage and the killing of Kennedy
and the behavior of all concerned about it, which
seemed to me beautifully done. However, I couldn't take
up the entire [*Saturday*] *Review* [*of Literature*]—wish
I could have.

I'm sorry if the Thackeray comparison was unjustified.
Particularly sorry because I am leery about that sort of
thing and hate it when it's done to me. I have a hard
time enough to keep away from imitating people I know
about without having people tell me I'm imitating somebody I never heard of. So I'll be warned and not do it
again. But I think you'd like Thackeray.

I'm glad you like *John Brown.* We were eight years in
Augusta when I was growing up and I can still shut my
eyes and remember the particular look of that country. I
hated it at first—I came from California and had been
very happy there—and then grew very fond of it indeed.
I spent one complete summer there, when I was tutoring
for college. And I still remember reading Conrad's "Ty-
phoon" at night in the middle of a typical Georgia thunderstorm. My!

Incidentally, I had much the same difficulty with James
Boyd's *Marching On* that you had with *John Brown.* I
was in Paris and around the middle of my own thing
when the American reviews of *Marching On* began to
come over. I'd liked *Drums* enormously and felt per-

fectly confident that Mr. Boyd could write a superb
novel of the Civil War. Well, he seemed to have, all
right. First I thought I'd read the reviews and then I
thought I wouldn't read them and then I'd look at one
out of one eye just to see what ground he'd covered.
Then people began arriving with copies of *Marching On*
they wished to present me—"we know you're interested
in the Civil War." And I would thank them and try to
deduce from that if my characters were going to conflict with Mr. Boyd's. I was bound not to read the
book, because I was deadly afraid if I did I'd steal or
be accused of stealing. Then I'd run completely out of
all literate reading-matter—and there, on the shelf, was
Marching On by James Boyd—and if I did steal from it,
nobody but God and I would ever know. And finally, in
fear and trembling, after my own book had gone to the
publishers, I read it—and discovered there were only
two very small points of likeness and I knew where those
came from. But I'll never forget the relief of finding out
that was so.

To return to *Gone with the Wind*—it's a fine book
and I hope you write many more of them. That probably
sounds rather portentous to you at the moment, but the
wish is sincere. I hope so not only because of your
veracity and your ability to get under the skin of a past
time and make it live—and I can run up a string of flags
for the research you must have done and the way you
were able to select—but also because the story moves,
and has fire in it, and the reader sits up, wanting to
know what happens next. There are lots of books like
that when you're young—*The Three Musketeers* and
The Cloister and the Hearth and all the good ones. There

aren't so many, now. I admire and respect the serious, high-minded, case histories—the technical jobs in the novel that are like a series of finely-stained slides under the microscope. But fiction is still fiction—and when a book keeps going on in your mind, even when you're not reading it, you don't need anybody to tell you it's good. It was that way with *Gone With the Wind.* Thank you again.

Very sincerely
Stephen Vincent Benét

TO CARL BRANDT

220 East 69th Street
New York, N.Y.
August 23, 1936

Dear Carl:—

I'm afraid this is a folkstory rather than a big strong marriage one. However, I will try to think some big strong thoughts during the next few days.

As ever
SVB

TO E. N. BRANDT

220 East 69th Street
New York, N.Y.
October [30] 1936

Dear Erd:—

Thanks for Mr. Pentler's missive. I'll write him.

As ever
SVB

I just got a beautiful letter from a New Hampshire gentleman who said he was sorry to disillusion me but that the Devil *has* been seen in N.H. recently and he thought it only fair to warn me.

TO SELDEN RODMAN [6]

220 East 69th Street
New York, N.Y.
[November 1936]

Dear Selden:—

My criticism on this would be the difficulty I feel in conveying ordinary, contemporary names, places etc. in normal blank verse. It seems to me that the beat of blank verse is against them and that you have to (a) go into rather false rhetoric or (b) write rather prosy verse of the "A Mr. Wilkinson, a clergyman" variety. This is, of course, merely my own feeling and it may not appear that way to others. But I notice in "Cherry Valley" that you have to split John Van Geld's name because of your beat—which is one of the things that happens. And another thing that happens—or happens to me when I try it—is putting in several-syllabled Latinized words (too many of them) because you have to fill out a line. "Peck the last vestiges of even lawn." Well, the hens weren't really pecking vestiges, they were pecking grass. And the danger with the medium is that eventually, if you don't watch yourself, you see a horse and don't talk about him as a horse but as "Four-footed pacer of the

6. Selden Rodman had graduated from Yale in 1931, where he was one of the founders of the celebrated *Harkness Hoot.* Since then he has been editor of *Common Sense* as well as a poet and anthologist.

vernal turf" because that sort of thing fits your beat better. To be perfectly frank, I don't think your medium
here quite fits your thought. I'd try a rougher and more
sinewy one. Or, if you are going to use blank verse—
take a look at Frost's for coming a little nearer our own
way of speaking—and also at Shakespeare's, in the trage-
dies. We were all of us brought up, unavoidably, in the
tradition of Tennyson's and Browning's blank verse—
which is a different affair. But Elizabethan blank verse,
for all its gorgeousness, has a masculinity about it that
Tennyson lost. I'd rough things up a bit.

Thanks for letting me see it.

As ever
SVB

TO VALENTINE MITCHELL GAMMELL

220 East 69th Street
New York, N.Y.
November [10] 1936

Dear Valentine:—

Thanks for the cookies, which will be greatly appreciated by all the Benét's! But I'm afraid I can't claim
much on prophecy—as I remember it, I conceded Lousi-
ana, and even the [*Literary*] *Digest* was righter than
that. Well, elections are queer affairs—I must say that
one thing that impressed me again about this one was
the quietude and order of the voting public in this rather
disorderly city. They don't seem to have the recipe for
that in Europe—wonder if they ever will!

I just saw another extraordinary thing—people coming to see the N. Y. *Times* Book Fair at the rate of a
thousand an hour. And paying a quarter apiece, too, just

to look at and hear about books! The place was as crowded as an automobile show—I wouldn't have believed it.

> . . . As ever
> SVB

TO CARL BRANDT

> 220 East 69th Street
> New York, N.Y.
> [December 1936]

Dear Carl:—

This is a nice little incident centering on Lincoln, but, somehow or other, I don't see it as [a] story. As it's written, it falls between two stools—it hasn't the homely veracity of somebody telling a true story and yet it isn't exactly a piece of fiction. If I did it, I'd have to rewrite the whole thing, which would be quite a job. It seems to me it would be more effective told in Mrs. Sprague's own words than as it is.

I may be entirely wrong about this—probably am. But it doesn't feel right to me somehow—for my doing it—I can't see my way around. Especially the finale. And why was that Lincoln's darkest hour? It was darker just before Antietam than just after. Somehow, to me, the fuse doesn't quite go off.

Well, I'm probably entirely wrong about this and somebody can make a "Perfect Tribute" of it. But it seemed rather tough to me—and I just got a new idea for a story.

> As ever
> SVB

1933–1940

TO J. RAYMOND DERBY [7]

220 East 69th Street
New York, N.Y.
[March] 1937

Dear Mr. Derby:—

Thank you for your interesting and flattering invitation to lecture at Iowa State College next Fall.

It sounds very interesting and, as you know, I like the State. But, this Spring I am coming out to the University of Iowa to carry out a somewhat similar program for them. I'm afraid if I tried to come back in the Fall for you that it would rather look as if I were trying to monopolize things. Wouldn't it?

I may be wrong in the matter—but it seems to me that the initial interest in such a course or program is usually aroused by the fact that the speaker does come from outside. But if the speaker had just been around in the State only six months before, doing a somewhat similar thing—well, wouldn't the natural reaction be, "Why do they always have to get him? Can't they think of somebody else?"

I'm writing this frankly because it seems to me that getting visiting authors to do this sort of thing is a very interesting and valuable thing to do. And I don't want to do anything to spoil it.

Very sincerely
Stephen Vincent Benét

7. Professor Derby was chairman of the Department of English at Iowa State College during the 1930's.

TO CARL LOHMANN [8]

220 East 69th Street
New York, N.Y.
May 12, 1937

Dear Carl:—

My goodness! I feel quite overwhelmed. Of course I accept [Yale's offer of an honorary doctorate] with pleasure. I thought I might be going West but I'll put it off.

I shall keep it entirely confidential, except for Rosemary—but will you let me know later what the etiquette is, as probably some of the rest of my family might like to attend.

I am really very pleased about this.

Sincerely
Steve

P.S. Incidentally, it seems only honest to say that I am still on the protest committee in the [Jerome] Davis business.[9] I don't imagine that makes any difference to the University, but it seems only fair to say so, in case they should want to reconsider the invitation.

8. 1887–1957. Secretary of Yale University, 1927–53.
9. Davis, a precocious and stimulating teacher and writer, was Gilbert L. Stark Professor of Practical Philanthropy in the Yale Divinity School from 1924 until 1937. His dismissal, which seemed to many to be connected with his militant presidency of the American Federation of Teachers as well as his outspoken interest in Russia, was followed by prolonged charges that Yale had violated academic freedom and tenure.

TO CARL BRANDT

220 East 69th Street
New York, N.Y.
June 6, 1937

Dear Carl:—

I enclose a revise on the Revere story ["A Tooth for Paul Revere"], in case Don Moore is still interested. On looking it over, I didn't want to give up the silver box— in the first place, it's the thing I like best in the story, and, in the second, it's a pretty definite symbol. However, I have gone through the whole thing, soft-pedalled the actual magic, tried to prepare for it, and tried to build up by incidental touches so as to make what there is of it convincing. I have also tried to make Lige a little less dumb—that was likewise Don Moore's suggestion. Will you let me know what you think?

As ever
SVB

TO HELEN McAFEE [10]

Killingworth, Conn.
[July] 1937

Dear Miss McAfee:—

Thank you for your invitation to review *Conversation at Midnight*. But I honestly don't think I'd better. I'm a little leery of reviewing contemporaries in my own field —Millay is a personal friend—altogether it just doesn't

10. 1884–1956. A member of the editorial staff of the *Yale Review* from 1913 until 1950, and managing editor during the last twenty-six of those years.

seem advisable. But I appreciate your asking me—try me again sometime with something else.

Sincerely
Stephen Benét

TO COLLIER YOUNG

Killingworth, Conn.
July 12, 1937

Dear Collier:—

As a matter of record, I have completed and sent in the radio version of *Much Ado About Nothing* that CBS asked me to do. It will undoubtedly have to be cut. The price on this is $500—will you get the check. The gentleman in charge at the moment rejoices in the Shakespearean name of Hole—Leonard Hole. Enter Hole and Peaseblossom, pursued by bears.

As ever
Stephen Benét

TO CARL BRANDT

Killingworth, Conn.
July 19, 1937

Dear Carl:—

As you know, I'm usually amenable to editorial suggestions—witness "The Blood of the Martyrs," "Princess Pauper," and a lot of others. But Mr. [Wesley] Stout's [editor of *Saturday Evening Post*] letter frankly has me stumped. It must have been a hot day in Philadelphia.

I have read it over three times and I still don't get the point. If I had written a violently political story, pointing out that the country would be teetotally ruined unless

                                        Killingworth,Conn.

Dear Carl:--

        As you know,I'm usually amenable to editorial suggestions--witness
"The Blood of the Martyrs","Princess Pauper",and a lot of others.But Mr.Stout's
letter frankly has me stumped.It must have been a hot day in Philadelphia.

        I have read it over three times and I still don't get the point.If I had
written a violently political story,pointing out that the country would be
teetotally ruined unless the Supreme Court Bill went through,I would understand it
better--though,even then,I'd expect the Post to accept it,if it were an
absolutely top-notch story.But my story is about the grasshopper and the ant--
and about a man and his son.The ant is,of course,a conservative and has the
habits and beliefs of a conservative--I don't see how I could have drawn him any
other way.And I can't see that he's an unlikeable character--far from it.He is
trying very hard to understand why he doesn't enjoy his success more now he's
got it--and why Schooner Fairchild has more fun out of life.That seems to me
human enough.While,as for the grasshopper,he hasn't any political convictions at
all.

        I have implied,to be sure,that most speeches are full of bunk.But that
is hardly spot news.And I've used contemporary catchwords in Parrington's
speech because this is a contemporary story--and they're the catchwords that
flowered in Commencement addresses this year.You can find them in any newspaper
file for May and June.The only other point I can see is the slightly pompous
series of questions asked by the liberal undergraduate.But that is the way they
talk,I've heard 'em.And if Stout doesn't believe it,he can go up to Yale or Harvard
or Princeton and see,When Dorothy Thompsin spoke at one of the Yale colleges
they fired questions at her for two hours.And,in my particular story,Parrington
is willing enough to argue with the undergraduate.But he hasn't Fairchild's gift
of getting people talking.The point is made clearly--or I thought so.
        As for the sentence in Stout's letter about Harry Hopkins,that simply
bewilders me.I don't know Harry Hopkins,he isn't mentioned in the story and there
is no character in the story romotely resembling him.So what? Nor,though I have
reread the story carefully,can I notice any particular moralizing in it--except on
the morals of getting on well with your son and getting some fun out of life.
Which seem to me allowable subjects for fiction.
        I suppose it boils down to this.I can't make any revisions--I wouldn't
know where to begin if I wanted to.I think Syout has read things into the story
that simply aren't there.The whole thing is pretty surprising to me--and pretty
disappointing.Becausenif the Post is going to want the opinions of its editorial
page stuck willy-nilly into its fiction--if you havexxxxx to class-angle a
story for the Post as you'd have to for the New Masses,only in reverse--there's
no point in my trying to write for them.I can't work that way.Any magazine can
make its own rules--but that seems to me a stupid policy for a general magazine.
Where does Stout think he gets his three million circulation? From the Union League
Club?
        I will be in New York Tuesday òr Wednesday with a new story and will
drop in at the office.

                As ever

                Steve

the Supreme Court Bill went through, I would understand it better—though, even then, I'd expect the *Post*
to accept it, if it were an absolutely top-notch story.
But my story is about the grasshopper and the ant—and
about a man and his son. The ant is, of course, a conservative and has the habits and beliefs of a conservative—I don't see how I could have drawn him any other
way. And I can't see that he's an unlikeable character—
far from it. He is trying very hard to understand why
he doesn't enjoy his success more now he's got it—and
why Schooner Fairchild has more fun out of life. That
seems to me human enough. While, as for the grasshopper, he hasn't any political convictions at all.

I have implied, to be sure, that most speeches are full
of bunk. But that is hardly spot news. And I've used
contemporary catchwords in Parrington's speech because this is a contemporary story—and they're the
catchwords that flowered in Commencement addresses
this year. You can find them in any newspaper file for
May and June. The only other point I can see is the
slightly pompous series of questions asked by liberal
undergraduate[s]. But that is the way they talk. I've
heard 'em. And if Stout doesn't believe it, he can go up
to Yale or Harvard or Princeton and see. When Dorothy
Thompson spoke at one of the Yale [residential] colleges
they fired questions at her for two hours. And, in my
particular story, Parrington is willing enough to argue
with the undergraduate. But he hasn't Fairchild's gift of
getting people talking. The point is made clearly—or I
thought so.

As for the sentence in Stout's letter about Harry Hopkins, that simply bewilders me.[1] I don't know Harry Hopkins, he isn't mentioned in the story and there is no character in the story remotely resembling him. So what? Nor, though I have reread the story carefully, can I notice any particular moralizing—except on the morals of getting on well with your son and getting some fun out of life. Which seem to me allowable subjects for fiction.

I suppose it boils down to this. I can't make any revisions—I wouldn't know where to begin if I wanted to. I think Stout has read things into the story that simply aren't there. The whole thing is pretty surprising to me— and pretty disappointing. Because if the *Post* is going to want the opinions of its editorial page stuck willly-nilly into its fiction—if you have to class-angle a story for the *Post* as you'd have to for the *New Masses,* only in reverse—there's no point in my trying to write for them. I can't work that way. Any magazine can make its own rules—but that seems to me a stupid policy for a general magazine. Where does Stout think he gets his three million circulation? From the Union League Club?

I will be in New York Tuesday or Wednesday with a new story and will drop in at the office.

As ever

Steve

1. "It is a tract," Stout had said of Benét's story, "worthy of the immaculately conceived Harry Hopkins. I care not how ridiculous he may make his Parrington, as long as he does not offer him as a symbol of the blasphemy of opposing those selfless, consecrated knights of the Holy Grail." The story—"Schooner's Class"—was bought by *Collier's.*

TO COLLIER YOUNG

Killingworth, Conn.
July 29, 1937

Dear Collier:—

How charming of the *Post!* [2] I am simply delighted. Please express the most cordial shake-hands and salutes.

I will write Lewis Titterton about *The Headless Horseman* [an operetta by Benét and Douglas Moore]. Also I will ask John Farrar to do his stuff about it, when the date of the broadcast is set. It would be nice if the broadcast could coincide with the publication of the score—or at least occur when the score had been published. We've read proof on the score but I don't know what Schirmer's date on it is—probably early fall, I should think.

Spurred on by the greed of gold, I will now try and write another story before I get too sunburnt.

As ever
SVB

TO WILLIAM TAYLOR, JR.

Killingworth, Conn.
August [7] 1937

Dear Mr. Taylor:—

Thank you for your very pleasant letter, which I greatly appreciated. Of course I was delighted to have them want to use *John Brown's Body* as a talking book, and glad to do anything I could to help.

2. The *Saturday Evening Post* had raised Benét's story price to $1500.

I was very much impressed, when I was down at the offices, with the intelligence, care and thought that went to the making of the talking books—also with the selection of readers, which seemed to me admirable. After my own little job was done, I stayed there for a couple of hours, listening to others read, and it was a fascinating experience. I had no idea that the thing could be done so effectively.

Thank you again—and let me assure you that it was a very genuine pleasure to me to have *John Brown's Body* reproduced in that way—and a very real honor for the book.

Sincerely
Stephen Vincent Benét

TO MARGARET WIDDEMER

Killingworth, Conn.
[August] 1937

Dear Margaret:—

How very interesting! I'm very much taken with "Ancient Lights" and, God knows, I wouldn't have thought "The Place of the Gods" had any influence on it, even if you hadn't told me. I don't see how that particular idea can help being at the back of a lot of our minds these days—it has suddenly come upon us that the works may blow up. I suppose Wells was the first to say it in our time—though it must go back to Macaulay's New Zealander brooding on the ruins of London Bridge.

Oddly enough, "The Place of the Gods" began as a poem—it was going to be a fourth nightmare for the *New Yorker*. Then somehow I couldn't finish it, dropped it, picked it up again and made a short story instead. I wish I could say I was writing it when you were writing "Ancient Lights"; then it would make a very nice case of mutual thought-transference, and we could both get a pack of cards from Dr. Rhine of Duke University. Or perhaps Mr. Wells' latest Martian is using us both as Cassandra—an unpleasant thought. When we get back to NY I shall have the cellar gas-proofed and practice up on my machine-gun.

We are having a pleasant time here in this nice house and the children are learning various things about the country, including how to get into poison-ivy.

With all the best from us both,
Steve

TO PAUL ENGLE

Killingworth, Conn.
September 16, 1937

Dear Paul:—

. . . I have been doing a lot of reading for *Western Star*—Pilgrims, Puritans, Virginians etc.—and at least know something more about early America than when I started, and hope it will come out some day. The diaries and letters and such are wonderful—why in hell aren't they better taught in most histories—why don't they let the people come through? Well, I will have a fist at a little of it, and pray I have the brains to make it come clear. Otherwise I've done a couple of short stories and will have a book of them [*Thirteen O'Clock*] out next month. But I am more eager than ever to try and see if I can do a long job again.

I wouldn't worry about the Oxford book—do it the way you want to do it. Or don't do it at all and have them put the advance on your next book. It'll probably be a good book, if you do do it—much better than you think at the moment. As for writing—the current always runs, sooner or later. It runs and stops, runs and stops—sometimes you can induce it by work, sometimes you can't. I haven't known a writer yet who didn't think he was through with writing, half a dozen times. The task seems impossible and one has nothing new to say. And six months later, you are trying like hell to say something you hadn't thought of previously. You exhaust certain forms and certain subjects—but others eventually arrive. A queer business—a never-ending one. But I like my trade.

. . . As ever
SVB

TO ELIZABETH MANWARING [3]

220 East 69th Street
New York, N.Y.
[September] 1937

Dear Miss Manwaring:—

I find I'm going out to Iowa the 16th and probably getting back around the 1st or 2nd of November. Any time after that up to Christmas would suit me. I'm afraid it can't be before the 16th as I have a lot to do here.

3. Elizabeth Wheeler Manwaring, a member of the faculty at Wellesley from 1907 until two years before her death in 1949. She conducted the Poets' Readings which have become an institution at Wellesley since Yeats read there in 1911.

As for the fee, I will come for $150—modestly between Mr. Frost & Mr. Eliot—if that will be of any assistance.

Sincerely

S. V. Benét

TO. J. RAYMOND DERBY

220 East 69th Street
New York, N.Y.
[September] 1937

Dear Professor Derby:—

I'm sorry not to have answered your letter before but I have been having some trouble with arthritis.

The lectures [at Iowa State College] would run about like this.

1. The Tools of the Trade (or the Use of Words)
2. Telling a Story in Prose
3. Telling a Story in Verse.
4. The Architecture of a Book
5. Writing and Keeping Alive.

I am not very good, I'm afraid, on titles—but that's the general idea.

I would be glad to be a guest at the tea on October 21st.

Sincerely

Stephen Benét

TO ROSEMARY BENÉT

Memorial Union
Iowa State College
Ames, Iowa
October 18, 1937

Dearest Girl:—

This is a funny place! I am quartered at the above—a handsome building with a lot too much steam heat in it. However, the windows in *my* room have been open since arrival & will stay open if I have to break the panes. There are 5300 students and the Head of the English Department explains about their being farm-boys and girls and not knowing much about the fine points of English Lit.—but to me, so far, they look just like undergraduates anywhere else. Some of the boys wear grey flannel trousers and brown jackets in the Yale manner—some of them look like Paul [Engle] when he first came East. The girls are pretty or not, and look like girls—the Union contains a beauty-shop, a barber-shop and a vast cafeteria, where I eat, very inexpensively, and where hordes of undergraduates are, but also family parties with children, old ladies, professors, God knows what all! . . .

. . . The thing I dread most is the Thursday lecture —which'll be big—350 people, all students—and also at 10 A.M., so I'll probably fall asleep on my feet. I think I'll switch lectures and give them the poetry one—I know it better.

There are 87 girls living in this Union & I hear feminine squeaks up and down the halls now and then and feel like

St. Anthony. But they go to bed early enough. Oh God how early everybody goes to bed!

> . . . Always
> Stephen

TO ROSEMARY BENÉT

> Iowa State College
> Ames, Iowa
> October 21, 1937

Dearest Girl:—

Your letter has just come and delighted my heart! Which needed delighting because this is the morning I talk to 350 of them. However, with that, the worst will be over.

It hasn't been bad. They've been nice people and Derby says I've had the largest undergraduate audience of anybody in this particular group. Probably every lecturer gets told that. The undergraduates are earnest about studies too. They all bring notebooks, which enchants me. The president's wife yesterday was describing a freshman reception at which she went up to a shy freshman & remarked politely, "I'm Mrs. Friley." The freshman, with perfect savoir-faire, replied, "Okay."

Yes, I was given a lunch by the woman's club and a sculptor on the faculty made a demonstration clay bust of me in front of a class of 80 co-eds, 4 of whom went to sleep. But in spite of these signal honors I remain true to Jane.

. . . I enclose a very pleasant letter from Uncle L. And the *Atlantic* has bought "A Tooth for Paul Revere." Which is incredible.

1933–1940

Darling, I love you with all my heart and soul. And, thank goodness, after tomorrow, I'll really be coming back to you! Love the children—I'm sending them some postcards. You don't know how grand it was to have your letter this morning, in the gloomy cafeteria! Love, love, love!

Always
Stephen

TO GEORGE ABBE [4]

220 East 69th Street
New York, N.Y.
December [29] 1937

Dear George:—

I have been meaning to write you but things have been pretty busy since I got back.

I've read Timmy Coward's letter [of Coward McCann] and talked to him on the phone. I think the main point is this—that first of all, you ought to finish the book. You see it really is pretty hard for any publisher to judge adequately of an incomplete manuscript. Especially in the case of a book like yours, which isn't a tightly woven plot but a series of threads, weaving together. If you leave out the final knitting, the reader is apt to get the impression of a series of rather pleasant individual incidents that don't get anywhere in particular. Because I can't tell—and no reader can—just what you're going

4. George Abbe, born in 1911, was one of a number of younger writers who relied continuously on Benét for professional help and counsel. Abbe, who won the Shelley Award for poetry in 1956, has taught English and creative writing at a number of American colleges and universities.

to do with the end until you've done it, and just what the final impression of the book is going to be. I can say, "I like this—it's promising—write the man a nice letter and tell him to go ahead and send in the whole thing when it's finished." But I can't do much more and I doubt if many publishers or editors can. I can't get inside your mind and see the book as you see it—it may be a whole in your mind but it isn't down on the page for me to see . . .

Well, that's about all. And listen. What you want, first of all, is a good book, not a contract. Honestly it is. I appreciate and understand how hard it is to wait. But a contract never made a novelist yet. And I think you have the makings of a good book here, if you'll work as hard and as well on the last part as you did on the first. It is a very great improvement on anything you have previously done. Try to get it in as good shape as you possibly can and wind it up consistently. Think what would have happened to Chet and Chuck and the rest of them at the end of the tale. And work toward that now.

As ever
SVB

TO CARL BRANDT

220 East 69th Street
New York, N.Y.
March 15, 1938

Dear Carl:—

I'm back [from Florida], without a story but full of vitamins.

No, I didn't like Hollywood—that must have been two other fellows. And I'm afraid any remarks I made about it would not be printable in the *Reader's Digest*.

Western Star is ⅛ done—about—but is not yet in a state to show. I want to start working on it again about May. And you'll be the first to see it, when it gets out of the amoeba-stage.

As ever

S.

TO CARL BRANDT

220 East 69th Street
New York, N.Y.
April 12, 1938

Dear Carl:—

This is a very interesting idea, but, unfortunately, not for me. It's very difficult for me to write on other people's suggestions—just one of those things like measles. And what poetic energy I have, I want to put on *Western Star*.

However, I know the person who ought to do it. John Andrews, who wrote *Prelude to "Icaros."* In fact he is doing some of it, right now. He is engaged on a long poem on the Lindbergh flight, parts of which would probably take out very nicely. He did a swell ballad on Blériot's first cross-channel flight, which I liked very much and couldn't get anyone to publish. And he's not only a dam good poet but a flyer and glider—one of the boys who goes up in thunderstorms because the air-currents are nicer.

Now, if the anonymous suggester here hasn't read *Prelude to "Icaros"* (F[arrar] & R[inehart] last year or year before) he dam well ought to. Because parts of it are just what he is talking about. I know perfectly well

309

that Andrews would be fascinated by the idea. He can be reached at 424 St. Ronan St., New Haven, Conn., or, if he isn't there at East Dover, Vermont.

If I may put in a word, however, don't ask the poet to do it in the Service technique. Say Kipling or Masefield. You'll make him feel better.

Glad you liked the Nightmare ["Nightmare for Future Reference"].

As ever
SVB

TO EDWARD WEEKS

220 East 69th Street
New York, N.Y.
June 3, 1938

Dear Weeks:—

The gentlemen of Phi Beta Kappa, while flattering, are inaccurate.[5] I mean—it's the kind of thing that sounds all right in a speech, but wasn't designed for reading. That's really true. They are different tones. So, in spite of your very gracious invitation, I'm going to keep it out of print.

By the end of the summer I hope to have more verse than I know what to do with, and will certainly send you some.

With all good wishes
Stephen Benét

5. "Friends in the audience," Weeks, editor of the *Atlantic*, had written Benét, "have told me that your address before the Phi Beta Kappa Association of Philadelphia will appeal to every poetry lover . . ."

1933–1940

TO WILLIAM MAXWELL [6]

Killingworth, Conn.
July 1938

Dear Mr. Maxwell:—

Thank you for your letter—and for the pleasant review of Johnny Pye in the SRL. I am still liable to nightmares and when I get another one I will certainly send it on to the *New Yorker*. Or anything else in the way of verse I can contribute. I don't do much if any short prose—short stories being my bread-and-butter—and when it isn't bread-and-butter I'd much rather do verse. But I shall certainly keep your friendly suggestion in mind.

With thanks again,
Stephen Benét

TO CARL BRANDT

Killingworth, Conn.
August 6, 1938

Dear Carl:—

Sorry, but I'm going to be busy on *Western Star* for the rest of the summer. Will you tell *Good Housekeeping* that, and express my thanks for their interest.

If I do any sort of story before Sept. 15th, it'll be one that has been in the back of my mind for a long time but never quite crystallized. However, I'm going to try to spend the next 6 weeks exclusively on the poem—it seems the sensible thing to do.

6. Novelist, and an editor of the *New Yorker*.

311

Glad you and the *Post* liked Doc Mellhorn ["Doc Mellhorn and the Pearly Gates"]. I had fun.

With always the best,

SVB

TO CARL BRANDT

Killingworth, Conn.
August 11, 1938

Dear Carl:—

Will you do a little job for me? The enclosed is the libretto of the musical version of "The Devil and Daniel Webster" for which Douglas Moore is doing the music. I'd like to find out if Houseman or Welles of the Mercury are at all interested in taking a look at it. Moore and I talked to Houseman about it last May, before the libretto was written, and he was mildly interested in the usual theatrical manager's way, but, naturally, made no commitment of any sort. Now most of the music is done, and it occurs to me that if the Mercury would be interested in such a thing at all, it might be worth while to have them take a preliminary look. I have written Houseman about it but gotten no reply—I suppose he's away somewhere—and, as I'm out of New York, it's a little hard to get hold of the people. There is no particular rush about it, and, if the Mercury isn't interested, there's another possibility. But if you could get in touch with them, and find out if they want to take a look at this, I'd be very grateful. It looks short, by the way, but the musical score is going to be pretty full and it ought to play between 1½ and 2 hours—maybe more.

Any contract of course that I would sign on this would

go through Brandt & Brandt. But I suppose Moore would want to handle his end of it independently.

I am going ahead on *Western Star* and hope to have a large chunk of it done by the end of the summer. God, though, I wish prominent historians wouldn't contradict each other as much as they do—how's a poor poet to know which is right?

This is a funny little job and I apologize for wishing it on to you. If the Mercury folks aren't interested, just drop it—as Moore has another possibility, if they aren't.

With all the best
Steve Benét

TO CARL BRANDT

Killingworth, Conn.
August 28, 1938

Dear Carl:—

Sure—send the script back—I thought it was a pretty long shot.

Has anybody gotten in touch with the Mercury people?

Conditions are rather unsettled here at Jamestown but with God's will we yet hope to plant a nation. And, boy, will I be glad when I get this second part [of *Western Star*] done.

As ever
SVB

TO CARL BRANDT

220 East 69th Street
New York, N.Y.
September 18, 1938

Dear Carl:—

I herewith enclose Book I and most of Book II of *Western Star.*

For God's sake take care of it! I have a carbon but this is the clean copy.

Book I will have to be very largely cut—probably reduced to Columbus's voyage and printed as a prologue. However, I am sending it along as it stands. Book II is not going to be as long as it looks. I land the Pilgrims immediately after the conclusion of the typed part and the thing will then weave together.

The entire poem will probably be in 6—or maybe only 4—long books as contrasted with 8 for John Brown. But it will probably be longer than John Brown.

I do not mind your showing this or a part of it to the *Post,* if you should think it advisable. But, if you do, I would appreciate it if they keep quiet about it. And I don't want anybody else to see it, outside, except yourself—and Bernice, of course, if she should want to. I always feel insecure about unfinished work.

As ever
SVB

1933–1940

TO ROBERT NATHAN [7]

220 East 69th Street
New York, N.Y.
October 17, 1938

Dear Bob:—

I raise upon my worn victrola
A hymn of praise for Tapiola.

He was no Lippmann, I can see,
Nor Heywood Broun, nor Dotty T.
But he seems rather more like me.

For he was liberally inclined
But lacked their comprehensive mind.

They know who's who. They know what's what.
But he and I, I fear, do not.
Who sniff the legs of grief and mirth
And run bewildered on the earth.

And if, at times, we run away
It is to sniff another day.
(Or so, at least, we always say.)

God makes mosquitoes and the saurian
And God, perhaps, makes Stuart Orrin,
Critics and war and Mr. Goebells
—In fact, God makes a lot of troubles.

7. Nathan had sent Benét a pre-publication copy of his new
novel, *Journey of Tapiola,* a fantasy about a Yorkshire terrier who
sets out from his sheltered household in search of heroic adventure.

315

But while there's mud at Pensacola,
I still vote for Tapiola.

Exalt his name and send his story,
The pride of Yorkshire, and the glory!

(Another Yorkshire's known to Priestly
But that, I think, is rather beastly)

For he was liberally inclined
But lacked the trained-dogmatic mind.
And yet liked living, wet or dry.
And so do I, and so do I!

TO PHILIP BARRY [8]

> 220 East 69th Street
> New York, N.Y.
> January 1939

When *homo sapiens* raised his head
And walked erect in Eden's vale,
There was a critic there, who said
"I liked him better with a tail."

When people first began to hark
To stories of the fall of Troy,
There was a critic to remark
"Is this obscure? Oh boy, oh boy!"

When Hamlet shook his trammels off
And darkness fell upon the slain,

8. Benét sent these verses after Barry's imaginative and thought-ful play, *Here Come the Clowns,* had received bad notices from the drama critics.

There was a critic there, to cough
"Why must he write about a Dane?"

"The tale's too old, the tale's too new,
The tale is one my uncle tells.
This, Mr. Keats, will never do.
He should have written something else."

Beauty and workmanship and fire,
All things that lift above the sod,
One works to make these things entire—
And then come critics.

        Oh my God!

                Respectfully submitted
                SVB

TO CARL BRANDT

                220 East 69th Street
                New York, N.Y.
                May 23, 1939

Dear Carl:—

This mild little number ["The Great Swinglefield Derby"] is about the best I could do in the intervals of putting on "Daniel Webster" [operetta, *The Devil and Daniel Webster*, with Douglas Moore]. It's awfully folksy but maybe you can do something with it.

                As ever
                SVB

TO GEORGE ABBE

220 East 69th Street
New York, N.Y.
May [25] 1939

Dear George:—

I am sorry not to answer you before, but we have been in rehearsal with *The Devil and Daniel Webster* and it's taken a lot of time. However, I have read over your outline and first chapter carefully and will tell you how they look to me.

In the first place, the book, as planned, will be to most reviewers and readers a college-novel and fall into that particular class. That isn't necessarily a defect—I'm just pointing it out. There have been a lot of college novels— some of them successful—some of them otherwise. If you can say something new and fresh about American youth at college, that will be recognized. If it's just another college novel—well, you've probably seen the reviews of Wells Lewis' *They Still Say No.* If you haven't, look up a couple.

In the second place, the problem of moral purity and character building that you raise is, obviously, very much on your mind. It is a genuine problem, but it is a rather difficult one to handle—particularly in terms of youth. It demands extreme skill. Or else the quality that Scott Fitzgerald was able to give *This Side of Paradise,* the young man who has rushed out into life, discovered, to his horror, that there is no Santa Claus, and run home immediately to write a book about it. This is not said in

318

dispraise of Scott, just to make a point. In general, you will find that virtuous characters are harder to do than vicious ones, and moral reform harder to portray than moral degeneration. This is probably just the natural cussedness of the human race.

I don't see, yet, very much plot. Perhaps your isolating the people in a college community will be enough of a frame to hold the book together. But, it seems to me, again, boiled down, the story of a young man and the influence of various girls upon him. I don't know whether that, and his moral reform, is enough to carry a book. I wish I did. How much time is this going to cover? Is it to run through one term or one college year or longer?

It would seem more logical to me for the professor's wife to affect the hero directly—though there I may be speaking out of turn. Otherwise it leaves her off-center of the story.

Where is your focus? On the hero and his love affairs, or on the professor and his wife? Think this out. And remember that, in a first-person story, everything has to pass through the narrator. He can be given a certain amount of information by others. But most of it has to come right through him.

Now, as to the writing. Some of it is good and some of it is bad. When you get into things such as, on the bottom of page 4, "I was cheap and filthy and low in those days. My blood swarmed with the maggots of thought-disease and lust," you are committing your old mistake—waving a large red flag in front of the reader, with "THIS IS A LECHER" on it in Roman capitals. And this in a prelude to a bit of mild necking. Suppose the hero really does something bad—what words will you have left to describe him with? In other words, do not use up all your shot on the first chipmunk that crosses your path. Or, when an elephant comes along, you'll have an empty gun.

Violence is not strength. Merely violent writing is not strong writing.

It is also NOT your business, as a novelist, to draw moral judgments on your characters for the reader's benefit. Particularly at the start of the story. It is your business to show them as they are—by this trait and that, by this incident and that, by this speech and that, to build up the character before your reader. If you want to paint a scoundrel, by all means paint a scoundrel, but do not make him enter with a villainous leer saying what a bad person he is. Thackeray drew a beautiful scoundrel, in the first person, in *Barry Lyndon*. But Barry Lyndon's own approach to himself is that he is an able, abused and much-misunderstood man. It is when, slowly and relentlessly, you begin to realize just the kind of things he is doing and saying, that the horror begins to come over you—a much more genuine horror than if Barry had been labeled a scoundrel in the first place.

. . . As regards your college background—well, what's it like? What's its chief characteristic to you? Think about it. Is there anything about the contemporary college generation that people ought to know and don't? I don't mean just campus-radicalism—but are they a new breed of cats in any way? If so, how? *This Side of Paradise* made a sensation because it was a new generation speaking— it did tell people some things they didn't know about contemporary youth. Is there anything new to tell today? If so, what?

Pardon this lengthy homily, and God be with you.

As ever

SVB

TO CARL BRANDT

220 East 69th Street
New York, N.Y.
May 28, 1939

Dear Carl:—

I am sorry if [Leo] McCarey [a Hollywood director] thinks I have offended him, but I really can't help it. He didn't call till a quarter of one and I had tucked in for an early sleep before getting Collier Young's telegram. Anyhow, it's under the bridge now, and Max[well] Anderson will do him a good job.

I don't honestly think I want to do the radio thing. Those things are an awful lot of sweat for a few minutes, and, now the show [*The Devil and Daniel Webster*] is off, there doesn't seem to be much point.

Glad you liked the little horse-story—I'll try to do another one shortly, now things have calmed down and I no longer have to worry whether the transformation-scene will work or the ghostly jury come on in broad daylight.

As ever

SVB

TO DOUGLAS MOORE [9]

220 East 69th Street
New York, N.Y.
June 1939

THE DEVIL AND DANIEL WEBSTER by Oscar Watts Brown.

This interesting and valueless experiment on the part
of the American Lyric Theatre shows what we have long
been waiting for and what we don't like now we've got.
Bright, gay and exciting, it is definitely America though
it ought to have dealt with contemporary themes or
maybe with Webster's reply to Hayne. We miss greatly
the character of Hayne, and why didn't Mr. Benét put
him in? It wouldn't have cost any more. However Mr.
Benét has done well, and while showing no sense of
theatre at all, has given us a dramatic evening, except for
Webster's speech which is out of "The American Way."
There should have been more or less music with the
speech or maybe Webster should have whistled it. As
for Mr. Moore's unobtrusive music, that should have been
more obtrusive. Then we could have said it was too obtrusive and called it a day. We did that with *Porgy and
Bess* but that was a couple of years ago and you can't
remember reviews that long. But Mr. Moore has done
well and shown skilful and delightful musicianship. Only
he ought to have been more operatic, except in Mary's

9. Benét wrote this parody of the evasive notices of *The Devil
and Daniel Webster* to comfort Moore. The composer had been
more optimistic than he about the production; although immensely
popular with audiences, it was the victim of poor management
and inept timing.

prayer which is too operatic and holds up the action. There is no excuse for the operatic in an opera. These experiments are doomed to fail. But if the opera had been more operatic that would have been daisy. Operas don't need librettos anyway, and why should a libretto have music attached to it? It's all very confusing, but, anyhow, *The Devil and Daniel Webster,* while not as good as *The Cradle Will Rock, Die Walküre* or *Getting Gertie's Garter* is just the kind of thing the American Lyric Theatre should do. That is, except for the score and the book.

TO CARL BRANDT

220 East 69th Street
New York, N.Y.
July 11, 1939

Dear Carl:—

I am leaving for the country this Wednesday the 12th and my address after that will be, believe it or not,

Whimsy Cot
Narragansett
Rhode Island.

I don't know the phone at the moment but it is the Irving Fisher house and central would know.

You will, God willing, have another story by the end of the month. I started in one and got stuck but I can probably get straightened out.

I like the idea of the Most Unforgettable Character but I don't know about an outline. It is practically impossible for me to do outlines and I simply would have to take a chance with the sketch itself. The one I should like to do would be my father, who was an army officer. You might see if this idea appeals to the *Reader's Digest.*

All the best.

SVB

TO BERNICE BAUMGARTEN

Narragansett, R.I.
July 24, 1939

Dear Bernice:—

I have read *Miss Bishop* [by Bess Streeter Aldrich]. It is a feminine *Good-bye, Mr. Chips.* It could be a good picture.

I would be willing to work on it if price and conditions were right, though it's not exactly my alley.

As ever
Steve

TO NORMAN ROSTEN

Narragansett, R.I.
August 1939

Dear Mr. Rosten:—

I am sorry to inform you that your manuscript, *Fragments for America,* has been found unavailable for inclusion in the Yale Series of Younger Poets.

As you know, we only have room for one book a year in the series. I wish we had more. I can tell you—if it means anything—that your manuscript was one of the three that I considered very carefully before coming to a decision. I like the whole idea of what you have to say. But it did seem to me that after page 24 or so—after Sacco and Vanzetti and Langley—the poem began to wander off. In other words that, except for certain fine things—the brother coming back from Spain, for instance —what you had to say about the past was more vivid and more telling than what you had to say about the present. Perhaps I am wrong—I don't set myself up as an oracle—and perhaps, also, it is in the nature of the material. I may be wrong about this and I feel a great deal of diffidence in trying to tell anybody how to go about his work. Please don't think I am trying, in any way, to tell you that. But it seems to me that you have the opportunity for a very fine poem there—and that the second half—the present part—is not up to the first. I wish you would think over the possibility of reworking it. In any case, I am very glad to have seen the manuscript and wish you all good luck with it.

Sincerely
Stephen Vincent Benét

TO CARL BRANDT

Narragansett, R.I.
August 3, 1939

Dear Carl:—

I have received the first letter from [Archie] Mayo and will ponder it.

When is the script [*Miss Bishop*] supposed to be finished?

I assume they want me to do a regular scenario, with scenes and dialog. Anyhow, that's what I'll do, unless otherwise advised. If they'd prefer me to do it as a novelette, of course I could do it that way.

Are they supposed to pay by the week, at the end of

the complete job, or what? Incidentally, will Frieda please deposit this dough to my account in the Park Avenue Branch of the National City Bank and have the bank send me a confirmation. All ordinary checks are to come on to me here as usual.

Thanks, old boy—I'll try to do a story.

As ever

Steve Benét

TO CARL BRANDT

Narragansett, R.I.
August 8, 1939

Dear Carl:—

Thanks for Collie [Young]'s letter and your own. I am going to do the Bishop story, writing the more important scenes in full, with dialog and stage directions, in play-form, and indicating the general outline of others. This is a good deal easier for me than to try to write it as a story—it gives me more room to move around in. I have to use a good deal of dialog or my characters won't come alive to me. Also making a book out of another book is pretty impossible for me—it'll stay dead unless I can get the new vitality on it that a new form will give. This is why I am doing it in this way—please explain it to them if there are any kicks.

I simply do not see the American Cavalcade idea in the story. Personally nothing is duller to me than one of those scenes when somebody says, "What's that funny little thing you have there, dear?" "They call it a radio." There is tons of background and you can use as much as you like. But it seems to me, if this isn't a personal story,

326

it isn't anything. Mr. ———'s suggestions I found frighteningly bad, though you need not pass that on.

In Collie's telegram the price seems to be $3750. Wasn't it $5000?

I would be delighted to see Miss Mason—probably in New York, at her convenience.

I am having quite a bit of fun with the Bishop story, though I may not sound like it, and will try to do a good job.

As ever
Steve

TO CARL BRANDT

Narragansett, R.I.
September 10, 1939

Dear Carl:—

"Nightmare for Future Reference" came out in the *New Yorker* about a year ago. It was done over the air by Basil Rathbone on whatever hour he appears on, and apparently made quite a success. Because, for the last six months or so, I've been getting occasional letters about it from people who heard the program and wanted to read the poem.

I haven't got a copy down here but you could probably get one from the *New Yorker*. The basic idea for a picture is there, though a fantastic and horrifying one.

Please tell Colly [Young], for McCarey, that of course I'd be delighted if he were interested in the idea. Also that, the day after the—ahem—unfortunate incident over the phone, I saw a McCarey picture and thought, "That's a swell job of directing." This is really so and not soft soap. That phone-call just happened to hit me the one night in the year when I'd have been brusque with the Angel Gabriel if he'd waked me out of bed.

As ever
Steve

TO CHARLES ALLEN [1]

220 East 69th Street
September 1939

Dear Mr. Allen:—

In reply to your letter of September 1st—I've never appeared in *Poetry*—I don't think I ever did in the *Dial*. The first poem of mine to come out in a well known magazine was "Winged Man" in the *New Republic*. I did contribute to the short-lived *Seven Arts*, to my brother's little magazine *The Chimaera* (which you ought to look up, by the way) and quite a bit to the *S4N*, which was founded by a bunch of us at New Haven. Then there was Danford Barney's *Parabalou*, though that wasn't precisely a magazine. But the *S4N* had an interesting history. Then there were also the years—around 1920 or so—when W. Adolphe Roberts was poetry-editor of *Ainslee's* and buying poems by Millay, myself and a lot of others. The stories in *Ainslee's* were very run of the mine, but the verse, if I do say so myself, was pretty good. And they paid cash.

The little magazines, of course, are absolutely indispensable. They give the beginning writer his first im-

1. A member of the English Department at the University of Arizona. He was collecting material for *The Little Magazine* (Princeton, 1946), of which he was, with Frederick J. Hoffman and Carolyn F. Ulrich, a co-author.

portant step—a chance to see how the thing looks in print. And there's nothing as salutary.

> With all good wishes
> Stephen Vincent Benét

TO PAUL ENGLE

> 220 East 69th Street
> New York, N.Y.
> September 27, 1939

Dear Paul:—

I am answering your letter with hideous promptness because we are moving around the block next week— to 215 East 68th Street—and, if I don't answer it now I'll probably mislay it.

I don't think you have any implied ethical obligation to Doubleday, if your contract has expired. So the decision's up to you. Malcolm Johnson is a better publisher than you think he is. But if he doesn't suit you, he doesn't suit you. If you want to go to Random House, I'd go.

I think the contract you mention would be a fair one, either for a book of poems or for your first novel. I would not tie myself up with a long-term, several-book contract. In my experience, these do more harm than good—unless you're the kind of author who definitely and regularly produces one or two books a year. If you want to stay with a publisher, you will stay—and if you want to leave him, you will leave him, no matter how many contracts there are. At least that's my experience. I have a contract with F&R for *Western Star*. But that's as far ahead as we go. Contracts on various other books have just been made as they came up.

We had a good summer—lots of sun and very little fog. Or rather we had a good summer till all this damn war came along. Jesus! I hope we stay out of it. On the other hand, I'd sell the Allies all the munitions possible —just selfishly, I don't want us to have to build a two-ocean fleet against time.

All the best to you and Mary and excuse the brevity. But painters, movers, carpenters, etc etc are jumping around—and so, I may say, are we.

As ever
SVB

TO PAULI MURRAY

215 East 68th Street
New York, N.Y.
October [25] 1939

Dear Miss Murray:—

Of course you didn't talk too much. You couldn't. I was in the room.

On the work you send me—"The Negro Worker Joins the CIO" is the better of the two pieces and the more developed. At least to me. From a purely technical point of view, I wouldn't mix free verse and rhyme—each ought to stand on its own feet. I mean, I think the four lines where you rhyme "bigger" and "nigger" would be better (a) if you put everything you had to say in rhyme or (b) if you took the rhyme out. It seems like a piece of another poem, with another beat, put in this one.

The sketch of your family, with the "rich Fitzgeralds" and "the poor Fitzgeralds," is perfectly fascinating material. It makes me wonder again, and not for the first time, why nobody has really tried to handle this sort of subject. As of course you know yourself, it's just material, in its present form. It is the nubbin, the germ from which a remarkable novel or a remarkable story might come. . . .

I don't know that you should try doing such a novel yet; you probably should practice more and write more first. Because that is the way—and the only way—with occasional criticism—that one learns writing. But this occurs to me—which might be good practice work. Take any one of the three sisters you mention and write 2500 words about her. Let's see the character, what she looks like, what she does, any little mannerisms, any ways of speech. Take your childhood's home or childhood's town —I think you said you were brought up in the South— write 2500 words about it and try to make it come alive— as Tom Wolfe makes Asheville come alive in his books. Take your first arrival in New York and write how it struck you. And make me (I'm using "me" for convenience, I mean the reader) see, hear, taste, feel, smell, be shocked or pleased, as you did and were shocked or pleased or both. There have been some rather good pieces in the *New Yorker* recently, about New York childhoods, from different points of view, by different people. Take a look at them, if they happen to come your way —see what details make the childhood seem vivid to you, what details don't. Try to see, think, hear, feel, reproduce as clearly and as intensely as possible.

It is a long road—it always is.

I don't know any short cuts—I don't know any easy

way. But, if you are bound and determined to be a writer, you frequently get there. You are more fortunate than most of us in having, in your background, and your own life, a fascinating, rich mine of material. I am not fooling about that, or trying to be courteous. It is merely true. For all art comes out of life and out of human beings, and the richer, more varied the life and the human beings, the greater chance for the artist. . . .

Meanwhile I shall always be interested to see anything you send me.

With all good wishes,
Stephen Vincent Benét

TO HAROLD G. RUGG

215 East 68th Street
New York, N.Y.
October 30, 1939

Dear Mr. Rugg:—

I feel honored that the Dartmouth College Library should be interested in the manuscript of "Daniel Webster and the Ides of March."

Unfortunately the manuscript, as frequently happens with my manuscripts, doesn't seem to be in existence. I generally write a story in longhand and then tear up the longhand version as I type. This seems to have occurred to this particular incarnation of Daniel. We've just moved and things aren't yet in order, so if the mss. does turn up, I will let you know. But I'm afraid Mr. Scratch came in through the window and flew away with it.

With many regrets,
Stephen Vincent Benét

TO MRS. WILLIAM VANAMEE [2]

215 East 68th Street
New York, N.Y.
November [3] 1939

Dear Mrs. Vanamee:—

Sorry, but I do not feel able to second Mr. ———. The woods are full of him.

Sincerely
S. V. Benét

TO ROBERT NATHAN

215 East 68th Street
New York, N.Y.
November 10, 1939

Dear Bob:—

Thanks for your good letter—I had just read a review of myself by an able young man and was wondering whether I couldn't write (a) because of native incapacity or (b) because the machine was running down.

You encourage me and maybe I'll write some more. Thanks for liking the tales.

As ever, affectionately,
SVB

2. An employee of the National Institute of Arts and Letters, of which Benét had been a vice-president for some time. Mrs. Vanamee had requested him to second the nomination to membership in the Institute of a well-known—and well-connected—but essentially commonplace writer of the period.

TO ARTHUR TRAIN [3]

215 East 68th Street
New York, N.Y.
November 18, 1939

Dear Arthur:—

In regard to the much-vexed question of Elections to the Institute, I have busied myself with a little collection of statistics which may be of service.

According to our Constitution, membership shall be restricted to those "qualified by notable achievements in Art, Music or Literature." Have we lived up to these qualifications, during the last few years?

I shall take the Department of Letters as an example.

From 1933–39 inclusive we have elected something like forty members to the Department of Letters. (As the new book has not yet been published, I have not the complete figures on the election of last January. However, 37 members were elected, 1933–38, inclusive, and I can remember some of those who were elected this January.)

Of these, 2 have been awarded the Nobel Prize for Literature (one previous to election to the Institute, the other after election).

3. Train, best known for the Mr. Tutt short stories in which he drew upon his legal background, was at this time treasurer of the National Institute of Arts and Letters and—along with such other members as Benét, Van Wyck Brooks, Henry Canby, and Archibald MacLeish—was active in the revolt within the Institute against its prolonged domination by Nicholas Murray Butler. For more on this internal conflict within the world of official American letters, see in particular Benét's letter of April 24, 1940, to the Board of Directors, American Academy of Arts and Letters.

5 have received the Pulitzer Prize for drama, 2 for poetry, 2 for biography, 1 for history, 1 for the novel. 2 have received the Roosevelt Medal.

Of course, prizes and medals do not necessarily mean immortality for the recipient. However, they are some indications, perhaps, of a man's contemporary position in his field.

Another indication—not a sure one, of course—may be found in inclusion in certain anthologies. I have therefore taken four widely-used anthologies of American literature—used in courses in literature at leading American Universities. They differ somewhat, both in purpose and editorship, but each attempts to cover the entire field of American letters from the colonial period to the present. Inclusion in such an anthology, for a living author, certainly shows some sort of standing. I will preface my findings by stating that, due to questions of permissions, these anthologies do not cover the field of contemporary drama, except for Mr. Eugene O'Neill, and they rarely include extracts from contemporary historians or biographers. They do try, however, to cover contemporary poetry, fiction and criticism.

The anthologies are *American Poetry and Prose* (Norman Foerster) (1934); *American Life in Literature* (Jay B. Hubbell) (1936); *The American Mind* (Warfel, Gabriel & Williams) (1937); *The Oxford Anthology of American Literature* (W. R. Benét & N. H. Pearson) (1938).

Of members of the Institute elected prior to 1933 *and still living at that date,* 15 are included in at least one anthology.

335

Of members of the Institute elected *from* 1933 to date, *14* are included in at least one anthology.

In other words, since and including 1933, we have elected almost as many members whose work rates their inclusion in these highly-selective anthologies as belonged actively to the Institute before.

6 names, those of Sherwood Anderson, William Faulkner, Robinson Jeffers, Sinclair Lewis, Archibald MacLeish and Carl Sandburg, are included in all four anthologies.

Two names, those of John Dos Passos and Thomas Wolfe, are included in two out of four.

All these have been elected since 1932.

The number of American authors still living in 1933 and included in these anthologies ranges from 21 in the Foerster book to 38 in the Oxford (which leans heavily on the latest contemporary). Let us take the Oxford book for a moment, since it is the most recent compilation.

We find, included in it, the following members of the Institute who were alive and already elected members in 1932.

> S. V. Benét
> Willa Cather
> Robert Frost
> William Ellery Leonard
> Edna St. Vincent Millay
> Paul Elmer More
> Eugene O'Neill
> Edwin Arlington Robinson
> Edith Wharton
> Thornton Wilder

10 in all.

We find included in it, the following members of the Institute elected *since* 1932.

> Sherwood Anderson
> James Branch Cabell
> John Dos Passos
> Robinson Jeffers
> William Faulkner
> Sinclair Lewis
> Ezra Pound
> Carl Sandburg
> Archibald MacLeish
> Thomas Wolfe

10 in all.

And, of course, this does not, as I have explained, really cover the field of contemporary drama, biography or history. It does not take into account the work of such men as John Steinbeck (elected this January) who are undoubtedly destined to play a large part in contemporary letters. But it would certainly seem to indicate that the elections of the Institute during the last seven years have been on the right basis, that the men elected to the Department of Letters in the Institute have been men of distinction, and that the Institute has been choosing its members in strict accordance to its Constitution.

That what is true of the Department of Letters is also true of the Departments of Art and Music, I have no doubt whatever.

That we have made omissions is also undoubtedly

true. A Melville or a Molière will, now and then, not be elected to an institution such as ours. Human judgment is fallible. However, in looking over the list of American writers in these four anthologies who are NOT members of the Institute, there are only three names which are included in all four anthologies. These are Messrs. Theodore Dreiser, Ernest Hemingway and H. L. Mencken. All three of these gentlemen have been nominated—all three have stated that they would decline an election. It is, therefore, not the fault of the Institute that they are not members of our body. The only man whose name appears in three out of the four anthologies, Mr. Conrad Aiken, is up for election this year.

The defense rests.

Sincerely,

S.V.B.

TO CARL BRANDT

215 East 68th Street

New York, N.Y.

December 24, 1939

Dear Carl:—

Thanks for your letter. I have been meaning to phone you, but, what with the merry Xmas season, things have been getting a little animated.

I think I could probably do the [*Ladies' Home*] *Journal* a Christmas story and it would certainly be easier to do it now than later in the year. The last Xmas story I did, I wrote in August with the temperature around 100 and it was a little hard to summon up the Xmas spirit. Let me think about this.

I am writing a rather gloomy, modern story, which you will probably have some difficulty trying to sell. Sorry, but it's the idea I had. Anyhow, it will probably be finished by the first of the year.

I have kept the *Country Gentleman* in mind, also the *Post*. I do not like to be out of circulation with the *Post*, and I am going to try to do some stories during the next few months. I will dam well have to, for one thing. But I have spent the last 2½ months taking notes for *Western Star* which really will have to get finished before I have a long white beard.

I'm not in the least worried about "All Around the Town." Somebody will buy it some time, if it has to be the *Forum*. As for the trotting story ["The Great Swinglefield Derby"]—I knew that was too slight, so anything you get out of it will be lagniappe.

We're leaving for Richmond Saturday and should be back around the 29th or 30th. Meanwhile, a very merry Christmas to you and the family, and all our best.

As ever

SVB

TO CARL BRANDT

215 East 68th Street
New York, N.Y.
January 4, 1940

Dear Carl:—

I'm afraid this ["No Visitors"] is highly unsalable but let's hope the next one won't be. All the best.

As ever

SVB

TO EDWARD WEEKS

215 East 68th Street
New York, N.Y.
January 10, 1940

Dear Mr. Weeks:—

That's extremely interesting. Now, let me see. Most of the young people I know are poets. However.

Joy Davidman (we published her *Letter to a Comrade* in the Yale Series last year) has, I know, written a novel. I haven't seen it, but I know that Bernice Baumgarten, of Brandt & Brandt, thinks well of it.

Reuel Denney (this year's Yale Series boy) has, I think, written a novel. Again, I haven't seen it, but he's a talented fellow. You probably have his address. If not, you can reach him through the Yale Press.

George Abbe, whom you know, has finished a first draft of another novel. I have seen that and it needs work. However, he might be able to do the work. His address is South Hadley, Mass.

Brendan Gill, an ex-chairman of the *Yale Lit,* is, to my way of thinking, quite a talented person. He has been doing short pieces for the *New Yorker.* Whether he has a novel or not, I don't know. But he is worth thinking about.

The Iowa boys I know who have written novels are mostly tied up with other publishers.

I should certainly suggest the negro writer, Richard Wright. He's in the last O'Brien book, I think. He has lots of stuff.

This is all I happen to think of, at the moment. But, if I happen to think of any more, I will suggest them to you.
With all good wishes,
Stephen Benét

TO THEODORA ROOSEVELT

215 East 68th Street
New York, N.Y.
January 21, 1940

Dear Miss Roosevelt:—

Thank you for sending me the poems. I've read them with a good deal of care. I think you have something. How much it is and how it is going to develop, I don't know.

You have emotion and you're able to convey it. You have to me a distinct individuality. That may sound lukewarm. It isn't meant so. Every year I read for the Yale Series about 50 book-length manuscripts by poets under thirty, who haven't published before. I'd say about 30 of them usually were by women. A great many of them are fluent, technically proficient and essentially pretty-pretty. Your work doesn't fall in that class. It is young but, at its best, it has what I keep looking for— the live nerve, the live person speaking.

I like the first poem least and should suspect, probably incorrectly, that it was written earlier than some of the others. Did you really mean "wean" there? Or did you use it because it rhymed with "clean." If you did, don't. Rhymes ought to look inevitable to the reader, no matter how much work they've meant to the poet.

. . . Now I really can't tell you what to do. Except to write some more—always trying to expand your range, always trying to see and hear more clearly, to get the things on the paper closer to the thing in your mind. To write in the heat, but to correct as coldly and ruthlessly as you are able—and not to be satisfied. With some people I would be able to say "Your free verse is pretty good but your rhymed verse shows lack of ear— if you want to use rhymed verse, try some five-finger exercises." Or "This sonnet has eight feet in the third line—don't you know about sonnets?" I can't do this with your kind of work and it would be silly of me to try.

From a practical point of view, you might try the best of these on magazines and see how far you get. . . . If you don't know all of [the little magazines], you can look them over at Brentano's and see what you think of them. But in general, it is worth while seeing your work in print. It looks differently. . . .

As regards a book, I think I would wait for a little. I don't know just what Mr. [Theodore] Spencer [of the Harvard English Department] means by an "endowed" publisher. Does he mean a college press or one of these publishers where the poet pays all or most of the cost of printing? If the latter—well, a good many people have started that way. But I'd try and find out as much about the publisher as possible. Some of them are gyps. In any case, I don't think I'd rush it—say for six months or a year. Because in that time, you may have written some more and some of the things you'd put in the book now you might not want to put in it then.

The rest of it depends, somewhat, on how much you want to be a writer. It is a tough job and a long road. It takes more work than you ever think it will when you start. And discouragements are frequent and copious.

. . . In conclusion, may I state, that I am not writing this letter because I know your father [Archibald B. Roosevelt] and mother. If your work had been of a different sort, I would have written a polite and amiable letter saying it was always nice to try and write verse because it didn't do any harm and helped your own appreciation of literature. As it is, I am forced to tell you to go ahead and do some work, because you have promise.

Very sincerely yours,
Stephen Vincent Benét

TO MRS. JAMES WALKER BENÉT

215 East 68th Street
New York, N.Y.
February 25, 1940

Dearest Mother:—

We went up to West Point on Friday—a beautiful ride on the train, with the long light of late afternoon on the snow-covered Hudson hills—got there in time for an early supper with the [Col. and Mrs. Clayton E.] Wheats —then I gave my lecture to the Third Class, who are just studying J.B.—went back to the Wheats afterwards and some of the younger instructors and their wives came in. The officers now, by regulation, have to wear either dress-uniform or a tuxedo in the evening and the new dress uniform is very handsome—not with the tight-fitting collar around the neck but more on the line of an English uniform, with lapels. A lot of the officers were artillerymen, so they had the broad red stripe down the trousers. The only trouble is, they wear the cloak with it—and they say that driving a car in a cloak—especially an open car—is just a terrible nuisance.

The Wheats were most kind, as they always are, and we had a very pleasant time. The Corps is a big one, now—they have over 200 officers stationed there as instructors—but the Point, of course, always looks much the same.

. . . Always
your devoted son
SVB

TO CARL BRANDT

215 East 68th Street
New York, N.Y.
March 6, 1940

Dear Carl:—

I'm afraid the person who most influenced me is still my father—an officer of the Regular Army who could write any fixed form of verse, was interested in everything from the Byzantine Emperors to the development of heavy ordnance, and was the finest critic of poetry I have ever known. He represented and represents to me integrity—and a sense of humor. However, I believe Sherwood Anderson has already written of his father— probably they don't want another.

I thought when you called me up, the task would be relatively easy. I see it isn't. I haven't, unfortunately, an Indian guide I went fishing with or a wise old priest who

344

changed the course of my life at seventeen. I couldn't write about the doctors I've known without embarrassing them—and the same goes for intimate friends. I could sketch a great teacher like Tink [Chauncey B. Tinker]—but that would be a profile, and from the outside. Most of the people who really influenced me are still alive. I could tell plenty of incidents about individuals—but they don't make a portrait. If I had known E. A. Robinson well—but I didn't—few people did. And I wouldn't want to try and do a make-up portrait—a phony

Well, I will keep thinking about this. However, it does occur to me that, in taking my father, I would take a kind of man most readers know very little about—the U.S. Regular. That life produces, at its best, a remarkably fine type of human being. At its best, I know—I have seen the worst of it also. But it can be at its best.

As ever

SVB

TO CARL BRANDT

215 East 68th Street
New York, N.Y.
April 2, 1940

Dear Carl:—

I will go ahead with somebody else for the Charles [River], but I am going to hold the Merrimac for John Marquand, when, as and if he would be willing to do it, as he seems to me the ideal person. There is no rush—we are clear on the Rivers [of America] Series for this year—but I should very much like to see him represented in it, and I think he might find it, at some time, an interesting change from other work.

The books have sold, so far from around 6000 to a little over 20,000, depending, of course on book and author. They have a continuing sale and we mean to keep the Series on as a Series, build it, possibly eventually sell sets—all that kind of thing.

I haven't thought of another Unforgettable Character but I will keep thinking. On the Christmas story, I would like to try and get another *Post* story done first, as I want to keep a little ahead there, and I'm trying to do that now. However, the Christmas story is in my mind.

All the best.
SVB

TO PAULI MURRAY

215 East 68th Street
New York, N.Y.
April [23] 1940

Dear Miss Murray:—

You know that I'm always glad to see your work, and I think you're getting ahead with it. You seem to be— well, loosening up a little is the way I'd put it—writing with more fluency and more freedom, with fewer places where the verse lets down with a bump, and more individuality. It's a job to be done, like any job—it's a profession to be learned, like any profession—it isn't learned in a month or a year—it takes time and practice. But it can be learned.

I'll make some criticisms, and, as you know, I make

frank ones. First of all on the Spring Morning in North Carolina.

This is well observed—it is the material for a poem, rather than a poem itself. It is the material for a poem because you have put in something like 20 characteristic details of Spring, but you've put them in so they're all the same size. The material isn't fused—there isn't any real progression toward a finale. The tomcat could follow the cardinals or the blue jay after the pear-leaves without much change in the verse. Now, in a great poem, let's say, that wouldn't be so. I see so many details here that I don't get a general picture—and yet a general picture is what you want. I want something that *is* Spring—the essence of North Carolina Spring, too. What's the difference between a Southern Spring and Northern Spring? Suppose you were doing a poem on Spring In Connecticut—what would be the essence that would make it different? Do you see what I mean? I don't mean this in harsh criticism—it is very valuable practice to write a description of something in front of your eyes, see how closely and truly you can come to it. But realism, by itself, isn't quite enough. Try it over, some time—try seeing, feeling, getting toward the way you feel about Spring in North Carolina, the way it's different from any other Spring, what makes it so. You can do it. . . .

Keep up the good work. And, as you know, none of the criticisms I make are intended in a harsh or depreciatory spirit. They merely concern the technique of writing, that we all have to learn, that we spend our lives learning, that, even after long practice, we must still try to improve and improve—to see more clearly, hear more faithfully—if we wish to be writers at all. And you have so much to write about. You have such rich material, once you have learned to smelt it out of the ore. And I think you are learning.

> With every good wish
> Stephen Benét

TO THE BOARD OF DIRECTORS,
AMERICAN ACADEMY OF ARTS AND LETTERS

> 215 East 68th Street
> New York, N.Y.
> April 24, 1940

Gentlemen:—

I am in receipt of your communication of April 23rd.

As a member of the American Academy of Arts and Letters, I wish to register my personal and emphatic protest against the action of the Board of Directors in passing the Amendment proposed on February 7th [under which the Academy would no longer have been restricted to choosing its members from the National Institute of Arts and Letters].

I wish to protest as well against the extremely disingenuous wording of the excerpt from the minutes submitted: "that there had been no criticism or protests received from any of the members of the Academy as a result of the announcement that this amendment had been proposed on February 7th and sent to each member of the Academy on February 23rd."

It is, or should be, well known to the Board of Directors that a large number of members of the Academy have protested against the passage of such an amendment. Whether the protests were made previous or subsequent to February 23rd is entirely immaterial to the issue at stake.

No valid reason has yet been given to the Academy in general for the passage of such an amendment; no general meeting of the Academy has ever been called to discuss it, though its implications are of the gravest moment to the Academy as a whole.

I am, therefore, forced to consider the action of the Board of Directors, in passing this amendment, as an arbitrary and undemocratic action, contrary to the principles on which the Academy was founded and contrary to the best interests of the Academy as a whole.

> I am, gentlemen,
> very sincerely yours,
> Stephen Vincent Benét

TO NORMAN ROSTEN

> 215 East 68th Street
> New York, N.Y.
> [April] 1940

Dear Rosten:—

It's a lot more important—and interesting—for you and Hedda to get married than for you to live a month in an art colony.

As a matter of fact, the only time I went to Peterborough [the MacDowell Colony], the birds bothered me terribly after the quiet El.

> Best to you both,
> SVB

TO ELLEN GLASGOW

215 East 68th Street
New York, N.Y.
May 3, 1940

Dear Miss Glasgow:—

I agree that the South should be better represented in the [American] Academy [of Arts and Letters].

I'd be glad to sponsor both Dr. Freeman and Mr. Cabell. But as I am somewhat persona non grata with the Directors of the Academy at present, it might be wise to have someone else nominate Mr. Cabell. Do you suppose Deems Taylor would be suitable? I remember his making a passionate speech about J.B.C. before the Institute.

We shall be in New York till the first of July and would love to see you.

Sincerely
Stephen Benét

TO CARL BRANDT

215 East 68th Street
New York, N.Y.
May 21, 1940

Dear Carl:—

Here's another one the *Post* won't like.

As ever
S.

TO BERNICE BAUMGARTEN

215 East 68th Street
New York, N. Y.
June 2, 1940

Dear Bernice:—

Thanks for Mr. [Wesley] Stout's pleasant letter. He knows that my personal feelings toward the [*Saturday Evening*] *Post* are always of the most cordial, as the French say.

As regards the point where we differ, I enclose an editorial from this morning's *Herald Tribune*. I didn't write it and God knows the H-T is not a New Deal organ. But it says, in essence, what I also tried to say in my story. Because I believe in that, I will go on saying it. Mr. Stout might look it over.

As ever
SVB

TO CARL BRANDT

215 East 68th Street
New York, N.Y.
June 30, 1940

Dearl Carl:—

I am leaving for [Killingworth, Conn.] Tuesday. . . .

When I get there, I'll get to the *Reader's Digest* piece. I am sorry to have delayed so on it, but this dam jury [duty] took a lot of time, and I have been doing the commentary for an REA film [*Power and the Land,* with Douglas Moore]—Government—which is fun but of course no money. However, in the country, I will get down to business.

All the best.
SVB

TO VAN WYCK BROOKS

215 East 68th Street
New York, N.Y.
[July] 1940

Dear Brooks:—

I am answering you in indecent haste as we are just leaving for the country.

I certainly agree about the Academy. I have already put my name to Miss Glasgow's nominations of Cabell and Douglas Freeman and I'd be very glad to forward MacLeish and Millay. Mrs. [Pearl] Buck, I suppose, ought to be in though I can't honestly say that I admire her work extravagantly.

Perhaps we could get a small bloc of votes, not only to further the just but to suppress the college-president kind of nominee. I should be happy to conspire on that basis.

Yes, by all means. The Howells Medal [for fiction] should go to Miss Glasgow. It is perfectly disgraceful that she hasn't had a major literary prize.

In haste,
SVB

TO WALTER DAMROSCH [4]

Killingworth, Conn.
July [20] 1940

Dear Mr. Damrosch:—

Thank you for your letter. I haven't forgotten either you or the Ode and I hope to get to it shortly. But my mother's recent death has made this a troubled month for me and I haven't been able to do all I should.

I shall get to the Ode within the next week or so and will send it on to you as soon as I finish it. I know the music will be fine—the only difficulty is the words.

With the best from both of us,
Stephen Benét

TO CARL BRANDT

Killingworth, Conn.
August 14, 1940

Dear Carl:—

No, sorry, there are a lot of people better equipped than I am to dramatize *The Man without a Country*.

As ever
SVB

4. Damrosch was president of the National Institute of Arts and Letters during this period.

TO GEORGE ABBE

215 East 68th Street
New York, N. Y.
October 1940

Dear George:—

I meant to write to you before about *Dreamer's Clay* but we have somehow been getting all the three children back to school and somehow the days have slipped by. I like it very much and I think with it you have successfully passed a difficult landmark—the second novel that stumps so many writers. I think, too, that the fantastic element in it works—at least it did to me. And the characters stick in the mind—particularly your Marathon Marcher . . .

I certainly hope you have luck with it—of course no one can ever tell how a book is going to sell. But 1500 is a good advance—very good and I think people are going to like it. And the whole thing is something that goes brick by brick. A durable reputation isn't built by one book or two—it grows. Then, at some point, there comes discovery by a larger public. That may not happen with this particular book—but that it will happen eventually I am perfectly convinced.

You have every right to be both pleased and satisfied with the work you have done this year and the results. May the next year be even better for you!

With every good wish,
SVB

354

TO HOMER FICKETT [5]

215 East 68th Street
New York, N.Y.
October 23, 1940

Dear Mr. Fickett:—

In regard to the suggested broadcast on "The Undefended Border."

I can't give you a detailed outline right now as I happen to be one of those writers who don't work from outlines. But my feeling about the story is that it ought to be as human a story as possible—the story of something which is exciting because it doesn't exist (a border without fortifications) told in human [terms]. Maybe a family on each side of the border—maybe one family—I don't know. But to realize the extraordinariness of something taken for granted—the continual passage back and forth between Canada and America—the likeness on the two sides of the undefended border.

I would want to do a good deal of this in verse—certainly the opening and the close. I may want to do some sort of choral thing in the close on the general lines of "We built a house for freedom here" (on both sides of the line).

There are certain historical incidents—such as the fact that over 50,000 Canadians enlisted in the Federal Armies in our Civil War—which might be used. I'd like to see about them. I want also to talk to a couple of

5. A program director in the Radio Department of Batten, Barton, Durstine, and Osborn, Inc.

Canadians I know here and ask some questions on background etc.

This probably sounds very vague. But I am not at all vague when I start writing something. I see this as a very exciting opportunity—a really big thing—and I would certainly do my best on it.

Naturally, the theme is good neighborship. But, as I see it, it won't be overloaded with propaganda, and I will keep strictly away from a "big brother" attitude. All the same, our relations with Canada are a matter of extreme importance and anything we can do to help understanding between the two countries seems to me well worth doing.

Sincerely

SVB

TO CARL BRANDT

215 East 68th Street

New York, N.Y.

November 24, 1940

Dear Carl:—

I don't know anything about this gent but he seems to write a good letter. The point about "Nightmare at Noon" is this—I made a little private bargain with myself that anything received from that poem was to go to charity. I'd be willing to sell it to him for $500 if that seems reasonable to you—and if he could do a good job. Will you give me a buzz on this? It certainly doesn't seem to me the sort of thing that the big companies would take a chance on.

I'd, of course, have to okay any version and the poem could not be changed.

As ever
SVB

TO WILLIAM DIETERLE [6]

215 East 68th Street
New York, N.Y.
[November 10] 1940

Dear Dieterle:—

Thank you for your very pleasant and cordial letter. It makes me very happy to think you like so much of what I have done and I know the story could be in no better hands than yours.

As regards the suggests you make for plot development and so forth.

I agree that the second half of the story—up to the trial—isn't quite as well tied together as it might be, and that it might be better to get the visit to Marshfield in earlier than we have it now. We lose a little by not having Jabez himself see the good way of life there—on the other hand, we probably gain more by having Mary actually do something and her appeal to Webster would give him a good reason for going to the fair. The only thing is that it shouldn't be suggested that Mary is motivated by jealousy. She is worried about Jabez—about

6. Dieterle, for whose ability Benét had considerable respect, was producing and directing the movie version of "The Devil and Daniel Webster"; Benét had written a preliminary scenario. The film was released in 1941 under the title *All That Money Can Buy*. See Benét's letter of August 4, 1941 to Dieterle.

her boy—about their life which is getting increasingly queerer. Webster promises to help and comes to the fair. We have the fair and the ram incident.

Mary's first idea has failed. She has gotten Webster there—but the ram—probably loosed by the devil—has spoiled things.

Now, shouldn't the trouble start there between her and Jabez? He is unreasonable—his attitude is "You got Webster here—the biggest man in the country—just to make a fool of me in front of him?"

But I think it might be better for Mary herself to make the decision to go to the party. Webster can offer to help her—at the fair or later. He can say that he'll stand by. But, if she herself says, "He's my husband—I know things are wrong but I must stand by him."—isn't that stronger for her? I am just a little afraid of getting everybody in on the party scene—and confusing the issue with so many characters. I may be wrong and the suggestion is tentative. But I feel there is also a slightly sour note for some of us in the suggestion of a conspiracy between a man's woman folks and his friends to Do Him Good. If Mary does it by herself, that's a little different.

I should, I think, prefer Mary by the force of her character to drive Belle and the guests away. Webster can, if necessary, then remove Mary and Ma Stone can then go on the line you suggest—that it's up to you now, Jabez. I like having Stevens danced to death—I wonder if it is better for the audience to know this and Jabez not, so there will be a sock when the devil tells Jabez of Stevens' death—or whether he had better die in front of Jabez. Anyhow, we go on from there.

I do not, frankly, like the idea of a drinking contest between Webster and the devil. It seems to me to weaken Webster unnecessarily. Webster is a hero. If he drinks at all, he ought to be able to drink anybody under the table.

. . . Please believe me that any suggestions I have made here are somewhat thinking aloud and I am not wedded to any particular phrase in the original story. I'm just trying to think of what is going to look best.

With every good wish
Stephen Vincent Benét

TO BERNHARD KNOLLENBERG [7]

215 East 68th Street
New York, N.Y.
December [24] 1940

Dear Knollenberg:—

My authority for stating that Kenneth Roberts did a lot of digging is Mr. Kenneth Roberts upon his own works, (vide *For Authors Only*, etc.) No, that is a dirty crack on my part. The guy does work. He is also as prejudiced as all get out—and demonstrates, it seems to me, in *Oliver Wiswell* that you can read a great deal about a period and still give a highly prejudiced picture of it if you start with a preconceived idea. However, God help us all, we do what we can with the modicum of brains we have. I am sorry to sound so prayerful—if anybody in the world had written even a competent and connected history of the Western frontier from say 1745 to 1815, I would feel better. As it is, I continue to take

7. Librarian of Yale University and an American historian with whom Benét often discussed the research for *Western Star*.

notes [for *Western Star*] in order to form judgments which will probably be wrong when formed. I wish I were writing about Lancelot and Elaine.

With every good wish for Christmas,
SVB

Writer at War (1941-1943)

Even before Pearl Harbor, as he had indicated in such 1940 radio scripts as "The Undefended Border," Benét had become deeply involved in the task of arousing Americans to their situation and responsibilities. All the multiple burdens of his diverse professional and personal life were now gathered during the last twenty-seven months of his life into a single mission of national service. He had come full circle, back to the Regular Army boyhood at Benicia and Augusta.

His concern over the fundamental issues of human liberty gave new dimension to his magazine fiction: sometimes he illuminated the American present by an evocation of the American past, as in the tale of a fugitive slave called "Freedom's a Hard-Bought Thing"; sometimes he dealt passionately and dramatically with a contemporary scene which in turn invigorated an ancient legend, as in "Into Egypt." Always he extended himself beyond his physical capacity, in committee work, in the laborious affairs of the Council For Democracy, in continuing leadership of the National Institute of Arts and Letters, in his generosity to young writers.

Bent with arthritis now and often tormented by pain, his spirit seemed to friends and associates to grow younger and more vibrant as he drove himself through a sequence of assignments. He was one of the major voices in the brief renaissance of the American radio, his imaginative and moving scripts an inspiration of technique to fellow workers and a tonic of intelligent propaganda for listeners. When he died on March 13, 1943, his heart literally exhausted from the punishment he had given it, the bromide of the orators and editorial writers was this time accurate—he had been killed in uniform as surely as if he had burned up in a B-17 or fallen at Guadalcanal.

TO CARL BRANDT

Hobe Sound, Florida
February [25] 1941

Dear Carl:—

That's a very amusing letter. I have reread the story ["Good Picker"] and it doesn't look so bad—there are a couple of spots that can be tightened up and there is one reference to speakeasies which shows its age. But I think it's a good story, though I had completely forgotten it. I wonder if "The Pacemaker" would be a better title? Anyhow, bless your heart! I'll be back Monday or Tuesday and, I hope, brown as a coconut though not quite so wrinkled.

With much entertainment,
SVB

TO THOMAS PIERREPONT HAZARD [8]

215 East 68th Street
New York, N.Y.
March 19, 1941

Dear Pierre:—

Thanks for your very pleasant letter which I would have answered before but I have been laid up with a foul cold. I'd love to come back to Rhode Island—and to the Homestead—but I'll tell you just what we're doing. Having acquired a certain amount of chips during the past year, thanks to luck and Hollywood, we are going out during the kids' spring vacation to look at a house in Stonington [Conn.] which Rosemary fell in love with last summer with a view to buying if the lady doesn't want too much for it. I don't know whether it will pan out but at least we're going to think it over pretty seriously—if we don't get a house soon we probably never will and Rosemary is bound and determined to have some place where she can put her back copies of *House and Garden* before we both die of old age. So if anybody else puts in for the Homestead in the next few weeks, you had better let them have it—if we do buy a house, I will let you know—and whether we buy one or not, we will hope to see something of you this summer, even if it has to be in a tank-trap. This is all very unbusinesslike and indefinite but you will recognize the usual Benét characteristics.

8. Hazard, a graduate of Yale in 1915, was a neighbor and friend of the Benéts for several summers in Rhode Island. A public-spirited member of an old Rhode Island family, he was active in Republican state politics during the 1930's.

How are you all? We had a pretty hectic winter for a while—I seem to have gotten mixed up in a lot of committees and a lot of extra work—then we did manage to get away for ten days at Hobe Sound with the Barrys which was unalloyed pleasure. The sun was warm and the jasmine scented the air—the nights were cold but starry—I swam every day even when the sea threw a rock at me—but we had a lovely time. Katharine Hepburn was down there too for a few days and of course when we came back we had to undergo hours of cross-examination from Stephanie on everything the lady had done, said and worn. As a matter of fact, she was very pleasant, with none of a star's mannerisms. No, we didn't see Mr. Willkie—but the Barrys' maid had worked for him and found him a very nice gentleman—so at least we touched the hand that touched the hand that etc.

Tommy Benét seems to have gained 10½ pounds at Exeter which makes us feel that at home he must be one of the underprivileged third of the nation. He seems to be able to maintain a gentlemanly average of C, and, as far as I know, likes being there, though I probably won't really know till he's 21. Stephanie is taller than Rosemary, has an evening dress and is thinking of going to Swarthmore. Rachel continues to draw pictures of animals and God. The cat, as usual, is in heat. Jinny is cleaner than usual as she has just returned from a nursing-home. The bulbs have come up in the back-yard just in time to get covered with a layer of ice. Life is quite normal.

We think often of you and Nancy and it seems perfectly silly that we don't see more of each other. It seems to be one of the penalties of middle-age that you spend a hell of a lot of time seeing a great many people you don't give a particular curse about and see the people you like about once a year. Well, however the summer turns out, let us try to fix that up.

With much affection from all of us,
Steve

TO WILLIAM ROSE BENÉT

215 East 68th Street
New York, N.Y.
March 29, 1941

Dear Bill:—

Thank'ee, old son. I feel flattered you ask me for advice. I don't know how good mine is, but I'll give it.

I have read your letter to Henry [Canby] twice very carefully and am sending it on to him. It's a swell letter, it is what you feel and I don't feel I'd have the right to suppress it, even if I wanted to. I will also, I think, phone Henry and get in touch with him.

I gather, however, from his second page that he isn't asking you for a revised version [of *The Dust Which Is God*] for the [Book-of-the-Month Club] judges to pass on at the next meeting but rather wants to talk about cuts that could be made, and would only be made if the book were definitely accepted. I think this would be worth talking over, whether you finally decided to make the cuts or not. And that it would be worth your while coming up here to discuss it, though I hate to get you back in this still unheated season. It's hard to tell from a general letter like that what sort of cuts people might want to make—and sometimes, when they've thought it over, they change their ideas. I have discovered from a long and nefarious experience with magazine editors that sometimes if you give them about one-tenth of what they ask for, the little dears are sometimes quite pleased and forget they ever asked for the rest.

Of course the cash would be nice—cash always is—but it would also get the book off to the sort of start that poetry, in this beautiful land, doesn't often get. And that this one deserves if ever any poem did. Well, you know that as well as I do, so why should I tell you? I think it's going to sell anyhow, because I think it's going to hit people between the eyes. But the selection would be a help—no doubt about that.

It boils down to this, with me. I would make slight changes, if asked. I would cut a passage here and a passage there if, after reasonable discussion, they seemed to impede the flow of the story. But I wouldn't cut by a quarter, by a third, by a half. I wouldn't cut to get the book into what is known as reasonable compass. It just isn't that kind of book. It isn't written that way. . . .

Of course I'd be glad to sit in on any conference. And, Lord knows, I think the whole thing is well worth discussing. Then, if you can't make the cuts, you can't, and that's that. Maybe Henry could give you a rough idea by letter, which would be a help. He sounds very genuinely enthusiastic about the book and eager to do something about it. So let's keep our fingers crossed and see how things develop.

If the BofM doesn't come through on it, it's certainly worth trying on the Literary Guild . . .

> All the love from us all, and a large and lusty prayer,
> Steve

If you do come up, why not take the enclosed and use it for the trip? I happen to be filthy with money right now—Carl sold two old stories while I was on vacation. And, as Alexander VI remarked on becoming Pope, "Since God has given us the Papacy, let us enjoy it!"

S.

TO EUGENE DAVIDSON

215 East 68th Street
New York, N.Y.
March 30, 1941

Dear Gene:—

Sure, shoot 'em along any time. I have two additional mss. sent directly to me, one by Eve Girdon and one by Martha Oliver-Smith which I will deal with in addition.

I'll be here till June 1st anyway. Ring me any time.

Nice about [Norman] Rosten and [Reuel] Denney getting Guggenheims. Also that Rosten has made such a hit with the Cavalcade of America folks.

As ever
SVB

TO JOHN FARRAR

215 East 68th Street
New York, N. Y.
April 3, 1941

Dear John:—

I like the looks of the selected edition very much. I think the dull blue and red are very handsome, and I like the box, and the kind of type on the binding-case. That is a fine job.

If I may make a criticism—I think the type-face used in the prose is rather hard to read and rather solid. This may be a question of leading. But it looks to me like an awfully solid block of type. It doesn't attract the eye. It may look well from a purely typographical point of view —but there is a difference between handsome type and readable type. And there seems to me far too little margin at the left-hand side of the page, as you look at the book. My instinct, on getting a book like that, would be to take it in both hands and break its back so I could actually read what is printed on the page.

My only other criticism is on the hand-lettered "Benét" on the title-page which seems to me unnecessarily fussy.

Now all this goes with saying that of course I am horribly pleased and impressed by having this sort of edition, and think of my latter end, and feel I probably don't deserve it. I also realize that editions of this sort have to look well—and I want it to look well. But the stuff, also, should be easy to read.

My God, have I done as much work as that? I should have done it much better.

As ever
SVB

TO H. EMERSON TUTTLE [9]

215 East 68th Street
New York, N.Y.
April 26, 1941

Dear Emerson:—

How beautifully and how charmingly sing the Sirens!

9. 1890–1946. Curator of Prints at Yale University and Master of Davenport College.

You know I'd like to oblige you and nobody could have put the invitation with more grace and tact—including the English boy with the flute. But, Emerson, no. School commencements are not my dish. It is tough enough talking to undergraduates but thirteen-year-olds floor me. I am afraid of them. As soon as I get up in front of them I begin to think how funny I look and wonder if all my buttons are properly fastened. I have done it, yes. But that was at the Brearley School and they were giving my children scholarships. I would like to see you—I would like to see your children. But not at a Commencement. I am old, I am arthritic—I am a ruined tower, like Wilkins Micawber. Ask me something else and I will do my best to comply. But the thought of addressing even the most charming and intelligent eighth grade at 10 A.M. fills me with pure horror. Already I hear them say "Who's that funny man?" And children always know.

With many regrets and apologies.
SVB

TO WALTER DAMROSCH

215 East 68th Street
New York, N.Y.
May 31, 1941

Dear Mr. Damrosch:—

I am a little dubious as to our [American Academy of Arts and Letters] participation in the Hemisphere Poetry Awards. There is an article on Mr. [Thomas J.] Watson [president, International Business Machines Corporation] in the May 31st issue of the *Saturday Evening Post* which gives him credit for good will and an interest in art but which states . . . [that IBM's cultural programs seemed to be connected with the development of new markets for its product].

This does not sound, somehow, very encouraging. Mr. Watson may be a very sincere man—but there seems to be an advertising tie-up.

Some other defects in the plan also occur to me.

(a) What a poet wants, most of all, is to have his work widely read and, if possible, to get his bread by it. Under the present set-up, the winning poet will get a free trip to N.Y. and Washington etc. for first prize—a hundred dollars for second, etc. But he gives up the copyright in his poem to IBM—the book to which he contributes is not to be sold but given away—and reprint requests, if granted, will be without fee. Now if, by some miracle, the contest should produce such a popular poem as "The Man With the Hoe"—the reprint and anthology rights, over the years, would be worth a good deal more than a trip to Washington, even from Patagonia. And, in general, I am very much opposed to an author giving up copyright under any circumstances whatsoever.

. . . These may sound like drastic criticisms but I am, frankly, very leery of getting the Academy into something which, with all the good will in the world, may turn into a publicity stunt.

As ever,

S. V. Benét

TO PAUL ENGLE

215 East 68th Street
New York, N.Y.
June 1, 1941

Dear Paul:—

No, dammit, it's just because I'm such a godawful correspondent. I did get *Always the Land,* read it and liked it very much. I liked all the horse stuff particularly, and the two fathers—and, as always, your feeling for earth and the people of earth. I meant to write you about it right away, and then this whole Winter and Spring has gone by like a runaway colt. I don't know what I have done with it—I seem to have done very little and yet I have been working all the time at one job or another. And, continuously, there has been the pressure of what is happening to the world. Well, that is the same for all of us, and it does not excuse me. . . .

We are trying to buy a house in Stonington, Conn— it's a nice house and, from the top windows, you can see water on three sides. . . . And, in spite of the fact that life, at the moment, is rather like living in the middle of a whirlwind, there are various compensations, such as watching the children grow. Give all our love to Mary and the baby and believe me, in spite of my tardiness,

Always affectionately
SVB

TO JOSEPH AUSLANDER [1]

215 East 68th Street
New York, N.Y.
June 1941

Dear Joe:—

How nice to be disbursed to by Mr. Rabbitt!

All the best
SVB

TO CARL BRANDT

215 East 68th Street
New York, N.Y.
June 22, 1941

Dear Carl:—

. . . For the record. I have done a 4th of July broadcast for the Council For Democracy ["Listen to the People"] which they will put on over the Blue Network July 4th at 2 P.M. It may also be used in *Life*. I have not bothered you about this as I am contributing it free—any *Life* money will go to the U.S.O.

For the record. The Treasury Department has asked me to write a song for *their* radio program, embodying the best features of "The Marseillaise" and "The Battle Hymn of the Republic." Perhaps God will assist me in this

1. A Harvard graduate who had been a lecturer in poetry at Columbia as well as a poet, editor, and novelist, Auslander was gift officer of the Library of Congress from 1942 through 1944. Benét's note was an acknowledgement of a $200 check for a reading he had given at the Library in May 1941.

372

endeavor—perhaps not. Anyhow, there is no money involved.

I seem to be becoming the Wendell Willkie of poetry —not entirely a happy thought.

I shall now, however, devote myself to writing a couple of stories as I need some dough—or will in the near future.

Bill was married yesterday to Marjorie Flack, which is very nice as she is an extremely nice person.

God be with you.

As ever
SVB

TO FELICIA GEFFEN [2]

Stonington, Conn.
June [30] 1941

Dear Miss Geffen:—

My address, by the way, is now just Stonington, Connecticut.

Now about the two requests. I never happen to have heard of ———— ————. I don't think she has been previously known as a writer. I am in favor, naturally, of books about democracy but it's hard to tell, from what she says, whether her book will be any good or not. You would have to look up her references and probably see the manuscript—on the hundred to one chance that it would be a first-class work. It might, perhaps, be easier

2. Secretary to Walter Damrosch in his role as president of the National Institute of Arts and Letters, Miss Geffen has continued her association with the group as Assistant Secretary-Treasurer.

to suggest that she get in touch with the Council For Democracy, 285 Madison Avenue, who are directly interested in doing that kind of job. I am perfectly willing to take a chance on somebody but I do feel that, with many well-known artists and writers who are really up against it, it is difficult to send money out into the blue. However, you might ask Henry Canby if he knows anything about this gal and has any line on her.

As regards _____ _____—well, we seem to have him on our hands. He is a talented young man whose work is not commercial. It is extremely advanced and experimental and I doubt if he ever makes any money. Nor does it impress me that he is a budding Joyce. Incidentally, [his current book] would give some of our more elderly members the screaming meemies. However, I consider it part of our duty to assist the young and experimental and I am willing, if Henry agrees, to allow him to borrow a further $200, if there is plenty of money in the Fund. But that is all we can do for him.

It seems to me that this whole business of the [Artists' and Writers' Revolving] Fund should be put on a rather more definite basis and I think we ought to have a meeting of the Council—or of the people most interested— as early in the Fall as possible. There isn't any doubt that, as the thing gets better known, we are going to have increasing calls—and there are also occasions where we ought to step in without any calls being made. It ought to be kept fluid, of course, but I think we ought also to have a more definite policy about it than we have now.

> With all good wishes,
> SVB

TO WILLIAM C. DEVANE [3]

Stonington, Conn.
[July] 1941

Dear Mr. DeVane:—

I'd like to be represented in the Thirtieth Anniversary issue of the [*Yale*] *Review* but I'm afraid you'd better not count on me. The apple-barrel is empty at the moment and it just depends on whether I happen to write anything worth reading before your deadline. If I do, I will send it along—but one can never tell, with poetry.

With every good wish,
SVB

TO CARL BRANDT

Stonington, Conn.
July 17, 1941

Dear Carl:—

That's a wonderful letter and, in spite of the fact that I can't remember one blinking thing about "Fireworks," I am delighted. Also the money will come in very handy. But do not be depressed. I have been sitting for the last four days, looking at the wall and trying to think of a story. I haven't gotten one yet, but I will in time. At least I hope I will. I always have. And I am racking the old brain.

God bless the B-file!

With love to yourself and Bernice
SVB

3. Dean of Yale College and, in 1941, a member of the Editorial Board of the *Yale Review*.

TO ROBERT NATHAN

Stonington, Conn.
July 18, 1941

Dear Bob:—

There are a couple of things you could do.

(a) Connie Ernst (she's Max Ernst's daughter, you may know her) is helping run the big Treasury Defense hour on the radio. You can get hold of her at CBS. She approached me about writing a patriotic hymn—and they're very anxious to get one or several. This is an all-star hour and you'd probably get it well sung.

(b) The Council For Democracy is just going out for a nation-wide contest for a patriotic hymn or anthem. This will start pretty soon. They may start with an open-air thing at Lewisohn Stadium where old anthems and new will be performed. They could also certainly get you sung. On this you could get in touch with Ernest Angell, the new President of the Council—or perhaps even with C. D. Jackson as this is C.D.'s pet project and he knows quite a bit about music. The address of the Council is 285 Madison Avenue, NYC.

Yours for a National Anthem
SVB

TO LOUIS FINKELSTEIN [4]

Stonington, Conn.
July 28, 1941

Dear Dr. Finkelstein:—

Thank you for sending me Mr. [Joseph Wood] Krutch's paper, which I have read with some care. It is clearly

4. Dr. Finkelstein, president of Jewish Theological Seminary,

presented and I am bound to agree with a good many of his conclusions, though, perhaps, I would state some of them differently. I don't happen to believe in the "madman" theory of the artist—not unless everybody who tries to bring some order out of chaos is, ipso facto, "mad." But it is true that he works as he works and has to be let alone a good deal. You can impose certain restrictions of space upon him, and even certain restrictions of subject. If you're painting the ceiling of the Sistine chapel, there is the very definite ceiling and you cannot cover it with a painting showing the triumph of Satan. But the limits should be largeish—you get the best work that way. When you narrow them and narrow them, you won't get the work—though artists have an uncanny way of getting around restrictions.

As for the propaganda side of it—great artists can write propaganda. They can point a moral, as well as adorn a tale. But the belief must be inside them—you cannot hand it to them like a tablet of benzedrine. However, I cannot agree that as soon as it becomes possible to state in abstract terms the lesson of a work of art, then the work of art becomes supererogatory. Milton states the "lesson" of "Paradise Lost" as he conceives it in the first few lines of his invocation—he is going to tell you about man's first disobedience and what a hell of a mess it made. If he had believed that man's first disobedience made little or no difference to mankind, or to him or to you, he wouldn't have written the poem. And the poem does assume and teach a very definite religious doctrine. I agree that you do not have to share

---

was also president of the Conference on Science, Philosophy, and Religion, to which Benét belonged and for which Finkelstein requested his comments on various papers delivered at its meetings.

Milton's particular brand of Protestantism to enjoy his magnificence—but that is another matter. I am merely saying that the artist can and does believe as well as rebel, accept as well as deny.

I agree with Mr. Krutch that the artist should not abandon his own function or the belief in the validity of his own processes—I believe he must remain to some extent autonomous. I believe certainly that many artists will continue to be, as they have been in the past, sometimes rebellious, perverse and generally unmanageable —and should be. I agree that artists should not all become "deliberate propagandists teaching what the philosopher and the scientist hand down to them for embellishment." I don't think they all ought to experience mass-conversion or all start writing against sin. I know they won't, for one thing.

Nevertheless, if the artist believes, I think he should state his belief. It will never be earlier. He ought to think and think hard. For neither his freedom of speech nor his liberty of action will automatically preserve themselves. They are part of civilization and they will fall if it falls. And he has a responsibility to his own art, and that is to make it great. I doubt if he can do so by blacking himself out.

Very sincerely

S. V. Benét

TO WILLIAM DIETERLE

Stonington, Conn.
August 4, 1941

Dear Dieterle:—

I saw the picture [preview, *All That Money Can Buy*] Friday night and am anxious to write you my impressions.

In the first place, I want to thank you for so much—the feel of country life—the singularly beautiful scenes of planting and sowing and harvest—the keeping of the story to its essential implications and yet letting it develop naturally in its terms of simply country folk—many delightful things, such as the handling of the band in the village—and larger ones such as the extremely effective handling of the trial. The main parts are beautifully cast and finely directed—I don't see how [Walter] Huston and [Edward] Arnold could have done better—and also the boy and the girl. I like the very end enormously—that's new and brilliant and effective. I was really astonished by the boy—[James] Craig—he is both sturdy and touching. In fact you all deserve—and you yourself most of all—a number of silver stars.

Now there are one or two things I would like to talk about and I know you would like me to do so frankly. John Farrar has already wired you his feeling about the beginning of the picture and establishing the devil so firmly that the audience can't possibly misunderstand him or be confused about the situation—and I have a very great respect for John's instinct for the line of a story. I think he is right about this and I think it can be done as he suggests. Moreover, I do think it would benefit the picture to do it.

I don't like the fox-hunting sequence at all or a bit. It just won't be believed. You cannot convince any New Englander that a New Hampshire Farmer in 1840 would go out in that costume and a velvet cap. It's against every idea we have of New England. And it really doesn't add a thing to the story.

In introducing Judge Hathorne, the line runs something like this—"a witch-*burning* justice." I know this is a very minor matter—but no witches were burned in Salem—no witches were burned in New England. They were hanged. And it is something that New Englanders are peculiarly sensitive about. I know, because once, in another poem, years ago, I referred, incorrectly, to "Salem witch-burnings"—and got letters of protest about it from all over the country.

On the title, I still stick to my guns. It isn't just personal feeling on my part—I simply cannot see, from a business point of view, throwing away the publicity value of a well-known title ["The Devil and Daniel Webster"].

Well, that is what I have to say and it comes, not from wanting to pick flaws, but from a very sincere desire to see this very fine thing you have done even more complete and perfect. I wish I could see the picture again, with you, before it opens. You have brought so much beauty and richness that it lingers in the mind.

With all good wishes
Stephen Benét

TO LOUIS FINKELSTEIN

Stonington, Conn.
September 8, 1941

Dear Mr. Finkelstein:—

. . . The question today is not whether a book may
or may not be banned in Boston—a good painter or a
bad painter hung on the line at the Salon. The question
is whether civilization, and art which is an essential part
of civilization, are going to survive or not. The issue is
not between the America of Rutherford B. Hayes and
the Florence of Lorenzo de Medici—in which case, a
good many people might vote for Lorenzo. The issue is
between life and a certain chance to do your work and
get it done—and death and no chance to get it done.
The artist—the writer—and the writer is the only person
of whom I am in any way qualified to speak—is a tough
kind of plant in general and will grow in unfavorable
soil. He can get his work done in poverty and ignominy
—he can get it done when he is living off a patron—
he can give his penny to Caesar or the church or to a
stupid middle-class society, as long as he gets the least
common denominator of freedom of thought for the
penny. Great artists have done all this. They have eaten
and will continue to eat a good many pecks of dirt in
order to get their work done. In exile in other lands, or
in self-imposed exile from the society of their time, they
have continued to get their work done. But when the
world reverts to a certain kind of barbarism—and that
does not necessarily mean the Cro-Magnons—they can-

not function. They cannot function because they cannot exist. As Mr. Justice Holmes once remarked (I am quoting incorrectly and from memory), "the machinery of government must be allowed a certain amount of play in its joints." When there is no play in its joints, the artist is one of the first people to be crushed between the cogs. He needs very little room, at least, but that much he must have.

What gives him that little room? A certain, admitted respect on the part of rulers and states for civilized things, for the work of the mind. A certain hard-bought tolerance—even a certain neglect. You may say that the United States of Grant neglected Whitman—so it did— but there were enough enthusiasts to keep him alive and going. Charles II may have been a bad king, but he did not hang Milton on a gibbet, though Milton had written "Eikonoklastes." The exile of Joyce may have been bitter —it was not haunted by spies and secret agents, when he had first left Ireland. It may be elementary to say so, but times have changed.

Because they have changed—because there is that abroad in the world which would take away from the artist even the minimum conditions he needs to do his work—the artist himself is forced to re-examine his position. That, as I gather, is part of the aim of this conference. It has led to various things.

Let me put it as baldly as I can. Having asked for very little from their writers, in the past thirty years, those who read them ask much. They ask for faith and hope and greatness of spirit—for the succour and fortitude great work can bring to the troubled spirit in troubled and dissolving days. And this they are right in asking—we are all asking that from somewhere. Yet, you cannot pull greatness suddenly out of a hat, you cannot create faith from a void, you cannot praise democracy unless you believe in it. You can get the tanks rolling on an assembly line—but great poetry, great fiction, are not made that way.

Nor is, I think, a great deal of recent criticism directed at modern writers because they wrote as they wrote entirely just. I am not willing to throw overboard some of the best work of the last thirty years because it does not match with our present mood. Those writers tried to tell the truth about life as they saw it, they broke old forms and made new ones, they cleared away a great deal of bunk and cant. It is the painful irony of their case that, even as they were winning for the writer complete freedom of expression, a political system was rising in the world which would make not only complete but even relative freedom of expression impossible for any writer of honesty. . .

It is obvious that modern poetry cannot remain in its present world of incoherent and private symbolism. It is obvious that mere painstaking realism in the novel can only go so far. But I do not think these things were obvious until they were attempted. Now the demonstration has been made. It is up to the writers, now, to see where they go next—what shapes they can summon from the ground. And the responsibility is not theirs alone. It is one that we all share. We all enjoyed the debunking and the disillusion. Now we are trying to go beyond that— we are trying hard, at long last, to find out what things have meaning, what things are worth keeping. The writer is a part of this endeavor but he is only part of it. We are all going to have to work for something rather larger than we ever thought could exist, and take responsibilities few of us dreamt of taking. I think that will have to mean larger and more genuine work in letters—primary literature, in Mr. [Van Wyck] Brooks' sense of the term —if we are up to the job.

Sincerely

Stephen Vincent Benét

TO LOUIS FINKELSTEIN

215 East 68th Street

New York, N.Y.

September 24, 1941

Dear Dr. Finkelstein:—

Thank you for your statement on the results of the Conference, which I have read with great interest. I was sorry not to attend in person and hope to do better in the future. But personal affairs got in the way.

I hope you will not think me advocatus Diaboli for making a few comments on that statement. I'm not trying to carp, I assure you, just to say what hits me as an individual.

. . . I notice on page 2 that "moral truths ... all of them" can be "implemented" in science. Well, implement is a vague word, a jellyfish of a word. Personally, I can find no relation at all between moral truth and either the discovery of insulin or the discovery of dynamite. What moral truth, if any, lies behind the X-ray? Perhaps I have misread the passage—very probably I have. But there is certainly a distinction between tools and aims.

3. My third criticism is on the language in which the

statement is couched. It is not first-class language. I know how difficult it is to draw up such a statement. The ideas are there all right—they repay careful study. But they are presented, in the main, without force or fire—in the pithless, indeterminate style that disfigures so much of American scholarship. If men are drawing up a new declaration of independence—a declaration of the independence of man's spirit—they should do it with at least as much care for the sound and sense and bite of English words as Jefferson gave to his own Declaration. I am interested—yes, and very interested. But if I should give this statement to a young man who wasn't an assistant instructor or a Ph.D.—how much would he get from it, what fire would it light in his mind? "The members of the Conference believe the most significant value of the discussion derives from the contribution made to the clarification of human ideas and the formulation of the truths underlying western civilization, and basic to all human happiness and endeavor." Well, to me, though I agree with the thought, and though I speak with deference, that is pianola-English. It does not remind me of the great beliefs men have held dear—it reminds me of nothing so much as a little book gotten out by the disciples of James Joyce and called "An Exagmination and Incamination of the Factification of *Work in Progress*." [5] Can't important ideas be stated so they stir the mind? They have been, in the past. . . .

> With every good wish
> Stephen Vincent Benét

5. Samuel Beckett, Marcel Brion, Frank Budgeon [and others], *Our Exagmination Round His Factification for Incamination of Work in Progress,* London, 1936.

TO ELIZABETH MANWARING

215 East 68th Street
New York, N.Y.
October 1941

Dear Miss Manwaring:—

Thank you for Miss Dixon's lines which I appreciate somewhat humbly, and wish I read aloud better.

Arthritis is a funny disease. Sometimes you get better, sometimes you don't. I'm getting a little better now and, if that continues, I'll go on as I am. If I don't, I will certainly remember Mr. Jeffery's doctor. Some day, they are going to dig up a specific and then all of those of us who creak at the joints will be a lot happier. Meanwhile, there is everything from chaulmoogra oil to radiotherapy. I have tried most of them, but am always willing to try something else.

It was a great pleasure to be at Wellesley and I enjoyed myself, as I always do. I want to thank you for a very delightful experience—because you made it just that.

With every good wish,
Stephen Vincent Benét

TO CARL BRANDT

215 East 68th Street
New York, N.Y.
October 10, 1941

Dear Carl:—

That sounds very handsome of the *Post* and I will hope to produce 4 short stories [at $2,000 per story] within the requisite year. I dropped in on Ted Weeks [*Atlantic Monthly*] in Boston and he was also saying that the hardest thing to get was fiction. Well, Lord knows, we all know why—every time I try to go back to my long poem, I think why the hell write about the early history of Pennsylvania with the world blowing up. And yet, work ought to be done.

As ever
SVB

TO CHAUNCEY B. TINKER

215 East 68th Street
New York, N.Y.
October 10, 1941

Dear Tink:—

In accordance with our conversation, I am sending you at the [Yale] Library, under separate cover, my copy of *Hike and the Aeroplane* by "Tom Graham." It was given me by Sinclair Lewis when the book first came out and I should now like to give it to Yale, on the understanding that it stays at Yale. You'll find on the inside cover three notes by Red referring to various pages. The last is self-explanatory, the other two refer to Benicia where my father was stationed and where Red used to visit us. "The colonel" referred to is my father, James Walker Benét, who had one of the finest collections of bad poetry in the country. You will not find the book in 'mint' condition—I read it, and reread it. But I should like to think of its being at Yale.

All the best,
Steve

TO CARL BRANDT

215 East 68th Street
New York, N.Y.
November 5, 1941

Dear Carl:—

I have, at long last, a few too many words to say ["The Bishops's Beggar"].

As ever
Steve

TO DOUGLAS FREEMAN

215 East 68th Street
New York, N.Y.
November 30, 1941

Dear Dr. Freeman:—

I am taking the liberty of sending you a condensed report of the first year's work of the Council For Democracy.

I don't usually do this sort of thing. I am doing it this time because I sincerely believe that the Council is doing really important work. It is the only civilian committee devoted exclusively to pro-democratic propaganda, both short range and long range. And, with a very limited budget, I think it has done a very fine job.

We do need money. We are asking the Rockefeller Foundation for money. If we can get it, we can expand our program and be sure of going ahead. I think we're needed. Will you read this condensed report and tell me what you think?

Very sincerely
Stephen Vincent Benét

TO ROBERT E. McCLURE

215 East 68th Street
New York, N.Y.
December 22, 1941

Dear Bob:—

I guess this is for the record. I was doing a piece on Carl Sandburg on Sunday, December 7 and, as usual, I was late with it. I finished it up about 6 P.M., called a Western Union boy, and sent it down to the *Herald Tribune*. We hadn't had the radio on all day. Then I poured myself a glass of vermouth and sat down to relax. And, ten minutes later, Ellen Barry called up with the news.

We went over to have dinner with them in their hotel and listen—with that curious thing that comes over you to get together with your close friends when something happens. And, as you listened, you could feel the country harden and come together, like ice forming on a pond. That may seem a curious simile when we were sitting in a warm, well-lighted room on the 10th floor of a New York building. But you knew that that was just what was happening. There wasn't any question about it or any discussion. You just felt it in your skin, like a chemical change.

Oddly enough, there were no extras—at least in our part of town—or if there were, we didn't hear them. The news came too quickly for extras.

All you heard next day in the streets was "Well, Roosevelt was right." "Well, we're in it." "Well, anyhow, we've got a great President." "Well, anyhow, this has united the country." And I'm not faking the last sentence. I heard

389

it, just that, from taxi-drivers and rooming-house keepers and the man who keeps the news-stand, put just that way.

The next day, Monday, I had to go to my doctor and get a shot of rheumatism serum—it seemed silly to cancel the appointment. He was late, of course, and I got to an emergency meeting of the board of a civilian committee I belong to late, around 12.30, I suppose. I walked into the committee-room late and saw six men I knew standing up, with their backs toward me, looking at a small, lighted box. Out of the box came the last bars of the "Star Spangled Banner." I took off my hat and stood with them. That was, of course, the moment after the close of Roosevelt's speech, asking for a declaration of war against Japan.

The next day, Tuesday, we had some air-raid alarms that turned out to be incorrect. There was no scare by anybody, anywhere, that I know of. People either went on with their business or did what they were told to do.

We have not yet blacked out—and that may be a somewhat difficult job in this particular city. However, if it has to be done, it will get done. In the New York way, probably—with a good deal of kidding and "why the bejeezus"—but it will get done. We have acquired black cloth, sand, tape, all that sort of stuff. There is just the possibility—that is the point.

It was fine to see you and I hope the novel goes well. And this little note goes with all our Christmas wishes— odd to phrase now and yet very real, because Christmas is going to last a dam sight longer than the Axis will, no matter what happens.

With all our love,
SVB

TO RUSSELL DAVENPORT [6]

215 East 68th Street
New York, N.Y.
[January 1942]

Dear Russell:—

I like the prospectus very much and its tone, which seems to me first-class. I like your two end-sentences particularly—a first-class slogan.

I have about two suggestions. The first one may be cockeyed. Would it be possible to work out your Commercial Memberships so that unions, as well as business houses, could take out Commercial Memberships if they wanted to? I am not clear as to whether commercial membership entitles a firm just to some space and a certain number of copies of *Bugle* as well. But I'd think, if you wanted to get the *Bugle* into plants in quantity, that workmen would be more likely to read it if it were distributed through their own unions or through their own CV [Citizens for Victory] groups than by an employer or a company. Probably you have already thought of this.

I object very much on page 5 to "So far as government is concerned we agree with Thomas Jefferson that it's a necessary evil; we only hope that it won't be any worse or any bigger than it has to be." Whether Jefferson said it or not, that seems to me completely outmoded think-

6. 1899–1954. A friend of Benét for many years and, at this time, chairman of the board of editors of *Fortune*. Davenport was active in several of the wartime propaganda agencies with which Benét was associated.

ing. If national government is merely "a necessary evil" why the hell should anybody bother trying to set up any sort of *international* government or world-order? It doesn't make sense. And any international government league or federation will have to be a lot "bigger" than anything we can at present conceive. I think one of our great troubles has been this idea that "government" is something high-sounding and far-off and scary that gets after you with a club—that it's outside of and removed from the normal life of the citizen—that it's something you yell to for help in a very bad jam and curse out the rest of the time. It isn't. Government is the people and the people are government. It isn't something some man from Mars called a "politician" does to you—it's what we do to and for ourselves to get the way of life we want and believe in. If we don't like the men who run it, we can get the men changed—if we don't like the laws they make we can get the laws changed—but we can't do either by sitting back on our rears and remarking, "The best government is the government that governs least." That never was true of any civilization more complex than that of the free hunter—and while I might like to be a free hunter, I know I can't be . . . I don't know how you get an ideal government—but I'm perfectly sure you don't get it by regarding it as a dose of salts or an inevitable doom overtaking the innocent taxpayer. To the men who founded this Union, the republic they envisaged and the government they devised meant something—a great and daring experiment and a roof for the people and a flag flung out on the wind. I want to get back to that idea and to the pride that was in that idea. I am tired of apologizing for the American experiment.

And I will remark, in addition, that American government is precisely and exactly a howling success by any standard now existing on this planet. It is full of defects, it is still what we make it. But it works.

No, I am really not running for Congress this year. But I think there is a point there. And with that impassioned cry, I will remove my fingers from the interior works of your watch and say, "Long may she tick!"

With every good wish and many congratulations,
SVB

TO FELICIA GEFFEN

215 East 68th Street
New York, N.Y.
February 4, 1942

Dear Miss Geffen:—

1. Florence Wilkinson was a rather minor figure as a poet but her circumstances seem to be very distressing. I do not think we are in a position to give her a regular pension—especially as the next year or so is going to be pretty hard on many artists and writers or I miss my guess. But I think we [The American Academy of Arts and Letters] could send her $250, if the committee approves. It might also be suggested to her sister that she get in touch with the Authors Club [League] which, I believe, also has a fund.

2. With regard to the musical awards. I see no reason why we should not repeat a grant of $500 to the Society for Publication of American Music. I should also be in favor of making a grant to the Society of American Composers, particularly for the composer's theatre project,

the program of outstanding works by young composers, and the other actual projects which get worked, played, or presented—rather than for exhibits or indexes, valuable as such latter plans are. Would it be possible for the League of Composers to earmark some such specific project, so the Institute's name would also be on it? As for the size of the grant—I suppose that should be discussed.

Sincerely
S. V. Benét

TO JAMES T. FARRELL

215 East 68th Street
New York, N.Y.
April [10] 1942

Dear Mr. Farrell:—

Thank you for sending me your paper on "Literature and Ideology" which I have read with great interest.[7]

With much of what you say I agree and am bound to agree. I do not believe in throwing overboard a lot of the best writing of the past thirty years because it was "gloomy" or "depressing" in tendency—if it was so. I think both Joyce and Proust were great writers and will remain great writers, no matter what is said for or against them. Nor personally can I find *Le Temps Retrouvé* depressing, any more than I can find the end of Mr. Bloom's soliloquy depressing. As for the writers of my own generation—well, they had one virtue, at least—they did try to tell the truth. They may not have told it all, they

---

7. James T. Farrell, "Literature and Ideology," *College English,* 3 (April 1942), 611. Reprinted, James T. Farrell, *The League of Frightened Philistines* (New York, 1945), 90.

may not have been wiser than the statesmen or more foreseeing than the prophets. But they did try to tell the truth—and the case can rest on that.

On the other hand I cannot agree that either [Van Wyck] Brooks or MacLeish wish to "politicalize" writing, set up a certain kind of State writing, put artists in uniform or do the various things of which they have been accused. I cannot see that that is so. It would seem to me they were asking for larger work, not smaller—and that was the essence of their argument.

Well, it could be a long argument. "Is a lyric poem the proper manner in which to predict historic events?" It is if it can—which doesn't mean that we should all immediately write nothing but poems on the downfall of Hitler. And you have quoted Milton to the point, but he also wrote, "I cannot praise a fugitive and cloistered virtue, unexercised and unbreathed." I don't think poetry should put its head in a bag—I don't think it should be the exclusive possession of an intellectual few. That is my only quarrel with the dogmatist intellectuals. But I would burn no books and suppress no writers.

Sincerely yours,
S. V. Benét

TO CARL BRANDT

215 East 68th Street
New York, N.Y.
April 15, 1942

Dear Carl:—

In God's name, what is the *Post* about? I have just read the Felix Morley article in today's *Post* and am amazed and horrified by its viciously anti-British angle,

its none-too-subtle sneers and smears at the Administra-
tion and its general attitude that it was we who attacked
the Japanese at Pearl Harbor.[8]

The Mayer piece was bad enough [9]—it would have
made George Horace Lorimer turn in his grave. But this
one is a calamity.

Is [Ben] Hibbs really running the magazine? Does this
sort of thing represent the *Post's* "new policy"? Or what?

I have always valued my connection with the *Post*—
and not merely and solely as a meal-ticket. It's been extremely fair to me—it has let me write the kind of stories
I wanted to write—and it has printed story after story
of mine that were way off the track of magazine fiction.
For that I am and always shall be most genuinely grateful. But, if it's going to turn into a glorified edition of
Scribner's-Commentator—well, that includes me out.

In sorrow and anger
SVB

TO CARL BRANDT

Stonington, Conn.
June 19, 1942

Dear Carl:—

That's perfectly all right. I want to establish the principle that I just don't go to Hollywood. They always
think that if you sit around and listen to a director's half-
formed ideas for a week or so, it will do good. Well, it
won't. Any director can put any ideas he has about a

8. Dr. Felix Morley, "For What Are We Fighting?" *Saturday
Evening Post, 214* (April 18, 1942), 9.
9. Milton S. Mayer, "The Case against the Jew," *Saturday Evening Post, 214* (March 28, 1942), 18.

picture on half a sheet of paper—that is, if he is able
to write.

My phone number here, by the way, is Mystic 991-J2.
There is one more ring on the J than last year, just to
confuse people.

As ever

SVB

TO CARL BRANDT

Stonington, Conn.
June 25, 1942

Dear Carl:—

No, I don't want to do that Miracle thing as a short
story. It is a movie idea, Carl—it is all right but it is
somewhat hammy. I just couldn't handle it as a serious
short story.

God knows I am as anxious as anybody to get that
$2000 [Benét's new *Good Housekeeping* price]. But I
want to get a good story for it, if I can. I am finishing up
the 3rd and 4th broadcasts of my series of 6 [*Dear Adolf*
radio scripts] this week. This puts me one ahead and
as soon as I get another one out of the way, I will try
and make some money.

I am still thinking about Western Star and the SEP
[*Saturday Evening Post*] idea. If the poem were to come
out anywhere in the near future, of course, I would be
crazy about it. If it won't be published in book-form for
2 or 3 years, I just wonder. On the other hand there
might be certain advantages in that section appearing
right now. Let me think a day or so.

As ever

SVB

TO C. D. JACKSON [1]

Stonington, Conn.
June [28] 1942

Dear C.D.:—

I am moved to write you a letter, having just finished revising the labor broadcast ["Letter from a Worker"].

The broadcast itself will be, I think, all right. But as you know and as Agnes Allen [research assistant] will tell you, the material we got in was inferior to that from any other group we tried and the cooperation pretty scanty. So much so as to be, to me, rather distressing.

So I am wondering why. Because I think there is a very genuine and national problem here. And that is labor not presenting its case to the American public. Particularly union labor.

They know how to exert *political* pressure—how to turn on that kind of heat. But explanation—communication—are different problems.

Yes, it's a new problem. For a great many years, all the emphasis, certainly, was the other way. Journalism, advertising, etc. were on the employers' side. But now, labor has grown up. The unions have money, they have power, they have ten million members. And yet their journalism, their means of communication, the means they use in which to talk, not to their own members but

1. Charles Douglas Jackson has been associated with *Time* since 1931, most recently as vice-president. He was a special assistant to the President of the United States in 1953–54. During World War II Jackson was an executive of the Council for Democracy; a good many of Benét's wartime radio scripts, as this letter indicates, were written for that organization.

to the American public—these seem to me, from a very limited experience, amateurish, unskilful, unsuccessful.

Take the *Nation's Business,* for which I hold no brief at all. But it is, for what it is, a well-dressed, readable and smartly-edited periodical. Is there any labor periodical that presents labor's case as well and persuasively? If so, I'd like to see it.

A couple of labor journals did come in, in the course of this research. Well, their local news is about up to the level of the Stonington [Conn.] *Mirror.* And I'm not sneering at that kind of journalism—far from it. It's highly necessary—but it remains local. But the general effect is provincial, amateurish in makeup, amateurish, chip-on-the-shoulder and blatant in editorial content. Again, take the farm field. Take all the various farm publications and papers, *Country Gentleman, Farm and Fireside, Capper's Weekly.* The labor press just doesn't seem to stack up. And yet there are more laborers than farmers.

Take the fact that a bitterly anti-labor columnist like Pegler is influential and widely syndicated. Is there any pro-labor columnist who stacks up with Pegler just in pungency and readability (he wouldn't have to stack up with him in being an SOB, because that is rather difficult)? Well, who have you got? Sam Grafton? He is good—he writes well—he is buried in the New York *Post*—I doubt if his syndication is worth beans.

Take the to me curiously pathetic bouquets received by *PM* from various labor organizations on its second birthday. Again, I am not sneering at *PM*—I am all for it. But that heads of large labor organizations should talk about *PM* as if it were a miracle, because it is pro-labor

—well, something is wrong. If labor has a case—and it has a case—there ought to be a labor periodical five times as good and five times as influential as *PM*. Where is it?

I am not talking about the *New Masses* or the *Daily Worker*. We all know the CP boys are smart, in their way. I am talking about something that really represents Union labor.

I am talking about this, too. If you go to the Department of Agriculture, the REA, the FSA—any of the agricultural government agencies—and ask them for human interest and background material, you will get it, and get tons of it, and it will be good. Because those boys know a human interest story when they see one. Well, I don't know if we contacted the Department of Labor or not. But I note we have no material from them —and I've never seen one of their releases that didn't look canned.

I don't know about the recent—the very recent—radio labor programs. They may be good and I will try to listen to them.

But, from a very cursory, hasty and probably inaccurate observation, I gather that something is wrong. There are ten million Americans who aren't presenting their case to their fellow Americans. And, apparently, they have no one who really knows how to present that case —not in anger and recrimination but at least as skilfully and persuasively as the case for a pack of cigarettes.

I don't know what *Life* can do about it. I wish I did. I wish somebody could do a real job of research on the labor press and labor communications with the public in general—just a factfinding appraisal. I am bothering you because the whole thing is on my mind. I may be all cockeyed. But—there are ten million Americans whose voices we really don't hear—the rest of us. Something is wrong.

Excuse this fervency—and with many thanks, old war-horse, for what you are doing for the *Dear Adolf* stuff—

As ever

SVB

TO ALLAN M. PRICE [2]

Stonington, Conn.
July 12, 1942

Dear Allan:—

Woody is, of course, quite right. It was shortly after that that the three wise men went West and found the Republican Party asleep in a manger.

It is cool here and blowing considerably at the moment. At night we are dimmed out but not blacked out—which is a hell of a sight more comfortable. The other night however, we went over to have dinner with Bill Douglas in Old Mystic and I attempted to drive back using only parking-lights but had to cheat once or twice when I couldn't decide whether I was on land or water. It is odd to see cars just crawling through pretty complete blackness.

I have been in NY just once for five hours on business and didn't get a chance to do anything but acquire prickly heat and snatch some things out of the house that Rosemary wanted ('in the little box in my dressing-room, no, not the green box, the little box, you know the little box.'). But if we do get up we shall certainly phone the Prices.

2. A neighbor of the Benéts in New York, and, with Mrs. Price, among their closest friends.

I enclose a pamphlet in which you will of course be interested. These are fine people but they do not go far enough. What good is a universal secondary language when they do not even mention that man's only health-ful diet is derived from the pure fruits of the earth, not from the diseased flesh of animals? There must be NO compromise with the powers of flesh-eating!

God and One Federated World be with you!

As ever
SVB

TO CARL BRANDT

Stonington, Conn.
July 15, 1942

Dear Carl:—

On the Blakeslee story [a Navy movie].

There is, of course, a very considerable story there, if it is done truthfully—say on the Mrs. Minniver, Pasteur line instead of the usual big whooping business. And I imagine that [Lt. Commander, USNR] Blakeslee wants the truthful thing.

The whole English complication seems to me entirely unnecessary—I think the classmates thing is conventional—and while the Liberty Bell thing is a tie, I think a better one should be found. The thing ought to be completely American home-grown, with no business about English lords etc etc.

Also there is a story which you get from the Fletcher Pratt book [*The Navy: A History*] of the struggle inside the Navy—the Reuterdahl report etc—which would be pretty dramatic.

Now the point is this—I have been thinking it over. I can try to set up a story line—maybe good, maybe bad. I can't actually write the script because the thing isn't in my bones. I could do a similar story about the Army with enormous enthusiasm and with complete self-confidence. I can't do that here because I'm quite literally at sea— the language isn't in my mouth. I've never been a sailor. But I could maybe try to work out a preliminary draft of plot.

One more thing—if this picture is going to be real, it is going to have to show some mistakes and controversies inside the Navy. It can't be all flagwaving.

As ever

SVB

TO CARL BRANDT

Hotel Windermere [3]
Chicago, Illinois
August [4] 1942

Dear Carl:—

Thanks for your note. It doesn't matter whether there's any pay or not—it'll have to go to Navy Relief if there is.

Yes I would do a picture about the Army—any time— and any picture—with of course a reasonable guarantee that it wouldn't be garbled.

I don't know that I could do a fiction serial on this. I could do, of course, a non-fiction piece very easily. Anything the Army itself would like me to do I would be extremely happy to do—that goes without saying.

3. Benét and his wife had gone to Chicago to help Mrs. Benét's mother through a difficult illness.

When we get this very sad situation cleared up—if it can be cleared up—and I get back to Stonington—I want to do a couple of stories. I had one started before leaving—dunno how good it'll look when I get back—but we'll see.

I'll call you when I get back unless we land in NY on Saturday or Sunday.

All the best
SVB

TO C. D. JACKSON

Stonington, Conn.
August [10] 1942

Dear C.D.:—

Thanks, massa, for the generous check which I am turning over to Army Relief as seems only appropriate. Well, the [*Dear Adolf*] series was fun, and [Joseph] Schildkraut certainly came through with a bang on the last one. Many thanks to you all.

The get-together sounds fine. I have to be in NY August 24 to read about Webster over the air for Freedom House. Maybe that would work in somehow. But I could come up any time.

I am now a trifle pooped, having just returned from Chicago. But I guess I'll be back at the old work-bench by tomorrow, praying for democracy again. After a week of reading the Chicago *Tribune* my glands of irritation are in first-class form.

All the best!
SVB

TO MARIAN L. JOEST

The Whistler House
Stonington, Conn.
August 11, 1942

Dear Miss Joest:—

Thank you for your very pleasant letter which I greatly appreciate. And thank you, as well, for your faith. This is a tough period now and it will get tougher. But this country has seen stormy weather before and ridden it out. And it was not a reformer or a dreamer who remarked, "Never sell the United States of America short." It was a highly capitalistic capitalist named J. P. Morgan. And, no matter what else he did, when he said that, he said a mouthful. Which may be worth remembering.

You belong to the generation that is going to make this country even greater than it has been. And that it is going to be greater I am utterly convinced.

Sincerely
Stephen Vincent Benét

TO JOHN F. HAGEN

Stonington, Conn.
[August] 1942

Dear Chaplain Hagen:—

Thank you for your letter which I greatly appreciated. The letter from Lieutenant Lee came to me from Mrs. Agnes Allen of the Council For Democracy who did the research work for the *Dear Adolf* series. I imagine that she must have obtained it from an Army chaplain.

My only regret was due to the fact that as we only had fifteen minutes on the air I was unable to use the whole letter in its entirety. It is a remarkably fine and moving document and something that should receive the widest possible circulation. As I have already written Mrs. Lee, I have taken the liberty of sending a copy to Archibald MacLeish, the Librarian of Congress, as I am sure he would be greatly interested in it.

Thank you also for your own letter to Dear Adolf. Our series is now off the air—we only contracted for a six weeks period—so that, unfortunately, will prevent us from using it. But I appreciate your good will and interest more than I can say.

With every good wish,
Stephen Vincent Benét

TO CARL BRANDT

Stonington, Conn.
August 16, 1942

Dear Carl:—

Well, anyhow, here is a story ["The Prodigal Children"]. I won't say anything else about it, because it stuck like cold glue.

As ever
SVB

TO CARL BRANDT

Stonington, Conn.
August 17, 1942

Dear Carl:—

I have written Commander Blakeslee telling him, what I very truthfully feel, that I am not the man for the Navy picture, and returning the material he sent me. It is just a question of my starting too far behind scratch. I haven't the feel of the sea—let alone the knowledge of the Navy—that the right guy for this picture ought to have.

I'd be glad, of course—though I didn't tell him so—to advise or criticize in any way that would be of help. And, if he wants to use any of the suggestions I made in my previous letter, I'd like him to be at complete liberty to do so. This may seem a little starry-eyed [4] but I simply cannot take money for anything in connection with the armed services. Anyhow, they were just suggestions.

All the best
SVB

4. Benét's "previous letter" to Commander Blakeslee was very nearly a preliminary scenario, its five single-spaced pages a compact working script of exposition, narrative, and characterization.

TO ALLAN M. PRICE

215 East 68th Street
New York, N.Y.
[1942]

Dear Allan:—

I have just found my favorite dedication. It occurs in *One Who Was Valiant* by Clarissa Young Spencer and runs as follows:

DEDICATION

To my beloved husband and children
I dedicate this book.
May it inspire you to emulate the life
of my dear father, BRIGHAM YOUNG.

As ever
SVB

TO FELICIA GEFFEN

215 East 68th Street
New York, N.Y.
[December] 1942

Dear Miss Geffen:—

I am sorry not to be able to attend the Annual Meeting of the [National] Institute [of Arts and Letters].

I cannot report on all the activities of the Committee on Grants, but I should like to say a few words in regard to the four grants given in the field of letters. At a joint celebration of the Institute and Academy, last spring, four grants of a thousand dollars each were awarded in letters—to Miss Muriel Rukeyser, Mr. Norman Corwin, Mr. Hermann Broch and Mr. Edgar Lee Masters.

The grant to Miss Rukeyser was made, not only in recognition of her distinguished work in poetry but to assist her in the completion of a biography of the American scientist, Willard Gibbs. This biography has since been completed and published. It has received the highest critical praise . . . and the general consensus of opinion seems to be that it ranks among the best American biographies of recent years. I think it's pleasant that we have helped a writer like that—and we did so effectively.

The grant to Mr. Norman Corwin was made in recognition of his contribution to the new medium of radio. Since then, Mr. Corwin has been on a government mission to Britain, produced a series of programs, explaining the war effort of the people of Britain to the people of the United States. He has just returned, and his programs, originally sent from Britain on short wave, are being rebroadcast here. There again, I think we have helped a good man to get on with his work—and I know from Mr. Corwin that the recognition given him by the Institute and Academy has meant a great deal to him.

Mr. Hermann Broch is still engaged upon his remarkable book. He is not the sort of writer who produces a book a year, but when he does produce a book it is an important and significant one. And we will have helped that book, when it appears.

That we have assisted Mr. Edgar Lee Masters, I know. The grant to him was made, not in the hope of work to come, but in recognition of his contribution to American poetry. And it seems to me that we did well in making it.

There are four very different people. We have given

them both money and the recognition of their fellow-artists. We can't weight the results precisely, in a balance. We can't say, "But for us, this book or that would never have been published—or, if published, it wouldn't have been so good." But we do know—all of us—what money and recognition mean to the serious artists—and these are serious artists. Money buys the time to do your work well. Recognition by people who know what work is gives you confidence to go ahead. I think we may all be glad that we have done what we have done in this field. For, if an Institute like ours is to mean anything, it cannot be just a pleasant club or a source of self-gratification to its members. It must help the body of art. It must help the new work coming along and recognize the good work already done, not always widely popular with the public, but done by the enduring people.

I have no doubt that we shall make mistakes with some of these grants. Any body is bound to do so. But, in all modesty, it does seem to me that we are better qualified to give such grants than almost any other institution. For our judgment is judgment by men who work themselves, and know what work is.

As the war continues, the problem of the creative artist will become and is becoming an increasingly serious one. Many, of course, are already in the armed forces. Others are working for various government departments. But there are and will be others, young and older, whose work is of great importance to the future of our art and letters and yet who don't fit into the direct and immediate pattern of the war-effort. Not every artist can write propaganda, for instance. Longfellow did —Melville didn't. It would be silly to ask for a propaganda novel from Jane Austen—and William Blake's comments on the great crisis of his time, the French Revolution, concern themselves with a revolution that may have occurred in his own mind but certainly never occurred in France. And yet, Heaven knows, if art and letters are to go on, we need the Jane Austens, the Melvilles and the Blakes. That is part of our duty, part of our responsibility as members of this Institute.

I am therefore recommending, as chairman of the Committee on Grants, that the Institute and Academy between them continue these grants and, should that be possible, increase them, either in number or in the sum of money to each grantee. And I think that, so doing, we will be of genuine and lasting service to both art and letters.

I will recall that these grants are given

(a) to older men and women who have really contributed something to the arts and whose work, for one reason or another, has not met with the sort of publicity which brings immediate monetary recognition.

(b) to younger workers, distinguished not only for promise but for definite achievement.

(c) a grant is not given on the basis of specific work, like a Guggenheim Fellowship, for which a particular work is to be done, and it is not given like the Pulitzer Prize for a specific work which already has been done— but for the whole work of the recipient.

These stipulations are very flexible. But we are the only body, as far as I know, which not only encourages the work that is going to mean something ten years from now, but recognizes the work of older craftsmen, who have worked with honor and distinction, but often without notable public reward.

I should therefore like to ask the members very seriously to consider the names of possible candidates for these grants and to submit them to the Committee on Grants. The Committee needs their help, advice and counsel. And it very much wants, not only the support, but the lively and personal interest of all members of the Institute.

Respectfully submitted,
Stephen Vincent Benét

TO CHRISTOPHER LAFARGE

215 East 68th Street
New York, N.Y.
December 10, 1942

SHORT BUT COMMENDATORY ODE ON THE BIRTH OF
MR. C. LAFARGE

A stork ... a nipper ...
December morn ...
Hello, Kipper!
We're glad you're born!

SVB and RCB

TO CARL BRANDT

215 East 68th Street
New York, N.Y.
December [14] 1942

Dear Carl:—

This is very cheap and conventional all the way through—hammy and unconvincing.

There might be a picture to be done on how English actors and actresses kept on through the blitz. But God

412

knows this isn't it—with a famous ex-singer married to a clergyman and her daughter inheriting her talent and all that sort of guff.

Nothing is motivated here, nothing is real. The whole thing is static, the characters step up and deliver speeches point blank. It is all a very bad rewrite of *Mrs. Minniver* without any of the small, illuminating touches that made that picture a success.

I would certainly not be interested in doing anything about it, despite my previous association with Mr. Rowland [of the *Miss Bishop* production]. You would just have to throw everything here out of the window and start from scratch.

Sincerely
SVB

TO GEORGE ABBE

215 East 68th Street
New York, N.Y.
[1943]

Dear George:—

Many thanks for your letter. I will now try to get my ideas in order.

As you know, I have nothing but respect for the sincere pacifist—always have had. But what we face today—well, it's a real crisis. If we lose this war, there isn't going to be any United States, there isn't going to be any pacifism, and that's that. If we win it, we have the chance of working out a better world. And that, to my mind, tips the scale. The alternatives are real—not argumentative. We know what has happened to Christianity itself in the Axis-occupied countries.

So much for the ideology. Personally, from some knowledge of your character, I do not think you would be either content or satisfied in a c.o. camp.

On the Army and Navy. They are different because the Navy is able, so far, to raise its men on the volunteer system. The Army, very much larger, has to draft. Just a practical question—if the Navy had to raise four million men they'd have to draft, too. But it makes a certain difference in the way they go about things.

What the Amy is trying to do, however—very much more than in any previous war—is not to put round pegs in square holes. They make mistakes—any big organization does. But most of the writers I know who have been drafted or enlisted as privates have ended up sooner or later in jobs where their particular skills would be of some use.

Now there is one particular branch of the service which might be worth your applying for. That is the Combat Intelligence of the Air Force—I think that's the correct name. What it boils down to, very roughly and inaccurately, is this. They send an intelligence officer out with each squadron. He isn't a pilot himself—what he does is to collate the various reports of the fighting pilots. Quite a few writers have gone into this—Thornton Wilder and Vincent Sheean among others—and, while I believe they prefer people with combat experience, that isn't essential. In any case, it is an interesting job. If this fits in with your ideas, it might be worthwhile to write a very simple letter to Colonel Arthur I. Ennis, Public Relations Officer, Army Air Forces, Washington, D.C., asking whether you could apply for such a commission and giving your teaching, writing and athletic background. I do not know Colonel Ennis, so do not use my name, but I understand he is the head of Public Relations for the Air Force. Naturally, if you had such a job and the Army decided that all ground officers would have to have machine-gun training, you'd have to take the training, and use the machine-gun, if, in a jam, you had to. But this seems to be a job which combines active service with a certain amount of writing—and they seem, at least, to want people for it who have some ability to write.

. . . There is one other consideration. You are a writer and, as you justly remark, all material is material. So, if you do get drafted, it won't hurt you any—you will be sharing in a very large human experience shared by millions of others and an experience that deserves the best a writer can give it. But—there are dull jobs in the Army as there are in any big organization. As a writer it would be a lot better for you to be with an anti-tank outfit than, say, counting blankets in a Quartermaster depot. So, don't if you can help it get into something that is nothing but desk-work and routine. Then you will be bored.

. . . With all good wishes

SVB

TO CARL BRANDT

215 East 68th Street
New York, N.Y.
January 18, 1943

Dear Carl:—

Of course I would be glad to talk to Lieutenant Boyer. I would be glad to look at air-gunners, or to look at anything else. I would like something kind of definite.

I will have to be thinking about a story, too, as it becomes increasingly evident that I will have to pay an income-tax. So think of me thinking.

As ever
SVB

Index

to Philip Barry, 316–17; rehearsing *The Devil and Daniel Webster* (operetta), 318; advises Abbe on writing college novel, 318–21; parodies notice of *The Devil and Daniel Webster* (operetta), 322–23; writing for movies, 325, 326–27; advises Pauli Murray, 330–32, 346–48; vice-president of the National Institute of Arts and Letters, 333 n.; concerned with elections to National Institute of Arts and Letters, 334–38; does commentary for film *Power and the Land,* 351; refuses to dramatize *Man without a Country,* 353; plans to do radio script on border with Canada, 355–56; writes scenario for movie version of "The Devil and Daniel Webster" (short story), 357–59; popularity of radio scripts, 362; buying house in Stonington, Conn., 363, 371; refuses to give commencement address, 369; fee for poetry reading, 372 n.; contributing radio scripts and broadcasts to war effort, 372 ff.; approves of, but criticizes, movie made from "The Devil and Daniel Webster," 379–80; criticizes Finkelstein's statement on results of Conference on Science, Philosophy, and Religion, 384–85; willing to help with movies of army and navy, 402–3; unable to write a Navy scenario, 402–3, 407; refuses pay for all wartime effort, 407; recommends Air Force Intelligence as good

branch of service, **414–15.**

ATTITUDE TOWARD: the artist, 377–78, 381–84, 410–11; censorship of Cabell, 22–23; conscientious objectors, 413; country vs. city, 118; death of father, 160–61; editors, 212; enlarging Yale, 133–34; events of *1934,* 237; Georgia, 287; government, 391–93; his ability to write, 75; his marriage, 39–40; historical fiction writing, 255; Hollywood, 192–203; ideological writing, 394–95; imitation and influence, 287; *John Brown's Body,* 166; little magazines, 328–29; modern poetry, 383, 395; movie directors, 396–97; North and South in Civil War, 143–44; Pearl Harbor, 389–90; poetic diction, 290–91; political events of *1935,* 280; publication dates for poetry, 147, 148; publicity pictures, 172; publishers, 133; rain, 72; revising in proofs, 148; revising stories for editors, 121, 122; Roosevelt (F. D.), 237; senior societies, 14, 17–25; tennis, 84; union labor, 398–401; the United States, 405; World War II, 330; writing of *John Brown's Body,* 147; writing poetry, 166; Yale, 13; young poets, 267–68, *see also* Abbe, George; Engle, Paul; Rosten, Norman; Rukeyser, Muriel.

OPINION OF: *Atalanta in Calydon,* 141; "The Barefoot Saint," 187; brother's poetry, 137; Chesterton's *Magic,* 9; Douglas (Norman), *They Went,* 56; editorial suggestions, 277–78, 296; Eliza-

Benét, Stephen Vincent (*cont.*)
bethan blank verse, 291;
Elmer Gantry and *Arrowsmith,* 139; Freeman's *Lee,*
257; *Gone with the Wind,*
286–89; help in writing given
by Yale faculty, 259–60; his
father, 344; historical fiction
writing, 216–18; Hollywood,
192–203, 219; *John Brown's
Body,* 142, 143, 147, 166,
182–83; Lewis (Sinclair),
boys' book by, 7, novels
of, 139; Lindsay (Vachel),
8–9; Marxism, 265; Newton
(A. E.), book by, 28; *Post*
editorial comments, 214; Putnam (Phelps), 150, work of,
35–36; Roberts (Kenneth),
258–59; Robinson (E. A.),
118, 123, 141; Rossetti, 9;
sister's poem, 30–31; talking
books, 301; Wilson (Wood-
row), 9; Yale, 133–35; young
poets, *see* Yale Series of
Younger Poets

WORKS

"All Around the Town," 339
"American Honeymoon," 211
"American Names," 135, 207
"Apollyon" (projected novel),
116
"The Bagpipes of Spring,"
229
"The Ballad of William Syca-
more," 99
"The Barefoot Saint," 100,
187–90
The Beginning of Wisdom,
2, 27, 32, 38 n., 61, 75, 83,
87, 90, 91, 97
"The Bishop's Beggar," 388
"The Blood of the Martyrs,"
296
"Bon Voyage," 126–27

A Book of Americans (with
Rosemary), 224, 231, 232
Burning City, 265, 272, 281,
284
"Chemical Analysis," 52 n.,
101
"Christmas City," 275, 279
"Cockcrow," 98
"The Curfew Tolls," 271
"Daniel Webster and the Ides
of March," 332
"The Devil and Daniel
Webster" (story), 27, 357–
59
*The Devil and Daniel
Webster* (operetta, with
Moore), 312, 317, 318,
321, 322–23
"Doc Mellhorn and the
Pearly Gates," 312
"Dulce Ridentem," 43 n.
"Into Egypt," 361
"Elementals," 91, 205
"Fiona and the Unknown
Santa Claus," 164
"Fireworks," 375
Five Men and Pompey, 2,
11
"Freedom's a Hard-Bought
Thing," 361
"In a Glass of Water before
Retiring," 101
"The Golden Bessie," 106
"Goobers à la Française," 96
"Good Picker," 362
"The Great Swinglefield
Derby," 317, 339
The Headless Horseman
(with Moore), 300
Heavens and Earth, 24, 26,
27, 28, 29, 167
"The Hemp," 16
"Hotspur" (projected novel),
116, 125, 149
"Invocation," 140

"Island and the Fire," 207
James Shore's Daughter, 224,
233, 239, 240–41, 251
Jean Huguenot, 38, 55, 61,
67, 69, 71, 75, 128
John Brown's Body, 27, 129–
90, 155, 156, 208 n., 223,
235–36, 249, 287, 314;
writing of, 130–42; criticism of, by brother, 145,
by mother, 142–43, by
John Farrar, 146, by E. A.
Robinson, 166; publication
date, 147, 148; SVB to
read galleys, 148; corrects
proof, 158–59; BOMC con-
siders, 163, and accepts,
164–65; well received, 169,
172–73, 175–85; size of
BOMC edition, 171; sales,
172; promotion for, 172–
73; praised by Hervey
Allen, 176; SVB's inten-
tions and purposes in writing, 178–79, 182–83; re-
viewed by Canby, 178–79,
in *Poetry,* 180–81; adver-
tised in *Saturday Evening
Post,* 179; nonpartisan,
181; two errors in, 184–
85; new printing, 185;
school edition, 189; royalties lost in stock market,
191; recited as monologue,
260–62; made into "talk-
ing book," 300–1; West
Point cadets study, 343
"Johnny Pye and the Fool-
Killer," 311
"July," 52–53
"A Keepsake Song," 43–44
"King David," 99, 108
"Litany for Dictatorships,"
223, 279
"Little Testament," 40

"Long Distance," 164
"The Main Street Camel,"
234
Man Is War, 133
"The Minister's Books," 282
"The Miracle," 272
"The Mountain Whippoor-
will," 99
"Mystery Train," 272, 276
Nerves, 99, 108, 110, 111,
112, 113, 114
"Nightmare for Future Ref-
erence," 310, 327
"Nightmare at Noon," 356
"No Visitors," 339
"Nomenclature," 89
"Notes to Be Left in a Cor-
nerstone," 283
"Ode to Walt Whitman,"
265, 279
"Old Man Hoppergrass," 283
"The Place of the Gods," 301
"Poor Devil," 89
"Portrait of a Boy," 89
"Princess Pauper," 220, 278,
284, 285, 296
reviews:
Dancing Mothers, 112
Gone with the Wind, 287
Marjorie, 112
"A Sad Song," 42
The Tall Men, 150
Trinc, 150
"Schooner's Class," 296–99
scripts (radio and movie):
Abraham Lincoln, 192 n.,
197–205
Dear Adolf, 397, 401, 404,
406
"Letter from a Worker,"
398
"Listen to the People," 372
Miss Bishop, 325, 326–27
Much Ado about Nothing,
296

267; letters to, 200–1, 203(2), 205–6, 206–7, 210, 212(2), 213–14, 214, 219–20, 220, 220–21, 222, 229–30, 233, 233–34, 254, 258–59, 263, 265–66, 271–72, 276, 277–78, 278–79, 282, 282–83, 283, 285–86, 289, 292, 295, 296–99, 308–9, 309–10, 311–12, 312–13, 313, 314, 317, 321, 323–24, 325–26, 326–27, 327–28, 338–39, 339, 344–45, 345–46, 350, 350, 351–52, 353, 356–57, 362, 372–73, 375, 386–87, 388, 395–96, 396–97, 397, 402–3, 403–4, 406, 407, 412–13, 415–16

Brandt, Erd N., 272; letters to, 210–11, 211, 289–90

Brandt and Brandt, 147, 153 n., 170, 176, 189, 196, 204 n., 210 n., 249, 269, 279, 313, 340

Breadloaf Writers' Conference, 173, 260

Brearley School, 369

Brion, Marcel, 385 n.

Broch, Hermann, 409

Bromfield, Louis, 200

Bronson, Francis W., 115 n.

Brooklyn *Daily Eagle,* 68 n.; reviews *The Beginning of Wisdom,* 97

Brooks, Van Wyck, 334 n., 384, 395; letter to, 352

Broun, Heywood, 97

Brown, John, Jr., 236

Browning, Robert, 291

Buck, Pearl, 352

Budgeon, Frank, 385 n.

Bugle, 391

Bull Run, Battle of, 159

Burlington *Magazine,* 104

Butler, Nicholas Murray, 334 n.

Byron, Lord, 108

Cabell, James Branch, 187, 337, 350; five books of, 22; Rosemary reads, 79

Calhoun College, Yale University, 14

Calvert Correspondence System, SVB educated by, 2

Campbell, Donald, 20, 37, 38

Canada, SVB to write radio script on border with, 355–56

Canby, Henry S., 14, 116 n., 125, 137, 173, 259, 334 n., 365, 366, 374; reviews *John Brown's Body,* 178; letters to, 178–79, 188–89

Capper's Weekly, 399

Carlisle, Pa., described by SVB, 82–83

Carpenter family, 12

Carr, Rachel (Mrs. Thomas), 403 n.; letter to, 109–10

Carr, Rosemary, 27, 37, 59; SVB courts, 39–64; letters to, 40–41, 41, 41–42, 42, 42–43, 43–44, 44–45, 46–47, 47–48, 48–50, 50, 50–51, 51–52, 52–53, 53–54, 54–55, 55–56, 56–57, 58, 61–62, 62–64, 66–69, 69–70, 70, 72, 72–74, 74–76, 76–79, 80–81, 81–83, 83–84, 84–85, 85–87, 87–89, 89–90, 90–93, 93–95, 96–97, 97, 98 (2). *See also* Benét, Rosemary Carr

Carr, Thomas, letter to, 109–10

Carter, Frederick D., 17

Carter, Henry, 13, 26, 35, 40, 47, 48, 57, 76, 95, 115

Carter, John F., Jr., 13, 17, 18, 20, 22, 23, 35, 45, 46, 61, 173, 175; letter to, 132–35

Cather, Willa, 336; *The Professor's House,* 221

Cavalcade of America, 367

Wirz, Captain, of Andersonville
Prison, 184–85
Wodehouse, P. G., 258
Wolfe, Thomas, 331, 336, 337;
Of Time and the River, 264
Wood, Kenneth A., 17
Worcester, Dean, 25
World War I, 9–10
Worthington, Lilla: identified,
249 n.; letters to, 249, 254,
276–77
Wright, Richard, 340
Wyeth, N. C., 102
Wylie, Elinor, 103, 130, 136

Yale Alumni Weekly, 24, 128
Yale Club of New York, 125,
132; letter addressed from,
111, 113, 114
Yale Daily News, 24
Yale Literary Magazine, 13, 20,
86, 340
Yale Record, 13
Yale Review, 83, 135, 204,
295 n., 375; SVB solicits
money for, 119, 121
Yale Series of Younger Poets,
SVB judges, 223–29, 243–50,
267, 269–70, 271, 324, 340,
341
Yale University, 133–34, 225 n.;
entrance exams, 11, 12;
SVB's affection for, 13, and
reputation at, 13–14; awards
SVB fellowship, 14; senior so-
cieties, 14, 16–17, 20; awards
honorary degree to SVB, 294
Yale University Press, 167, 225,
340; SVB published by, 162.
See also Yale Series of
Younger Poets
Yeats, William Butler, 303 n.
Young, Brigham, 408
Young, Collier, 321, 326, 327;
identified, 275 n.; letters to,
275, 296, 300

Zell (by H. G. Aikman), 67